The Pleasure Was Ours

For Phyllis and Ken,
whose friendship,
thanks to Doug, we have enjoyed
for some time cordially

Milton Katims

June 17, '04

For a great Couple –
Love –
Virginia K.

Arturo Toscanini • *Pablo Casals* • *Arthur Rubinstein* • *Igor Stravinsky* • *Yo Yo Ma*
"Munio" Feurermann • *Jascha Heifertz* • *Van Cliburn* • *Leontyne Price* • *Isaac Stern*
Rudolf Serkin • *"Lenny" Bernstein* • *Byron Janis* • *Roberta Peters* • *Glenn Gould*
George Bernard Shaw • *Fleur Cowles* • *Henry Kissinger*

The Pleasure Was Ours

Personal Encounters with the Greats, the Near-Greats and the Ingrates

by

Milton Katims
Conductor-Violist

Virginia P. Katims
Violoncellist

Overture by Isaac Stern

Itzhak Perlman • *"Slava" Rostropovich* • *Yehudi Menhuin* • *Ravi Shankar*
Georg Szell • *Dimitri Mitropoulos* • *"Pinkie" Zukerman* • *Eugene Istomin*
Leon Fleisher • *Elizabeth Schwartzkopf* • *Eugene Ormandy* • *Oscar Shumsky*
Aaron Copland • *Arthur Judson* • *Sol Hurok*

Vision Books International
2004

Library of Congress Control Number: 2003110031

ISBN: 1-56550-094-6

Published by Vision Books International
Mill Valley, California
www.vbipublishing.com

Book Design by Illumination Graphics
Grants Pass, Oregon
www.illuminationgraphics.com

For information, please contact:
Milton and Virginia Katims
8001 Sand Point Way Street C-44
Seattle, WA 98115

First Edition
2004
Printed in U.S.A.

Dedication

Dedicated to these great artists who provide inspiration for us all, young

and still young.

With affection,

Milton and Virginia

Appreciation

We wish to thank Lou Guzzo (former *Seattle Times* music critic, and former managing editor of the *Seattle P.I.*) for his initial editing of our manuscript, and for offering so many valuable suggestions throughout the adventure.

Also to Jo Ann Ridley for her time spent with our book and giving us the benefit of her writing experience.

Thanks to Barbara & John Erling, program annotator, for their constructive comments and for their affectionate friendship.

Special thanks to Isaac Stern, long-time friend and esteemed colleague who found just the right words with which to introduce our book.

Many thanks to Patrick J. Steele (our gifted son-in-law) for introducing us to and guiding us to within hailing distance of our computer.

Heartfelt thank yous to Liz Cope for her tutorial in grammar, her carefully crafted list of needed or unneeded commas, periods, quotations and question marks!

And a bouquet of thanks to all our family and friends for their constant loving support and their many nudges, which finally brought closure to this very pleasurably nostalgic project.

Contents

Prelude

We have written this book because we wish to share our incredibly good fortune and joy in having spent our two lives in music with so many superb, profoundly gifted artists who have touched and electrified the world with their artistry. We have been privileged to be a part of the lives of the greats and the near-greats, from A (as in Claudio Arrau) to Z (as in Pinchus Zukerman). We have been blessed by the hours and days spent with re-creative geniuses like Maestro Arturo Toscanini, Maitre Pablo Casals, pianist Arthur Rubinstein, violinists Jascha Heifetz and Isaac Stern, cellists Emanuel Feuermann, Gregor Piatigorsky and Yo Yo Ma, sopranos Leontyne Price, Birgit Nilsson, Roberta Peters, and many, many more. Our travels the world over have also brought us into close contact with extraordinary talents in other arts as well, and with royalty, political leaders, and the movers and shakers of our own and other countries.

With these personal reminiscences we hope to convey some of the same excitement, creative fervor, and joy all of these wonderful artists have stirred in us. Perhaps all is not complete beauty and consonant harmony, however. A few foibles, frailties, warts and wrinkles appear here and there in these remarkable personalities, as we are quite aware is also true of both of us. We have engaged in a duet, taking turns to tell our tales which, after more than 50 years of living music, seem to us like an unbelievably impossible, but beautiful, dream. Don't awaken us!

Virginia and Milton Katims
Seattle, Washington
2004

Overture

There are very few musicians who have the eye, the ear, and the writing ability to comment with the kind of personal association, wisdom and humor that Virginia and Milton Katims have put into their book *The Pleasure Was Ours*. They have had the opportunity, given to very few people in this country, to have met and to have known truly as friends some of the seminal musical figures of the second half of this century.

It is particularly fitting that this clear-eyed and humane glance at the world of music, its great figures, (and its would-be great figures) should be available to all young musicians studying today, as well as to those hundreds of thousands who find music a daily necessity of life. It is so important that all young people entering the field today should know the history and art of performance and realize what riches have been granted them by the efforts of so many great music makers.

I applaud Virginia and Milton Katims for completing a task that few would undertake, providing vital and valuable knowledge to both performing musicians and audiences, taking these wonderful memories into the twenty-first century.

Isaac Stern

The authors in the lobby of the Seattle Opera House (1962)

Chapter 1
Hisstory – Rhapsodic Start in New York

Milton: From my beginning there was music. No! From before my beginning! I can't really boast that I actually remember hearing music when I was in my mother's womb, but something must have stimulated my appearance two full months before I was due. My mother often told me that as she was being wheeled to the delivery room of the Williamsburg Hospital in Brooklyn, New York, she heard the familiar sounds of Liszt's "Hungarian Rhapsody No. 2" being played on a gramophone. Of course, she decided that it was a special omen.

The records kept by the hospital at that time leave much to be desired as I discovered years later when I needed a birth certificate to obtain my first passport. (I was going to France to play viola at the Casals Festival and then on to the Middle East to guest-conduct the Israel Philharmonic.) In response to my application for a birth certificate the Brooklyn Hall of Records sent me a document which read: "Milton Katims is said to have been born on June 24, 1909." That didn't do much for my ego. I wasn't even a vital statistic.

Milton and Virginia Katims

Our family was not affluent, nor was it indigent. We were a typical middle-income family. My mother, whose maiden name was Caroline Spiegel, had been brought to the U.S. from Austria-Hungary when she was six months old, and my father, Harry, had come to the U.S. from Russia with his mother and four older sisters when he was six. He went to work when he was 12!

The family name was originally Katimsky, but an Ellis Island official decided the name was too long and sounded too foreign, so he shortened it to its present length. What effect it had on my professional career I'll never know. My name should have been Michel Katimsky, but I do know that "Milton Katims" has made my ethnic origin ambiguous, and it has caused no end of trouble to those who have tried to pronounce it correctly. (Perhaps I should have spelled it "Kaytims" to assure proper pronunciation.) Unfortunately, my parents did not speak the language of their homelands. My father soon forgot the little Russian he had known and, of course, my mother had not begun to talk when she was brought to New York. Her parents spoke only German, so I can't even regret not having had the opportunity to learn Hungarian.

From the beginning, there was never any doubt that our household was a matriarchy. Mom ruled the roost! At 5 feet 3, she may have been short in stature, but she had a powerful dominating personality, accustomed to having her own way. My father had relinquished authority in the home early on. He wanted peace at all cost, and was content with ruling the comparative tranquility of what we called "Papa's York." (His place of business in Manhattan).

Mom had unlimited energy and many talents, but her first love was music. In addition to playing the piano, she had a delightful lyric-soprano voice, and sang well enough to get into the chorus of the Friends of Music and then the noted Schola Cantorum, which performed often with Maestro Arturo Toscanini. Years later she teased me with the reminder that she had made music with that legendary conductor long before I did. It was Mom who ignited a passion for music in all of us children and, in concentrating on us, probably denied herself a career she might have had. Curiously enough, when my father was courting her she would frequently ask him to take her "to hear many violins." It wasn't till a bit later that she came to call the "many violins" an orchestra.

Mom also loved to paint. She studied at the Art Student's League on West 57th Street in Manhattan, and would sit for hours in the Metropolitan Museum of Art copying the paintings of such masters as Rembrandt. Planning and preparing meals for the family might easily have kept her from her music and painting, but she refused to be bound to the kitchen stove. The stove, she determined, needed some kind of timing device which would turn itself on and off automatically. With that in mind she went to the Brooklyn Union Gas Company, described her idea to management, and their engineers picked it up from there.

Friday was "bake day." In addition to the occasional very special Hungarian strudel, the creation of which called for the talents of a virtuoso (which Mom had in spades) she would bake other cakes and bread. As proof of my childish stupidity I confess swapping slices of Mom's home-made bread for an equal number of slices of Wonder bread with Helen Foster, my five year-old playmate next door. But that wasn't all I swapped with her. One day we decided to exchange intimate knowledge of each other and I must say I was very disappointed because I didn't see anything. I felt cheated! – and I suppose she did, too!

My father was a gentle, kind man from whom we seldom heard a harsh word. He never raised his voice. Before he married, his ambition had been to go on the stage as a monologue artist, but one failed attempt put that out of his mind. Then too, at that time he was courting Caroline, and had to face the reality of supporting a wife and a family. With little schooling and no training, he had to start at the bottom in the business world. He began as an errand boy, rose to the job of salesman, and then became the general manager of a large textile firm, Freiberg Brothers. His annual salary was $15,000 a year, a very good stipend in 1914. But when his hope of becoming a partner in the firm was thwarted by the presence of so many Freibergs (sons and brothers), he decided to go into business for himself as a cotton converter in the textile industry. (A cotton converter buys goods in the raw from the factory, and then decides on the color and finish of the goods which he then sells to the garment manufacturers.)

Although he was not a musician himself, he loved music and loved to show off his musical family whenever we had visitors. Ordinarily a shy person, he never hesitated to talk to strangers when he thought they might be helpful to one of us. One Sunday morning, he returned from a stroll to tell us excitedly about his walking along a neighboring street and hearing a violin being played beautifully. He listened for a while, entranced, then summoned enough courage to ring the apartment doorbell. He introduced himself and suggested that it would be wonderful if this fine young violinist would play sonatas with my brother Herman, who was already very serious about being a concert pianist.

That's how we met Joseph Sherman who was studying with Leopold Auer, the teacher of Jascha Heifetz and Mischa Elman. Thanks to Pop, Joe and Herman became good friends and spent many hours together making music. When we moved to our new home in Flatbush, we lost contact with Joe, hearing only occasionally about his progress as a concert violinist. (Years later, as I walked on-stage for my first rehearsal to guest-conduct the Cincinnati Symphony, I was delightfully surprised to find Joe Sherman sitting at the first desk of the viola section. He told me that I was responsible for his switching to the viola. Joe had been tuning in every Sunday afternoon to my viola-piano hour on WOR, Mutual Broadcasting System, the series of broadcasts that played quite an important a role in my career.)

I was in my early teens when I decided that the Golden Rule, the foundation of all religions, was to be the guiding beacon in my life. In the years we lived in Brooklyn's Bushwick section we belonged to a reformed Jewish temple on Putnam Avenue about a dozen blocks from home. I always looked forward to attending services there because of the wonderful pipe organ in the large sanctuary. It was played by a fine organist named Richardson. He introduced me to the chorale preludes of Bach, Händel, Telemann and other great Baroque composers. I loved them. Then when I was eleven we moved to Flatbush. The closest temple to our new home was a conservative congregation with no pipe organ and no music! Although I did go through the ceremony of a Bar Mitzvah at 13, I lost all interest in what the temple had to offer.

I had already been playing the violin about three years when we moved to Flatbush. At six I had barely made a nodding acquaintance with the piano when I decided I would never succeed in getting my two hands to work together on the keyboard. Besides, we already had three pianists in the family – my mother, brother, and sister. I wanted to be different and play the violin. When my mother told me I was to start on the piano it didn't occur to me to rebel because I just thought that everybody in the world played an instrument. I was too young to realize that musicians, and others for whom music is one of the most important parts of life, are very much in the minority.

Soon after switching from the piano to the violin, I discovered that I had absolute pitch. When I heard a note I could determine its pitch immediately because of the mental image of where on the fingerboard I would have to put my finger to produce that particular pitch. I soon began making sounds that didn't repel the family and, after a while, even I began to like the sounds I was making. Perhaps I wasn't a normal youngster because I never had to be reminded to practice. I was an underweight, scrawny kid who had made slow progress from my two pound start and wasn't good at any sport except one. I could run pretty fast. In high school I held the record for the 50-yard dash – six seconds flat. That meant I was a fast starter, (not a bad skill for a performing musician). At any rate, there was never any serious distraction from my violin-practice after school hours. Radio broadcasting was just beginning, television was still quite a way in the future, and I wasn't quite ready for girls.

Milton and Virginia Katims

One of the most vivid memories I have of those early years were the countless times Mom took the four of us (Seymour, my younger brother, had arrived) to concerts and lectures at the Brooklyn Academy of Music. She always carried a large paper bag full of assorted snacks that she kept passing along to us. One of those concerts was particularly memorable, because it was my introduction to the superb Spanish cellist, Pablo Casals. We sat in the balcony and, in my mind's eye, I can still see that shiny bald head as he leaned lovingly over his cello. I thrilled to his warm glowing sound and his unique way of making music that seemed to talk to me in a language I yearned to understand. He played one of the Six Bach solo suites. Mesmerized as I listened to him, I couldn't possibly imagine that one day I would be performing and recording with him, that I would be dedicating my own viola edition of those same Bach suites to him, that I would get my chance to tell him in person that he had been the first great artist to turn me on to the wonders of the legendary master of Leipzig.

Unfortunately I also have traumatic memories of those years. In addition to Mother Caroline's manifold gifts, which I have already described, there was a severely troubled side to my very amazing mother. Without warning she would often fly into strident vocal hysterics, usually in the middle of the night, after she had been shouting at and nagging Pop. The outbursts apparently were caused by her own physical and psychological frustrations, which my brothers, my sister, and I could hardly have been expected to understand. Her hysterics affected everyone but Seymour and me in some way. Seymour was spared because he was too young to understand what was happening. I was not affected because I withdrew into a world of my own, building a protecting wall around myself.

Herman, on the other hand, became frantic. Mom's hysterics would cause him to threaten to leap from the fourth story of our house if she didn't stop immediately. I'm quite sure that the psychological problems he developed later could be traced to these experiences. Many years later my sister Frances developed a brain tumor the

Milton at age 13 playing with older brother Herman at the piano

Milton Katims at age 20 about to receive his B.A. from Columbia University

size of a small grapefruit, and it, too, probably had its origin in the hysterical, middle-of-the-night eruptions. Fortunately the tumor proved to be benign, and was removed successfully, but the surgery took with it a large segment of her memory.

When we moved to Midwood Manor in Flatbush, I finally had a room of my own, and it proved to be just what I needed to insulate myself further from any unhappy situation. I just closed my door to disturbing events. My wife, Virginia, insists I'm still doing that! Our home looked and sounded like a scene from "You Can't Take it with You." The only thing missing was Grandpa manufacturing fireworks in the basement. Visualize and add sound: Herman is practicing on the Mason & Hamlin grand piano in the living room. Frances is at an upright piano upstairs in the back bedroom. Mom is vocalizing in the kitchen. Seymour, a beginner, is scratching on his cello in a front bedroom. And I am practicing my violin in the enclosed porch.

Is it any wonder that all of this finally proved to be too much for our next-door neighbor one day? He called the police to make us stop. A handsome young officer rang our doorbell and told us about the neighbor's complaint. At the same time acknowledging that because our household cacophony was taking place during the daylight hours he could not order us to stop. Like a typical Jewish Mama, my mother invited the nice young man to come in to our living room, gave him a glass of her best home-made wine and a large piece of her elegant strudel, and invited him to have a seat and listen to us play.

I finished high school in three and a half years with average grades, which made it necessary for me to take college entrance exams to get into Columbia University. There I surprised everyone– most of all myself – by the change that came over me as a student. My grades improved dramatically, and I made the Dean's list every semester, earning my degree in three and a half years. I majored in psychology – why I'll never know – with a minor in music. It was obvious that I was a somewhat mixed-up young man.

Milton and Virginia Katims

The combination of my youth (barely 20) and my indecision as to what I wanted to do with my life (psychology, music or something else) led me to take a trial run in my father's cotton-converting business. He said he was delighted at my decision, but we both very quickly realized it was a terrible mistake. I resigned at the very same time Pop fired me. My ill-advised attempt at converting cotton had one very positive effect: It made me realize that the only path I really wanted to follow was music.

I returned to Columbia for graduate studies. In glancing through the university catalogue my eyes lit up as I came across an entry announcing that Leon Barzin was offering a course in conducting at the National Orchestral Association. Of course I signed up. After a couple of sessions I realized that I had to know the C-clefs in order to read directly the notes of transposing instruments like the clarinet and trumpet. The viola was the natural C-clef instrument for me to turn to. Leon loaned me his beautiful Gaspar da Salo viola and I began to play the viola, sitting at the last stand in the viola section. As I became more proficient on the instrument he moved me forward in the section. At one point Leon told me that as a violinist I played as well as 300 or so other violinists in New York, but if I concentrated on the viola I could be part of a much more elite group. I loved the rich, mellow sound of the instrument. It was love at first sound! The switch caused me to forsake the violin completely. And, as an aspiring conductor, I quickly realized the advantages of playing viola, sitting in the middle of the orchestra with excellent sight lines to the conductor. Another benefit was that the viola part was in the middle of the score; and because the viola usually played a subsidiary role, I could devote my attention to what was happening above and below my part.

I am reminded that when Mozart "sat in" on chamber music sessions, he preferred playing the viola for the same reason. (But I also recall that when Mozart was very young and he offered to substitute for the absent second violinist in his father's string quartet, he was told that he didn't know how to play the violin. (With apologies to all second violinists] the very young Mozart said, "You don't have to know how to play the violin to play second violin!")

It was during this period that I was courting beautiful cellist, Virginia. It was she who succeeded in getting me my first professional position. She had been studying cello with Alfred "Wally" Wallenstein, and one day he told her that he had just been appointed music director at WOR, the Mutual Broadcasting System, and was looking for an assistant conductor and solo violist. Virginia, always on her toes, recommended me to Wally and gave him my phone number in Woodstock, New York, where I was playing string quartets. Immediately after her lesson, Virginia rushed to a phone to alert me to the possibility of my being offered a job by Wally. I didn't wait to hear from him. I immediately jumped into my old jalopy and drove the 100 miles to New York as fast as the car could move. When I phoned Wally, he said with amazement:

"Gosh, you're fast! I just wired you a half hour ago."

Virginia certainly knew what she was doing. I started the job in September and we were married in November.

In my eight years with Wally, we covered a lot of interesting musical territory – most of the Bach cantatas, (which became part of the Sunday services in churches reached by WOR), all of the Mozart piano concertos with Nadia Reisenberg (wonderful Russian pianist, colleague of mine on the faculty of the Juilliard School of Music), and the Wallenstein "Sinfonietta," the varied repertoire that permitted me to conduct and perform as viola soloist many times, and the vast literature played by the Symphonic Strings in an extended series of programs.

Wally was most generous, giving me the opportunity to guest-conduct many of the programs, in addition to my being able to program performances of my own. Two of them stand out in my memory. One was conducting the American premiere of the "Poulenc Concerto for Two Pianos" with Rosina and Joseph Lhevine. The other memorable program was a scripted series in which "Les Miserables" was dramatized. I enjoyed the responsibility of selecting and conducting the bridge music for that series, but most of all it gave me a firsthand look at the tremendous talent of the young director and leading actor, Orson Welles.

The WOR years gave me the experience I could not have found in any university or music school to prepare me for my career as a conductor. Rehearsal time was limited and expensive, so that I was forced to learn how to be efficient and to make every minute count. I can truthfully say that I learned to conduct at WOR. Those incomparable, highly disciplined years convinced me that the only way to become a conductor was to have the actual experience of conducting. On the job training!

Chapter 2
Herstory Beginning in San Francisco

*V*irginia: My Mom told me the fog was rolling in from the Bay at three in the morning when I was born that day in a San Francisco hospital. If all she could remember about my birth was that it was a foggy day in San Francisco, I guess my arrival was hardly a headline event.

Although my mother came from a very poor family, she was a born aristocrat, at least as far as her interests and ambitions for her children were concerned. Her name was Vincentia, a beautiful name for a beautiful lady. Dad, Carl Peterson, was born in Sweden, and lived much of his boyhood in Rowley, a small Massachusetts town just north of Boston. He and his mother had arrived in Rowley with no father, a fact duly noted by Rowleyites. Years later when Dad learned that they thought of him as illegitimate, he dropped out of school, and started to work his way west, doing odd handyman jobs in a number of cities across the country. Eventually he arrived in San Francisco.

Vincentia and Carl met at a picnic, fell in love, and were married soon afterward. As fate would have it, their marriage took place on the night of the colossal 1906 San

Francisco earthquake. The newlyweds, who were both 16, were in each other's arms in bed at a boarding house on Union Street when the quake struck. Their bed fell to the floor below. Despite the one-story drop, they were still safely locked in an embrace. (Ah, the power of love!)

My father (how I loved him!) became a successful builder and contractor in the Bay Area. Always regretting that he had not had much of a formal education, he spent every free moment in the Mechanic's Library in downtown San Francisco. If I wanted to become a truly educated woman, he would often tell me, I should read the Wall Street Journal for at least an hour each day. But at that time I couldn't have cared less. Today I devote a couple of hours every day to this great newspaper about America's business. I realize now how important his advice was. If only I could tell him!

I called Mom an aristocrat for good reason. Despite her humble beginnings she saw to my manners and behavior, and insisted that I study piano, voice, and drama. The drama lessons began at the Reginald Travers School of Acting. In my teens I felt that I might be a better actress than the musician I became. In fact, I thought the same thing about ballet. I once danced with a youngsters' group in a production of Verdi's "Aida," staged by the San Carlo Opera Association at the San Francisco Opera House. A small group of us performed as Nubian slaves of the Egyptian princess, Amneris. We each had the responsibility of applying our own black makeup. At one performance I was late in arriving at the Opera House and hurriedly applied the black makeup. During the performance when I rose from my kneeling position at stage front, I couldn't understand why the audience started to laugh - until I glanced down at my knees. They were both snow-white!

I loved school. In my first year at high school, an all-girls school, I found out that if I studied an orchestral instrument during my lunch hour I could earn extra credits and graduate in three and a half years. I immediately went to the music office to pick out an instrument. Alas, by the time I arrived only two instruments were left, a tuba and a cello. Because of my violinist brother, Harvey I chose the string instrument, the cello. All through high school I acted in plays and was always assigned the role of a man. One of the reasons was that I was extremely slender and completely flat chested. Something happened in the course of the years – I'm now better endowed! Whatever else I did at school, I must have done something right because I was named valedictorian of my class.

Harvey became a gifted violinist, sponsored by the Crocker banking family of San Francisco. They bought him a beautiful Italian violin, and sent him to Belgium to study with the famed Eugene Ysaye, and then to New York to continue his studies with the equally famous Hungarian-born violinist and teacher, Leopold Auer (teacher of Heifetz).

I'm sure my Mom had more ambitious plans for me in many directions. Time after time she insisted that I try out for this or that contest. One, for whatever reason, was a competition to find a girl whose feet were the same size as Greta Garbo's. Thank God I lost.

Another contest offered a prize for singing. I knew I didn't have much of a voice, but try telling that to Mom. "You have studied voice, and besides someone has to win," she kept insisting. She arranged for me to sing with a big band at the NBC studios, where Harvey was now playing a program of violin solos as "Ricardo and His Violin." The fateful day arrived. I was to sing "My Future Just Passed." The band struck up the introduction to a souped-up orchestral arrangement. I had been tapping out the tune with one finger on the piano, but now, suddenly I couldn't for the life of me find the first note of the melody. My future didn't just pass by. It ignored me completely!

It was time to get a job and bring home some money. Why me? I wanted to practice the cello, just as Harvey was doing with his violin. I found a job modeling furs, and occasionally running the elevator at Louis Gassner, which later became I. Magnin. With my rotten luck, it seemed that whenever I was running the elevator the swank, wealthy girls from my school showed up to buy furs. And how I loathed having to go up to the top floor to model them. There the fur salesmen were showing their coats to the head furrier, an old German fellow, who fondled me all the way down the front of each garment.

"See how fine these skins are," he said, as he pressed unnecessarily and I blushed a beet red. When I had filled out my application for the modeling job, I listed the name of a Boston store I had heard about, in an effort to impress my prospective employer. It backfired. I was called into the boss's office.

"Miss Peterson," he said, "you are a high school graduate, aren't you?"

"Oh yes, I was valedictorian of my class."

"How then could you spell Filene's as Phyleens on your job application? You're fired. Learn to tell the truth. If you had been honest, you would have kept your job." It was a lesson I never forgot! During all these experiences, I practiced the cello madly.

Soon scholarships began coming my way, and they led to studies with noted teachers. I couldn't wait to practice each day. My wish to become a good cellist and my passionate love of music filled my very being. I was also learning the string-quartet repertoire with two fine violinists and a very capable violist, all of whom returned home to San Francisco each summer from their studies at the Curtis Institute in Philadelphia.

In the meantime I had acquired a couple of boy friends who usually waited for me outside the rehearsal studio. One was a second-rate fiddler, who always reeked of cheap cologne. The other was John Thomas, an engineer with a large oil company. He loved classical music and sent me wonderful books like "Cyrano de Bergerac," in which he had marked Christian's lines as he shyly related his love for Roxanne. John took me to the opera one night (I, in my pink tulle party dress and long white gloves and he, very handsome in white tie and tails). The opera was Donizetti's "Lucia di Lammermoor." I swooned with ecstasy during each scene, but John stared at me

Virginia and brother Harvey – ages 4 & 8
in Stonehurst, CA (near San Leandro)

Virginia, ready to take on New York after her first year at the Royal College in London

throughout the evening, the perspiration pouring down his face. I was too stupid to realize that this was "Love." For him, at least. He wrote me passionate letters for years thereafter, addressing me as "My Princess."

How innocent I was! One night Harvey, who was now playing in the San Francisco Symphony (the youngest member of the orchestra), took me to a big party with many of the musicians. My Mom had made me a new sapphire-blue dress, and I was confident that I looked like a worthy date for my handsome brother. What a party it was! An extraordinary amount of alcohol was consumed, and I worried that many of the guests would not be able to drive home safely. Drinking harmless punch and being so young, I thought no one would be interested in me. I told Harvey I wanted to go home.

"Here's Ed Harris. He's a fine pianist. He'll drive you home."

At that moment, a well-known San Francisco music critic took my arm and pulled me into a small side room. He sat me down on a couch and proceeded to tell me all about the famous cellists he had met. I was fascinated. Then, suddenly, he pushed me down on the couch and jumped on top of me. In my naiveté, I thought at first that he was just horsing around. But when the horsing around took a serious turn I decided it was time to do something. Besides, the fine hairdo for which I had paid hard earned money was now terribly mussed up. That was too much! I took off one of my new pumps and conked him on the head. Leaping from the couch, I dashed out of the room, pausing at the door to shout at him, "It was an honor to meet you!"

Not all my experiences with men or "boys" were distasteful in those days. One beautiful interlude in my life was the joy of being introduced to poetry. On several occasions I was invited to hike up Mt. Tamalpais, across the Bay from San Francisco, with Harvey and other symphony musicians. I usually found myself walking with Lajos Fenster, the orchestra's assistant concertmaster, because he was so much fun. In addition to having a keen sense of humor, he seemed to know every plant and rock on the mountain paths.

19

Milton and Virginia Katims

Lajos was married to a remarkable, lovely woman, Elizabeth, who had just given birth to a son. That son, now a brilliant physician, Dr. L. F. (Fritz) Fenster, is one of our best friends, and a leading doctor at the Virginia Mason Clinic in Seattle. One of the reasons I loved hiking with Lajos was that he would whip out a volume of poetry whenever we reached a promontory and read aloud from Shelley, Keats, Byron, and other greats. I was transfixed. Noting my deep interest in poetry, he gave me one of his collections, The Weekend Book, which has given me immense pleasure throughout my life.

One of the greatest opportunities of my life lay immediately ahead. A lovely English woman, Lady Vestey, the wife of Sir Leonard Vestey, had arrived in San Francisco Bay on her gorgeous yacht, the Anandorra Star, built especially for her by the family's Blue Star Lines. She had come to visit my mother. Mom explained, "Hilda – that's Lady Vestey's name – has a sister Dorothy, who was maid of honor when your father and I were married. Hilda was a true brunette, with a full bosom. I thought her quite glamorous. Wonder of wonders, she invited me to spend the summer with her in England!

"I have two children," she said. "Joyce is almost your age. You can sail on one of our freighters, the Gothic Star, and you'll be the only passenger with Captain Fielding taking good care of you." I was thrilled of course. She told me I could take my cello with me and practice to my heart's content. The day of departure came and all my friends were on the dock to see me off on the super, but unglamorous, Gothic Star. My mother had sent Capt. Fielding a huge basket of California fruit topped with a perfect avocado.

And so, with family and friends waving goodbye, we sailed away to Richmond across the Bay, where we spent three days taking on fuel and cartons of canned goods. I could have spent those three days at home - or at least phoned home - but I didn't. I was assigned a neat cabin and was soon practicing madly. Whenever I became aware that sailors were peering into my porthole, I played only "pretty" pieces so they would think the cello a beautiful instrument. Which of course, it is.

As we sailed through the Golden Gate my excitement took me to portside to watch the flying fish and even a whale. My reverie was broken by the words of the first mate, Percival Hunt, who introduced himself and said, "You don't want to spend any time with the Second Mate. He's not a gentleman."

Hmmm. The old English caste system had reared its ugly head.

It took six weeks for our old tub to reach England, and I had fun playing volley-ball with the officers and going up to the captain's quarters every evening to listen to the wireless and play cards. I watched the fruit in the huge basket disappear until only the avocado was left. It looked quite forlorn - but it too was gone the following night. I asked the captain how he liked the avocado. "So that's what it was Miss Peterson. Cook and I didn't know what it was, and this morning he prepared it with sugar and cream. It was delicious."

By now I had become well acquainted with First Officer Hunt. When we sailed through the Panama Canal, and I saw him in his "whites," I thought him very handsome.

"Call me Jummy," he told me. "I loathe my name, Percival." I agreed. Earlier he had informed me that his brother, John, was a concert pianist who had studied with Artur Schnabel in Berlin.

"Will you go dancing with me when the ship reaches Liverpool?"

"Why, thank you," I said. "I'd love to."

When we docked at Liverpool, I rushed off the ship to find a beauty salon to have my hair done. The salon operator was quite candid: "You know," she said, without hesitation, "your hair is really a dirty blonde. May I put a lightener on it?"

"If you think so, please go ahead."

It was one of my better decisions. I liked the new, brighter, "clean blonde" look. And so did Jummy when he saw me. "I say, Gin, you look quite smashing."

We dined and danced at a lovely little café, and in my mind I saw headlines that might have been written if I were anyone important: "Young S.F. Cellist Seen Dancing With Handsome Officer; She Had Stars in Her Eyes."

The last leg of the trip began the next day and ended at Gravesend, London's port. I was packed and eager for the next phase of my new adventure in the new to me 'Old World.' There, waiting on the dock, was Lady Vestey in a beautiful Humber with a smartly dressed chauffeur at the wheel. The chauffeur, who bore the unbelievable name of Belcher, took my single suitcase and I climbed into the back seat with my cello. Did I imagine it, or did Hilda cast a somewhat baleful eye at the big instrument as I lugged it in with me?

We drove past the Elephant & Castle — what a strange name for a pub — and through the little town of Dulwich, up a colorful road to Sydenham Hill, where the Crystal Palace once stood, and finally to Oakover House, the impressive Vestey home. The front door opened and Hilda's children, Joyce and Polly, poured out. I loved them on sight and I knew in short order that the feeling was mutual. Hilda introduced me to Joan, my maid, to Lucy the housekeeper, to the cook, and to the rest of the staff. I also met the children's governess, realizing quickly that they were taught at home. In minutes, I also learned there was no Sir Leonard Vestey. Hilda was divorced.

Although I didn't quite know what to do with my maid because I had never had one, I thought she was cute. She giggled a lot, mostly because she was amused by my American accent. My room on the second floor of the mansion was marvelously large and well appointed. On my first day there, Hilda took me up to still another beautiful room on the third floor and said in her best British accent:

"Vuhginneeah, you can do your practicing up heah in this room. It ovuhlooks the gahdens, and I'm suah you will love it, Deah."

I did, even though the thought flicked past my mind that a "thuhd-floah" site for cello-playing would put it safely outside of listening distance from the rest of the huge house. Almost every night of the year the Vestey home reverberated with the sounds of a dinner party. I had to borrow gowns from Hilda, since she insisted that everything be formal. My first job every morning was to gather flowers for the dinner table.

Jummy came to visit each time his ship was in port, but his presence wasn't enough to keep me from getting restless. I was practicing three or four hours each day. Summer turned into fall, but I remained at Oakover House, happily. I had been invited originally for the summer only, but Hilda never spoke to me about it, nor did my mother write to remind me that my time was up.

One day I phoned the Royal College of Music in London and asked to speak to the director of the cello department. My call was routed to Sir Ivor James. In a wonderfully cultivated voice he graciously made an appointment for me to come to his home with my cello. Two days later, Belcher drove me into town and waited for me while I played for Sir Ivor. He was extremely complimentary when I had finished playing. When I told him I didn't have enough money for lessons, he graciously offered me a scholarship. I was thrilled and began lessons with him. He was an excellent teacher, and I progressed rapidly. His musical menu for me: All of the Goltermann and Romberg concertos.

It was during that period of study that I had still another inspiring experience. On a visit to the incomparable Tate Gallery, I saw the stunning Augustus John painting of Madame Wilhermina Suggia, a famous Portuguese cellist. Deeply impressed, I just had to meet her. I'd heard she was in London and on an impulse, after finding her phone number, I called her. Boldly, I introduced myself as an American cellist and asked if I could play for her.

"Of course," she said and gave me her address on Birdcage Walk. I fairly flew there with my cello. I found her stunning in dress and manner, even more impressive than she had appeared in the painting. Maybe I should have been shy and inhibited, but I surprised myself with my aggressiveness, and that seemed to delight her. After I played for her, she said without hesitation:

"You are a fine talent. Can you come to Lisbon where I live? I will give you a scholarship, of course." I couldn't afford the trip and will always regret that I could not accept her kind offer, but I was thrilled to have her expert opinion.

In the meantime, I finally realized that Lady Vestey was not terribly happy with my all-day practicing. She began leaving the house more often. When she was out I would put aside my instrument and join Joyce and Polly in tearing through the house like three subteeners on the loose. The girls were happy to break away from their school lessons.

I had been warned that Polly was epileptic and often fell down. "If that happens Vuhginneeah, put a spoon in huh mouth so she won't swallow huh tongue."

The idea was a constant worry to me, but fortunately she never had an attack while I was there. Once in a while Hilda would come home in a rage, especially if she had been into town to have her hair tinted and the result displeased her. She would scream and swear at the help.

"Why are you all so bloody stupid!" Sometimes in her fury she would throw dishes at the housekeeper. A few times she would turn on me without provocation. Early one morning I phoned Jummy, whose ship had just arrived from India.

"I want to leave here Jum. I'd really like to be in London where I can go to all the concerts."

"Good, Gin. I'll pick you up on Saturday and you can stay at my Aunt Kate's flat."

I left Lady Vestey happily, but not before thanking her as best I could for her hospitality and for all she had taught me, particularly in the art of entertaining, and for putting up with me all that time. Regretfully, I had gained many pounds. We seemed to be eating all day, beginning with tea and biscuits in my room at 7 a.m., a hearty breakfast at 8:30, milk and cookies with the girls at 11, a huge lunch at 1 o'clock, high tea at 4:30 or 5, a lavish dinner party at 8, and finally tiny sandwiches and chocolate in my room at 11 o'clock.

The two girls never dined with us, which was just as well. Hilda seemed to throw caution to the wind when they weren't around. At the dinner parties she was a practiced flirt, batting her eyes and thrusting her ample bosom at the gentlemen at every opportunity. She was quite an artiste, at least in that department. I had an inkling of why Sir Leonard had deserted ship.

One weekend Jummy rented a car and we drove to the little town of Ayot St. Lawrence in Buckinghamshire, where his mother had a cottage. The town's main claim to fame was that it was the home of George Bernard Shaw, author, playwright, and critic. As we walked around the town one day Jummy pointed to an elderly, white-bearded man across the street.

"Why, he looks as if he has a lot of rouge on his cheeks," I said.

"It's Shaw himself," Jummy whispered. "It is rouge. He's a vain old fellow. You might be surprised to know he also wears a corset."

"Oooh, I'd love to meet him. Would that be possible?"

Jummy told me his mother was planning a tea party in my honor before we left town and that she would invite the famous old man because she knew him well. The tea party came off as promised, and Shaw did attend. I had a few moments with him, and he did most of the talking. Naturally.

"Miss Peterson," he said after we had been introduced, "this is a horribly dull little town. The main activity of the people here seems to be going to church. It was hardly a surprise comment coming from one of the world's best-known agnostics. Later Shaw wrote Jummy's mother a thank-you note in which he mentioned that he was pleased to meet an American girl who spoke the King's English. By that time I had acquired a broad British accent, thanks to my long exposure to Lady Vestey and all her family and friends. Of course I asked if I might keep Shaw's note. I still have it among my most cherished possessions.

Next to Mrs. Hunt's cottage was a very large duck farm. On the night before we were to leave for London, those damn ducks quacked and quacked all night.

Milton and Virginia Katims

The next day we drove back to London. Jummy was a terrible driver and we landed in a ditch twice. Back at his flat Jummy produced a small velvet box and handed it to me. It contained a beautiful topaz, my birthstone, set in 24-carat gold, that he had brought from India. On an impulse I said,

"Well Jummy, I suppose this means we're engaged, doesn't it?" " It seems to me that I was always quite nervy and never hesitated to speak my mind. We made plans to meet when I returned to San Francisco and his ship was next in port.

"Gin, did I remember to tell you that I've been made president of the Blue Star Lines? (I quickly sensed that Hilda Vestey may have had a hand in this.) When we're married, we'll live in Ceylon. That's where the head offices are," he continued. "By the way, it's hellishly hot there and it would not be a good idea to bring your cello because the humidity would wreck it."

Hmmm. That did it. I wasn't about to marry anyone if I couldn't have my cello with me.

But I didn't say a word. Jummy left for his ship, the old Gothic Star, and the very next day. I packed and bought a steerage ticket for the SS Manhattan that would soon sail for New York. My passion cooled, but I loved my ring, and still do. He never asked me to return it.

As the ship cleared the Southampton harbor I fell into a pensive mood. It wasn't Jummy who was on my mind. That chapter in my life had already ended. Instead, I could think only about how lucky I had been to have such wonderful parents who had shown me how to realize my potential. Mom had been 100 percent right when she told me, "Music would open every door." It always has and always will. Heavenly classical music, beautifully performed feeds my heart, my soul, and my mind. How I wish all others might enjoy the same rewards!

The Arion String Quartet
Harry Farbman and Bernard Robbins, violins, Milton Katims, viola, and Sterling Hunkins, cello

Virginia, in Birmingham, Alabama, 1982

Chapter 3
A Duet in the Making

Virginia: I had mixed feelings as I sailed from Southampton board the S.S. Manhattan bound for, where else, Manhattan, and a week's visit to the sights, sounds and characters of New York. I had spent a most enjoyable and rewarding year at Lady Vestey's and in London. Perhaps most important of all, I had studied and practiced the cello with such fervor that I was now a far better cellist than before.

Although I would miss the many friends I had made during that happy time, I was thrilled to be returning to the U.S. and eventually to my home in San Francisco. Also, I had acquired a broad English accent and couldn't decide whether that would be a help or a hindrance in the States.

My ticket read "Steerage" which corresponded to today's "third class." With all of $125 stashed away in a zippered pocket I felt quite rich and anxious to take on the Big Apple. What a ball I had on that voyage! Every night one pianist or another sat down at the ship's terribly beaten up spinet immediately after dinner. They played polkas, czardas, mazurkas and other dances from every country represented on the passenger list. I danced every night until at least 2 in the morning. The mood was hilarious. Virtually all of my Steerage-mates were on their way to realizing a dream – the dream of becoming a citizen of the fabulous U.S.A.

One of my dance partners was a fellow named George Balnitis, a Lithuanian en route to Troy, New York, to join the friends who had preceded him. George was a fun-loving happy-go-lucky fellow who worried about me and my $125 on the streets of Manhattan. Although he had heard about the gold lining the streets of the Big Apple, he had also heard about the bad apples. I wonder what he and his friends think about the streets of New York today!

George was pretty handy with a needle and thread and persuaded me to let him sew the $125 into the hem of one of my skirts. I produced one of my favorite skirts and handed it to him. "No one will think of stealing your money if it is hidden here," he said as he stitched away.

As soon as we debarked from the Hudson River slot at New York's West 23rd Street, I grabbed my suitcase with one hand, my cello with the other and began traipsing up 23rd and down 22nd looking for a room to rent for a brief period. I came upon a fairly decent looking brownstone building with a "rooms for rent" sign in a window – and rang the bell. A woman I presumed to be the landlady let me in and led me to a third floor room with a large bed, a sink and a toilet. I unpacked, picked up my cello, and began to practice.

Within minutes I heard a knock at the door. A man I can only describe as ordinary was standing there. He looked askance at my cello and said, "Oh, I guess I have to have an appointment, don't I?"

I remembered that I had told the landlady that if I stayed on, I would be happy to give cello lessons to pay my way in Manhattan.

"Yes," I told the man at the door. "You need an appointment. Come tomorrow morning at 10 o'clock. Do you have a good instrument?"

He grinned widely, turned and left. I wondered why he was grinning.

A short time later, another man appeared, equally undistinguished, and we went through the same routine. When I suggested he come with his instrument the next morning at 11 o'clock, he too grinned broadly, turned and left without another word.

After a third man appeared and the same dialogue was repeated I went downstairs to find the woman who had rented me the room.

"Well Dearie," she said, "you're sure to have lots of customers. I can see that."

Customers! Good Lord! What had I done? Those guys at my door weren't prospective cello students.

The brownstone building was a brothel! And they thought I was a brand new girl. I blushed deeply as I recalled what I had said to each of the men. Now I understood the instant grins when I asked them if they had a good instrument! I waited till nightfall to pack my suitcase and cello and stepped gingerly and quietly down the three flights of stairs to 22nd Street. That was a close call.

A bit farther down the street I spotted a sign on a fine looking building that read: Women's Federation Club. This sounded more like it. At the reception desk an attractive young lady gave me a warm greeting and told me her name was Miss Ince. I told her that I had just returned from a year's cello study in England and was looking for temporary lodging. Before she could answer I burst into an explanation of what had just happened to me, including my visitors and asking them about "their instruments." She was warm and charming thank God, and laughed along with me.

One phone call was all it took. She turned to me with a broad smile and said,

"Miss Peterson, this is a residence for working women, and we would urge you to stay with us. We charge $7.50 a week and that includes a private room with breakfast and dinner."

I reached across the counter and gave Miss Ince a big hug. New Yorkers could be warm and helpful. Maybe that was why I was encouraged to lengthen my stay from the two or three weeks I had originally intended. In fact I discovered that job opportunities were there for the taking. I answered an ad that resulted in my modeling lingerie for the Sears catalogue. One of the reasons I wanted to spend a little time in New York was to look up my very first cello teacher, Sterling Hunkins, who had moved here from San Francisco. Then I thought I would be on my way back to California. I found Sterling's name in the phone book and called him.

"I'm thrilled to hear from you! Can you come over this evening at about 7 and listen to my string quartet rehearse? I can't wait to hear about your experiences in London." With his directions I had no difficulty taking the subway and finding his apartment in a brownstone building on West 86th Street. As I approached the apartment I could hear the strains of a Beethoven quartet in the midst of a fortissimo. No one heard my knock at the door, so I tried the knob and the door opened. I walked in very quietly. There on a large sofa were three very attractive young ladies who were listening intently to the music making of the four men on the other side of the room.

Sterling spotted me and stopped playing. He put his cello down and came over to me and gave me an embrace that was more like a bear hug. In the years since I had last seen him he had added many pounds to his once elegant frame and was now a giant of a man in all directions.

"You found your way," he said with the same contagious smile I remembered well. "You look great with your rosy English complexion."

Playing the viola was a rather handsome young man named Milton Katims. He played beautifully but I was disturbed by his take-charge attitude. The three other performers were clearly talented professionals but he kept interrupting the flow of the music to make suggestions about phrasing, bowing, dynamics, and tempo. By the time they had finished rehearsing I was convinced that this viola-player was one of the most conceited men I had ever met!

After attending several more rehearsals of the Arion String Quartet (the two violinists were Harry Farbman and Bernard Robbins) I discovered that the dictatorial Milton Katims was nothing like that at all. He was actually quite shy. Was it music making that produced a Dr. Jekyll-and-Mr.Hyde in him? Maybe Congreve had it

The Katims on delayed honeymoon – cruising from San Francisco to New York via the Panama Canal

Virginia in betweeen tour concerts, in the garden of their Jamaica home, circa 1947

backwards when he intoned that "Music has charms to soothe a savage breast, to soften rocks, or bend a knotted oak." I wonder why the old English dramatist said nothing about what music does to the person who produces it.

One day a very reserved and quiet Milton asked me, hesitatingly, if he could take me to dinner and the theater afterward. Since my opinion of him had warmed dramatically, I said "Yes." He lived uptown and I downtown, so we arranged to meet in front of Carnegie Hall on West 57th Street. I arrived in a long gown and silver slippers since I had been accustomed to dressing for dinner each night at Lady Vestey's. On the subway ride I had been the object of considerable staring and whispering.

Milton, no captive of polite British society, was waiting for me and I gulped when I saw him. He was wearing a bright-blue T-shirt and casual clothes. I said nothing but thought: "Oh, well, just another New York musician!" He took my arm and guided me down the street to, what else, the Automat. I was embarrassed but tried to hide it. My mind was shouting: "All these assorted characters who are staring at me must think I am going to Carnegie Hall to give a concert! So let 'em!"

After the dinner (?!), we went to the theater, all right. A movie. It was my initiation into a small segment of the inner Milton Katims. How he loved movies! Good or bad. He does to this day. One date led to another and many of them were to concerts, of course. We also "cruised" often on the Staten Island Ferry (the fare was 5 or 10 cents). But through it all, Milton rarely talked. I mean no mind-exploring conversations or even thought-trading. He was sweet, gentle, kind, and seemed to have the disposition of a saint. Maybe the fault was mine. I still bore the strong influence of my London experience and may have put him off with my ersatz English accent. I had not told Milton that I had very recently been engaged to an Englishman who was an executive with the Blue Star Lines, and that it was a brief romance that didn't take. I also didn't tell Milton that I had always hoped to marry a musician because of my love for music and my deep affection for my violinist brother, Harvey. (How I adored my big brother who had been my musical inspiration throughout my growing-up years.)

Now I had met an enormously gifted violist. Was he "my musician" and should he be my choice of a lifetime partner? The next time we took the Staten Island Ferry - after more than a dozen such trips - I waited patiently to hear some words of endearment from my bashful violist. Hearing none and trusting my intuition, I took matters into my own hands.

"Milton, I think we should get married." There. I said it, and I was glad.

Instead of the shy, reserved, or at least shocked response I expected, he said almost nonchalantly, "OK. When?"

"How about tomorrow?" I blurted out, no longer worried about how it sounded. Besides, I wasn't going to give him a chance to back out. My mind turned on a picture of my marvelous Mom, who would always say after each date I had: "Marry him. He's a nice boy."

The next day we went to City Hall and obtained a marriage license. On an impulse I said, "OK. Let's elope to Greenwich. It's a beautiful town. So romantic."

What I didn't tell him was that I mistakenly thought that getting a divorce in Connecticut would be easier than getting one in Manhattan, if needed. It was noon and we drove through beautiful scenery to Greenwich, checking in at a lovely inn. Milton found a Justice of the Peace who told him that she would be free in a few moments. Suddenly I felt a wave of doubt so I retreated to the ladies' room to think things over. Sitting on the throne, I meditated:

"Is this what I want to do? I respect this man for his wonderful viola playing. We have music and careers in common. He is kind to me and he is very handsome. But can I awaken the sleeping giant within him?"

My painful reverie was interrupted by someone banging on the door. It was Milton and was he in a state!

"Come on, let's go. The Justice of the Peace has another couple waiting!"

When I saw the J.P., an enormously overweight, completely unromantic woman who was to perform this most important ceremony of our lives – this quickie wedding! I almost backed out. But the Justice was all business. She would have none of my delaying tactics.

"Do you take this woman? Do you take this man? That will be ten dollars, please." Maybe that's what I needed - a martial Brunnhilde who would brook no procrastination. There. The deed was done. Milton and I embraced and he kissed me without stopping for what seemed like five minutes. The J.P. was long gone. She had no time for these five-minute romances.

At the inn the reservations clerk escorted us to our room where he had placed a huge bouquet of flowers on the table next to the bed. After a warm handshake and good wishes he left. I looked at Milton and he looked at me. On what must have been a Freudian impulse, I said, "Did you notice the movie theater as we came into town? There's a good film there. Let's see if they have a matinee."

We jumped back into our jalopy. Yes, there was a matinee. And there we were sitting in a movie house on our wedding day. Now ordinarily when you go to a movie with Milton he is so completely absorbed in what is happening on the screen that you could drop dead next to him and he wouldn't notice. This time, however, the film had been running only a short time when he began to squirm and blurted out:

"Come on let's get out of here." And it wasn't such a bad movie, either.

We returned to the inn, had a martini, and went to bed early. Very early!

The next day, exhausted, we headed back to New York and checked into a hotel near Carnegie Hall, naturally. Milton had a quartet concert to play that night at Columbia University and he left for a rehearsal. I took a subway down to Klein's on Union Square and bought a white satin wedding gown, with a train, yet!!! I think it cost $25. I wore it that night, and, holding up the train with one hand, arrived at the concert hall, found a seat and immediately became completely absorbed in the music.

Milton and Virginia Katims

After the concert Milton came for me, took my hand and led me into the artists' Green Room. I had met the members of his family on previous occasions, but this gathering was different. I was now a Katims and enjoyed a different status. His entire family was there. I clung to Milton as he led me to his mother.

"Mom, I want you to meet your new daughter-in-law."

She didn't say a word but took my arm and pulled me into a small dressing room adjoining the artists' room. Mama had only one quick question for me, "Do you believe in circumcision?"

Unfazed, I quickly answered, "Of course, my two brothers were circumcised." That was it. Dear God, I thought, how romantic are things going to get in La Famille Katims?

We rented an apartment at 315 West 57th Street, but we had no furniture. Milton said, "Let's go to a hotel until we get our place furnished. I'll get a room at the Hotel Taft."

"Darling, ask for a room with a large double bed. You register alone and later on I'll bring my things and join you. That way, we'll have to pay for only one person."

I thought my idea was brilliant. That night after I went to a movie I phoned Milton and he gave me his room number. I went to the elevator as quietly as I could and joined him in the room. We were comfortably settled in bed when we heard a loud knock at the door. It was the hotel detective. Through the door, he asked:

"Are you entertaining a woman in there?" I fled to the bathroom as Milton opened the door. He tried to persuade the detective that nothing was wrong. I couldn't stand it any more. Opening the bathroom door, I pleaded, "But we're married!"

"Lady, I couldn't care less. You owe the hotel another $5."

As I came to know my mother-in-law, I began to love and respect her. She was incredibly gifted but a bit "off the wall," too. I suppose talented people have a right to be.

The Pleasure Was Ours

But God, dear God, in spite of the interesting lives Milton and I embarked upon, one terrible thing intruded (and still does). Dear God, I married a Democrat!

Milton: When Sterling Hunkins, the Arion String Quartet's cellist, told us he had invited one of his former students to come to our rehearsal, little did I realize how much that visit would affect my future, my whole life. He said very little about the young cellist except to tell us she had just arrived in New York after a year's study at the Royal College of Music in London and was now on her way back to her home in San Francisco.

When Virginia Peterson walked into our rehearsal room the next day my mouth fell open in unabashed admiration. She was the most angelically beautiful young woman I had ever seen. I must add that she was also the healthiest looking angel I had ever seen. When she sat down on the couch I was sure I heard it groan as it sagged under the weight of her 180+ pounds. Her year at Lady Vestey's in London had certainly been a carnival of food, as she later confessed to me.

Although I was mightily attracted to this beautiful young cellist, I made no advances because I assumed she was Sterling's girlfriend. (Believe it or not, there is honor among musicians) I kept my hormones in check! In time however, I discovered that she and Sterling were just good friends. I quickly unleashed those hormones!

Sterling and I persuaded Virginia to delay her return to San Francisco, to stay in New York to continue her studies. With a severely limited amount of money she was eating sparingly and rapidly losing weight. She was fast becoming slim and trim and as her weight went down my interest went up. I finally summoned up enough courage to invite her to dinner.

When I met her in front of Carnegie Hall I was not surprised to find her wearing a long gown. She had told me about her very proper formal-dress dinners at Lady Vestey's. I'm not proud of the fact that I took the beautifully gowned young lady to the Automat on our first date, but, after all, my financial resources were severely limited too.

Milton and Virginia Katims

My experience with girls was even more limited. That doesn't mean that I hadn't had my share of puppy love and college days (and nights) of necking. I wasn't so busy practicing and studying scores that I had no time for sex. God knows I had all of the requisite male yearnings. (My favorite Greek myth has always been the one about the race of perfect beings who incurred the wrath and jealousy of the gods. The gods cut them into two parts, one half male and the other female. Ever since, as mythology has it, each half has striven to be joined to the other half in order to recreate that original perfect being.)

After my first and potentially disastrous dinner date with Virginia she filled my mind all day, every day, as well as my dreams at night. I wanted to be with her, to touch her, to tell her how she had captured my heart and soul. However, the sad truth is that when I was with her I was tongue-tied. Her beauty and charm were such that my mind shorted out, refusing to function. I couldn't think of a single thing to say. She must have thought I was a dumb mute, with the accent on "dumb." All the brilliant words and phrases I had planned remained in the planning stage. I desperately needed a Cyrano to plead my case.

One star-filled evening I invited Virginia to take a drive with me in my new pre-owned Model A convertible. We drove across the George Washington Bridge and parked at the edge of the Palisades looking down at the Hudson River and across at the myriad twinkling lights of Manhattan. Can anyone conjure up a more romantic setting? But my muse wasn't merely out to lunch - she was on sabbatical. I couldn't think of a thing to say,

We sat in the car for almost two hours and I did nothing but gaze longingly at this beautiful vision like a lovesick dummy. Although I was dying to touch her, I didn't even reach for her hand. (If I had she would have probably given me her right hand because she was very self-conscious of the large calluses on the fingers of her left hand due to her years of cello playing.) It's a wonder that she ever went out with me again.

The Pleasure Was Ours

You'd think that I would have learned from the experience. But no. The following week we went for a walk in Central Park and, although I did hold her hand and I did find my voice. I'm embarrassed to confess what I talked about. I told her in great detail about the geology course I had taken in college – a course which enabled me to identify the rocks in the park – Manhattan schist! I should have been identifying the rocks in my head.

Virginia at an evening of chamber music

Chapter 4
Marriage Knot in Greenwich

Virginia: With Milton's career as a violist and conductor rising fast, it was time for me to tend to my own career in New York. To establish myself and also to earn some much needed income, I began playing concerts in the schools. I loved playing for children and if I could beguile them with good music and some interesting words about what we were doing, I felt that I could be helping them become fans of classical music.

The school engagements had been obtained for me by Hans Letz, who was a fine violin teacher at the Juilliard School of Music. I had met him when I auditioned for Felix Salmond, the great English cellist who offered me a scholarship when he heard me play. "You play like a Gypsy," the sedate cellist said with, I thought, admiration. After giving some thought to the scholarship offer, I decided that it wasn't more study I wanted, but to get started on my career playing cello professionally. When Letz discovered that I adored performing for children, he secured me a fine contract playing school concerts. I was grateful to him.

Milton and Virginia Katims

One day, soon after Milton and I had tied the knot, I decided to try out for the Naumberg. The winner would be offered a New York recital, all expenses paid, plus an opportunity to secure a professional manager and thus open the way to booking concert engagements throughout the U.S. As I walked onstage at Carnegie Hall, where the auditions were held, I took a quick look at the judges. One of them was Hans Letz. When I saw him, I thought, "Wow! This is going to be a cinch!" I thought all had gone quite well when I played the first two movements of the "Dvorak Cello Concerto." Then, to my dismay, the judges asked me to play the last movement and I had to confess I hadn't memorized it. In spite of the presence of my "friend," I received only an "honorable mention." The judges handed me my critiques. Only one of them was glowing. The others called me "very gifted, but unprepared." They were right.

All was not lost, however. My experience with school concerts led to an audition, along with three other fine young women musicians, for C.A.M.I. (Columbia Artists Management, Inc.), the largest and best known of the concert agencies in New York. Ward French, former president of C.A.M.I., had organized Community Concerts under the C.A.M.I. banner, concentrating on smaller towns in the U.S. and Canada. Many of the artists who performed on that circuit were at the height of their careers and still found time to tour for Community Concerts.

Those years in New York provided me with many great memories. One of them was the night I was engaged to play at the Waldorf Astoria Hotel as soloist with the Mendelssohn Choral Society. After the concert a lovely lady, who was well along in years, came backstage. She introduced herself to me and invited me to play a concert in her home with her private organist as accompanist. Of course, I accepted immediately and thanked her warmly. She was Alta Rockefeller Prentice, of the famous American family.

I performed for Mrs. Prentice at her musicales for the next several years, both in her Manhattan home next to what is now the Modern Museum of Art, and at the

The glamorous Bary Ensemble –
Virginia (cello), Mary Becker (violin), Lorna Wren (flute) and Gertrude Bary (piano)

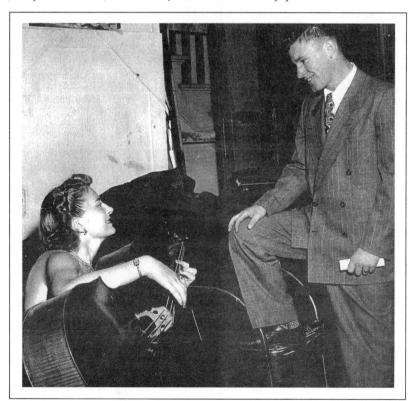

Virginia,
after a concert,
with admiring
young fan

Rockefeller summer estate in Williamstown, Massachusetts. Her husband, a very conservative lawyer, insisted that I was not to wear any lipstick when I performed, but Mrs. Prentice was not so stodgy and had no such hang-ups.

She was very kind and considerate and always wanted to do things to help my career. After one of the musicales she asked if there were "something special" she could do for me. I told her she already had. She reminded me that I had once mentioned to her that I longed to buy the cello I was playing, an instrument I had borrowed from Mischa Schneider, cellist of the Budapest String Quartet. Mrs. Prentice asked me to find out what the cello would cost. I did so and she bought it for me! It was a Grancino, a beautiful cello with a mellow, rich tone. She couldn't have given me a finer gift, and I thanked her again and again until she asked me to "hush."

Mrs. Prentice knew me as Miss Virginia Peterson. I had never told her I was married because I feared she would lose interest and stop inviting me to play at her musicales. Milton laughed at my little secret and shook his head in disbelief. Several months later Nature took a hand in revealing my little secret. It was a warm day in early summer. I was in the third month of my pregnancy and playing at the Rockefeller summer estate, when I suddenly became very nauseated. I'd been playing Saint Saens' "The Swan." What else? The bird started to sink as I slumped to the floor in a faint. A butler hurried to assist me and guided me into the adjoining library to recover. Mrs. Prentice came in, alarmed.

"Miss Peterson, what seems to be the matter?"

Not only had I not told her I was married, here I was pregnant. In a panic, I improvised while holding my stomach.

"Uh, oh, uh, I think I must have a little tumor."

"Oh, you poor thing. Now, let me see. Yes. I'll have my car call for you on Monday morning and we will take you right up to our hospital, Presbyterian Hospital, and we will have that little tumor removed!"

Dear God, what was I to do? I had made a terrible mess of things. The only thing left for me to do was tell her the truth.

"Mrs. Prentice, I don't know how to tell you this. You've been so wonderfully kind and generous to me, but I have to tell you that I am married and also pregnant."

I don't know which bit of news bothered her more, but she looked perplexed and wounded, looking first into my eyes, then at my figure, which, at three months, showed no sign of the impending event. Then, as if she had thought it all out, she gave me a brief hug and said, weakly,

"I must see to my guests," and left the room.

The chauffeur drove me back to New York. I never felt so shabby in my entire life! As soon as I was home, I wrote her a heartfelt letter of apology and asked her to forgive me. She responded with a gracious, but very brief, note. I was never engaged to play for her again.

Our son Peter was born on Pearl Harbor Day, December 7th, 1941, at exactly the same moment the Japanese were bombing Pearl Harbor. All of this may sound to some like a footnote reference to history, but to me the event was a wondrous miracle.

During the summer I often played trio engagements at beautiful resorts in Pennsylvania's Poconos. My pianist, Paul Sargent, was a fine musician, very dependable, clean-cut, and always well-dressed. Each summer we engaged a different violinist. Early on I became aware that after each concert Paul seemed to be surrounded by good-looking, older gentlemen. One was an athletic director from a nearby college. Others were prominent businessmen. To me they all seemed to have a really great love of the piano. I finally realized that it was Paul they loved!

I found the national concert trail rewarding and exciting. The Bary Ensemble, with which I toured under the auspices of Community Concerts, was organized by Gertrude Bary, a stunning, gray-haired woman, a gifted pianist from Germany. She had studied with Edwin Fischer. Our violinist, Mary Becker, an attractive brunette, had been a pupil of Albert Spaulding and Paul Kochanski. Red-haired and equally attractive Lorna Wren, our flutist, had studied with Georges Barrere. I, the blonde in the group, had studied with Sir Ivor James and Alfred Wallenstein.

Our Bary Ensemble was so popular we could have toured the year 'round. We played solos, trios, and piano quartets and ended each program with light pieces designed to send our audiences home in a happy mood. And it worked like a charm! Alas, I was the only married one with small children at home and it was a situation that caused me to feel great guilt. Gertrude was married to a doctor, but her sons were in college, leaving her all the time she needed. Mary and Lorna were both divorced and made it quite clear they were "down" on all men. I was the only one who had to make elaborate plans to care for my two offspring whenever I went on tour, and being away from them made me miserable much of the time. On the other hand, the touring finally gave me a chance to find out who I truly was as a musician. The reviews of our concerts were especially kind to me and to my artistry as a cellist. Even my personal appearance drew praise. It was all very rewarding and helped soften the pain of being away from my children.

We performed mostly in relatively small towns, but many of them boasted a university or college. Most of the time our accommodations were not quite up to Waldorf Astoria standards. Mary would take a look at a dingy hotel lobby and say to Gertie, "A mousetrap, I promise you." She was invariably right, as we discovered on arriving in our rooms.

One particular experience stands out in my mind, It was in Sylacauga, Alabama, and we had been booked into an extremely small rundown hotel. My room was dingy. Oh well, no matter. I decided to relax and forget about it because we wouldn't be there long. At least my accommodations included a bathroom. That's what I needed: a nice warm bath. I was soaking my tired body and enjoying myself when I opened my eyes and idly looked upward. Peering through a wire transom, which probably connected my bathroom with the one next door, was a man looking down at me. He was apparently enjoying himself as much as I had been enjoying my bath – 'til now. I slithered out of the tub, grabbed a towel, reached for the light to turn it off, and rushed to the phone.

"I've been using the tub," I reported to the front desk angrily, "and there's a man watching me through the transom!"

"Oh, don't mind him," the desk clerk said nonchalantly, "that's Mr. Goldberg. He's one of our permanent guests. He is not a transient."

I couldn't believe what I had heard. Suppose someone knocked on my door in the dead of night. Was I supposed to open it and ask whether the knocker was a permanent guest or a transient?

The voyeuristic Mr. Goldberg aside, the Sylacauga audience was marvelous and gave us an ovation. Afterward, a gentleman came backstage and told me he had many of the cello recordings of Pablo Casals. I was impressed –until he spoiled it all by saying, "It was fascinating for me to watch the muscles of your chest jump as you played!" I had worn a strapless evening gown. He may have been amused. I was not. I was disappointed that he hadn't mentioned my playing at all!

A concert I remember well was one we played in the nuclear city of Los Alamos, New Mexico. Our audience included many physicists, chemists, and engineers, all brilliant men and women who evidently knew the classical music repertoire well. A very attractive man met us at the Santa Fe airport to drive us to a Los Alamos hotel. I'm usually impressed more by brains than looks in a man, but this fellow had both. He seemed to ignore my colleagues. He introduced himself,

"My name is Rector. I'll be by at 7:20 to escort you to the concert."

Later, bathed, practiced, and dressed, I rode down in the elevator. All afternoon, I had told myself,

"When you see him again, to remember his name. Just think of a church. Yes, a church."

49

Milton and Virginia Katims

I swept out of the elevator and there he was in full dress and even handsomer than I had remembered. I concentrated. Just think of a church. A church.

Beaming, I said to him, "Good evening, Mr. Sexton."

He corrected me politely. Embarrassed, I said to myself, biting my lip, "Thanks a bunch, Mr. Freud!"

No matter how difficult the travel conditions, how small or unkempt the hotel accommodations, or how rotten the weather, we always felt it was immensely worthwhile when we played a concert. Performing for audiences had another important advantage for me, it helped subdue my guilt feelings over my frequent absences from my family. My five-year-old son, Peter, didn't realize it, but he contributed to my guilt feelings with letters like this one:

"Dear Mummy, I am so happy you are coming home Saturday. When you come home, we will kiss and have fun. I learnt to play on the piano an Indian chief peace, and I can play it by hart. The first night you come home, can we sit at the table with the candles. I hope you will never go away again."

He didn't realize what a remarkable letter-writer he was at only five, but I almost wished he weren't. After one of his notes, I wanted to pack up and head for home. I restrained myself, of course, but I would lie awake afterward loathing myself and cursing my ambition. Thank God for the music that sustained me.

When I finally returned home after a long tour, the thrill was indescribable. I became the perfect mother, the perfect housekeeper, and the perfect wife – for a while. Then, particularly when I was doing something like scrubbing the bathroom, vacuuming, or cleaning the kitchen, I would stop and ask myself, "Why am I here doing this when I could be playing beautiful music for crowds of people somewhere in this vast land?" I would shake my head slowly, realizing that I was caught in the trap set for herself by the modern professional woman who wants both a career and a family, and can never really make a choice. Perhaps she shouldn't have to?

The Pleasure Was Ours

So many times my mind brings back vivid pictures of what my musical life with the Bary Ensemble was — having *Life* magazine follow us on several concert dates, as if we were world celebrities; enjoying a wonderful Texas breakfast at the home of former Vice President John Nance Garner; having water glasses full of bourbon at our place settings (at 10 in the morning!); forgetting to turn off the bathtub faucet in my hotel room in Pittsburgh one night in my hurry to go down to dinner and later discovering, to my horror, that my concert gown, which was steaming, was now drenched because it apparently had fallen off the hanger and into the tub, and trying to hitch-hike a la Claudette Colbert (in "A Night to Remember") while lugging my heavy cello down a highway when our bus broke down in the midst of a dust storm in Arizona. For better or worse, these adventures, plus my music and my family, were what sustained me.

If I were in a complaining mood while on the road or at home, it wouldn't take much to shift gears and find a silver lining. For example, I would sometimes receive a letter from a fan that would bring out the sun, like this one from a music lover after a concert and a party at his home:

"Dear Heart, Your playing enchanted me. Is that what causes pounding of the heart, shaking of my pen, and reeling of the brain? Or have I fallen in love?"

I didn't care if he meant it or if he was just a kook. Letters like that were a balm to my ego and served as worthy antidotes that I could retrieve and re-read whenever my ever-loving spouse yelled at me!

Peter, Virginia, Pam and Milton at the LaJolla Beach & Tennis Club

Chapter 5
Milton Remembers Toscanini

Milton: Arturo Toscanini, the most wonderful maestro of them all, had a tremendous influence on me as a musician and as a conductor. For me, the title of Maestro is synonymous with his name and belongs to him alone, so profound was his impact on music – and on me.

As a schoolboy I frequently attended concerts by the New York Philharmonic when Toscanini was its conductor in the glory years of the late 1920s and early 1930s. My sister Frances and I had seats in the top balcony of Carnegie Hall (the Family Circle). From that viewpoint, Maestro Toscanini and the orchestra were about the size of a 9-inch television screen. When I grew a bit older and had been studying the violin a few years, I would sneak into Carnegie Hall when I knew Toscanini would be rehearsing the orchestra. I would lie very quietly on my stomach in a box just left of the stage, so that I could hear everything Maestro said.

One of my many vivid memories is of a rehearsal of the Beethoven Ninth with Toscanini singing at the top of his lungs. In the fourth and fifth measures of letter A in the first movement, the first violins and the violas have a downward rushing passage. When the players didn't give him the furious quality he wanted, he shouted, "Leone! Leone!" (like lions). At the time I wondered why I had bothered to find a hiding place near the stage. I could have heard his roaring voice up in the top balcony. Even in later years, when he was in his 70s and 80s, I was impressed by the tremendous voice that emerged from this short, barrel-chested man.

My mother and sister sang in the chorus of the Schola Cantorum, which was engaged by the N.Y. Philharmonic for such choral works as the Verdi Requiem and the Beethoven Ninth, conducted by Toscanini. After a rehearsal I would hang on every word describing their experience. I remember clearly one special instruction Maestro gave the chorus. He asked them to sing absolutely pianissimo (extremely soft), but to pronounce every word fortissimo (very, very loud). Adding to their enthusiastic comments about the rehearsal, my father would report on another aspect of the experience. He, like a stage door Johnny, would remain in the anteroom while the chorus began the rehearsal under the direction of Hans Lange, assistant conductor of the Philharmonic. When Maestro Toscanini arrived my father would watch him pause in front of a large mirror before going into the rehearsal. He wanted to make sure that his coiffure was just right.

For years I had been watching Maestro from the back and from the side. Now I wanted to see him as his musicians saw him. Little did I know that in just a few years I would have that opportunity – that my dream would be realized. I tried to sneak in and substitute for an absent tenor at one Sunday afternoon performance of the Beethoven 9th, but the secretary of the chorus spotted me and firmly escorted me off the stage. Fortunately, she didn't do a complete job and throw me out of the hall. When the performance began, I stood in the wings, an ideal spot from which to watch and listen.

What a revelation! Toscanini's face was electrifying. Every facet of the music, every fleeting emotion seemed to be reflected in that photogenic face – his expressive mouth and those active, piercing eyes glancing quickly at a player or a section of the orchestra, not when the players and chorus played and sang, but just before they played and sang. It was clearly his intention not simply to give them a cue, for which there was usually no need, but to guide the way they were to play and sing. The musicians and singers couldn't help but perform with the special quality desired by the "Old Man," as he was called with affection and respect – and perhaps a bit of fear, as well. It seemed impossible for one man to have his eyes and ears directed to so many places at one time.

Sitting way up in the top balcony for so many of his performances, I was impressed in a number of ways. The visual elements were unforgettable: his fluid use of the baton, the expressive control of dynamics with his left hand (its unique functions lost on so many conductors today), and the meaningful twists and turns of the upper half of his body. I felt that I could literally hear the music in the flow of his baton, as if he were choreographing it. If the orchestra were suddenly muted I felt that I still would have been able to hear the music.

I think I appreciated most his sensitive molding of phrases, the extraordinary orchestral balance and the ensemble he achieved, and over all, the tremendous dramatic, dynamic quality of his electrically charged performances. However, a more mature and complete appreciation of what I was responding to instinctively and with admiration did not come until years later, when I began to play viola with him and was also striving, as a conductor, to achieve the same goals.

I had never met Toscanini before I began to play in the NBC Symphony, the orchestra that had been created by Gen. Sarnoff expressly to take advantage of Maestro's genius. For several years I had been solo violist and assistant conductor at WOR, Mutual Broadcasting System. At the same time I played in a string quartet with violinists Erica Morini and Joseph Gingold and cellist Frank Miller. Erica was a celebrated concert violinist and Joe and Frank were members of the NBC Symphony, the former as assistant concertmaster and the latter as solo cellist.

Milton and Virginia Katims

One evening after a quartet session in Erica's apartment on Park Avenue, Gingold told me that British violist, William Primrose, had just resigned from the orchestra to pursue his solo career. He suggested that if I really wanted to learn something about conducting, I should replace him at the first desk of the viola section, right in front of that fantastic "Old Man." I heartily agreed! The next day I called H. Leopold Spitalny, the orchestra's personnel manager, to apply for the Primrose chair. He promised to let me know when I could play an audition for Toscanini.

I was a nervous wreck as I waited for his call. The very next day Spitalny phoned to tell me that the chair was mine! When I asked him about auditioning for Maestro, he told me that I had already played for him! For a couple of years I had been playing a series of Sunday afternoon viola-piano recitals on WOR with pianist Milton Kaye. Maestro had been listening to the broadcasts. He knew my name and my playing. There was no need for an audition. He wanted me to join his orchestra.

Before the first rehearsal that fall, I was sitting beside Carlton Cooley, principal violist at the first desk of the viola section, waiting expectantly and excitedly for Maestro to appear. When he stepped on the podium at precisely 10 A.M. I was overwhelmed – not only by the realization that I was about to play with my idol at long last, but by the overpowering scent of strong Italian cologne with which he had evidently doused himself. It didn't take me long to learn that the cologne had a specific purpose. When he conducted, Toscanini perspired profusely; and, being a very fastidious person, he had a great need for the cologne, and plenty of it. At the end of each rehearsal there was a large wet spot on the stage in front of him.

In the 11 years I played with Toscanini, I never knew what the back of my chair felt like (I was always sitting on the front edge), and I never lost my fascination for the way large beads of sweat would form high on his forehead, roll slowly down, hang for a moment or two at the end of his nose, then silently drop to the floor. Sometimes the perspiration would get into his eyes and sting. He would rub his eyes until they were red with irritation. Maestro's son, Walter, who devoted his life to serving his father, was always nearby. He neatly solved the stinging eye problem by covering his father's eyebrows with mustache wax. He also used it to form a protective bridge just above Maestro's nose. After that, the beads of sweat would bypass his eyes and flow harmlessly down his cheeks. Immediately after rehearsals and concerts, Maestro would slip into a terrycloth robe, and if he hadn't had time to apply his powerful cologne, he would be extremely embarrassed if anyone came too close to him.

Although my first olfactory contact with Maestro's strong cologne had me reeling, I quickly recovered and learned to take it in stride. I found from the very beginning that I didn't have time to be nervous playing with this legendary conductor. I was so absorbed and excited to be making music with him that I felt as if I had been playing with him all my life. His positive way of bringing the notes on the printed page to life was so persuasive and so perfectly right for me that I felt compelled (very willingly) to follow his every wish.

Toscanini had the uncanny ability to draw the best performance out of his musicians. I remember Harry Berv, one of the three brothers playing French horn, telling me that two or three bars before an entrance he would look up and find Maestro looking directly at him. Before he realized it, he was playing, almost as if some unseen hand had reached out and had drawn the music from his instrument. Don't ask me to explain it. I can't.

Dr. Isadore Lattman, a friend of mine and also a close friend of Toscanini's, said of him, "Toscanini is a biological sport, a freak of nature."

I would add that Maestro was one of those rare men with tremendous, personal magnetism, men that come along only once in centuries. Great religious leaders like Jesus and Moses, as well as military geniuses like Napoleon and Alexander the Great, must have had it. When Toscanini stepped on the podium and lifted his baton I couldn't help but feel the power of that magnetism. Those piercing eyes and his entire being and regal bearing, as he began to conduct, persuaded us to play precisely as he wished.

Milton and Virginia Katims

One of my friends, a psychiatrist, tried to explain it by saying that we were in a trance of the Maestro's making and that we loved every minute of it. I reject this Svengali explanation. For me, he was simply a great musician with an instinctive feeling and understanding of the music, which he translated instinctively into the ultimate art of conducting. There was never any question of our complying with his musical will. We were quite aware and quite willing. He was able not only to draw the best from us and his soloists, but had the unique ability to inspire us to perform over our heads.

The Toscanini genius had many components. He used every trick in the book (and a number that were not in the book) to achieve the results he wanted. He exhorted, demanded, shouted, cajoled, pleaded, and begged. Once he actually got down on his knees to ask for a musical result he wanted. If such entreaties didn't work, he would resort to browbeating or scornful sarcasm. On one occasion that has become a legend, he desperately wanted a certain passage played extremely softly, pianisisimo.

"Play it," he said, "as if it's coming from Brooklyn."

We were once rehearsing a work by Debussy, and Maestro wanted a particular passage to have an ethereal quality. Unable to express himself adequately with words, he reached into his pocket to pull out a very large, white, silk handkerchief. He tossed it into the air, and, as it floated slowly and gently to the floor, he said, "Comme ca."

His French was almost as good as his Italian. Whatever language he used, his meaning was always clear, even his limited English. Toscanini rarely, if ever, resorted to a wordy analysis of what he wanted. His approach to music was in no way cerebral; it was completely instinctive. He also felt that he should be able to achieve everything he sought through his conducting and was very self-critical if he failed. In most instances he would resort to singing a phrase. Despite his very croaky voice, his musicality was unmistakable, and we couldn't help but understand his musical wishes. But he didn't sing only at rehearsals, he also sang during performances.

The Beau Brummel of the Baton

*Acolyte and the
Master in the
latter's studio
at NBC*

Milton and Virginia Katims

At the end of one RCA recording session, Richard Mohr, the RCA director, reminded Maestro that he was singing during the taping. Toscanini clapped Mohr on the back, and said, "With Toscanini tenore, you sell more records!"

Maestro never went into the control room during a recording session in order to listen to a playback. He performed this necessary chore in his home at his own leisure. RCA would set up five large speakers in a semi-circle in his study. Toscanini would sit about five or six feet from them and turn the volume up to rock-music levels. He wanted to hear the music exactly the way it sounded to him on the podium. Very often Virginia and I were invited to join him at one of these listening-sessions, and we would sit right behind him. After two or three hours of listening at hyper levels, our heads throbbed and we couldn't hear anything for hours. But Maestro took it all in stride.

Talk about stick technique! This incomparable baton-wielder had a technique that was truly a translation of his instinctive and aural images of the music, a translation from the subjective to the physical objective. Of course, he always gave us an unmistakable downbeat at the beginning of every bar, and we always knew where the beginning and the end of each beat was. But much more important was the way he indicated the style, the character, the quality of the music within his beat.

I'm quite certain that his having been a cellist had much to do with this gift, because it could not be taught. I'm sure he could not explain what he was doing. I'm also quite sure that there is a natural affinity between the use of a bow and a baton (and how often he vibrated on his heart with his left hand, as if it was the fingerboard of his cello). I am also quite certain that the translation of his mental and emotional concepts into visual physical motion was completely instinctive, something which could only be felt. Only once in his studio did Maestro pick up his baton to show me how he conducted a particular passage. He went through the motions for about three beats. Then he stopped, and with a sheepish grin on his face, he said, "Isn't this a silly thing for a grown man to be doing?"

The Pleasure Was Ours

The large number of facets he could express simultaneously was extraordinary. For example, my viola part was usually a subordinate line. Nevertheless, I could almost always discern the rhythm of the viola's voice in some subtle movement Maestro would make – perhaps in the way an elbow was turned, or a shoulder, or his head. It was a phenomenon I could never understand, let alone explain. But it was definitely there.

In one of the very first telecasts in the early 50s, Toscanini conducted a concert performance of Verdi's "Aida." I was offstage conducting the small band and chorus heard in the distance. From where I stood it was impossible to see Toscanini, making it difficult for me to coordinate my offstage beat with his. Without telling Maestro, I asked the director for a small monitor screen and requested that the camera be pointed at Toscanini during the time I had to conduct the offstage band and chorus. Although I knew he had nothing to conduct during my bit, I was sure that he would unconsciously move or twitch in a way that mirrored the music I was conducting. And sure enough he did! I followed him precisely. He never could understand how I was able to follow him so exactly. I never confessed!

Perhaps one of the greatest facets of Toscanini's genius was his ability to make me feel that no matter how often I had played or heard the music at hand –be it the Schubert "Unfinished," the Dvorak "New World," or the Beethoven "Fifth" – this was really the first performance, the first time we were playing or hearing it. His interpretations always had the freshness and spontaneity of a first performance. He was constantly restudying each score, no matter how many times he had conducted it. At the end of the final recording session of the Beethoven "Ninth," Toscanini came over to me and said, "You know, young conductor, I have played this symphony for 50 years – 50 years! – and finally I think I understand something."

Over the years there was much talk about Toscanini's legendary explosions of temper. Yes, they happened. Not often, but they did occur. They came perhaps because his expectations were so high and his demands for results were so great that he lost patience. Or perhaps he knowingly manufactured an explosion in order to achieve the result he sought.

There were a number of occasions when I was convinced that Maestro knew exactly what he was doing when he blew his top. At one rehearsal, after sounding off at the top of his voice for about four or five minutes, he paused to take a breath. Slowly he looked at each of us sitting at the front desks closest to him to see what our reactions were – from Eddy Bachmann and Bernard Robbins (2nd violins), Carlton Cooley and me (violas), Frank Miller and Benar Heifetz (cellos) around to Max Hollander and Mischa Mischakoff (1st violins). Like the rest of us, Max Hollander sat stock still; but because the left end of his upper lip turned up slightly, he gave the impression that he was sneering. Toscanini fixed a very stern glare at him (in complete silence) for what seemed an eternity. Poor Max's face turned beet red! Then Maestro very quietly asked, "Why do you look at me that way? You think I am crazy? No! I am not. I am very sensitive – very intelligent. Do not look at me that way!"

At another rehearsal, in an apparent rage over what we had or had not done to his satisfaction, Maestro broke his baton and threw the pieces on the floor. Then he reached for the score, with the intention of tearing it apart. But he remembered that this particular partitur was one of a kind– extremely rare and almost impossible to obtain. He laid it down very gently.

On the other hand, it is seldom mentioned that Toscanini could also have the patience of Job. If he felt that a player was aware of a mistake and had the musical intelligence to correct it, Maestro would ignore the error. I'll never forget the time I biffed in with a loud wrong entrance, all by myself, during a performance of the Beethoven "Fifth" in Carnegie Hall. Toscanini whirled around and gave me a quick glance. He saw that I was mentally casting about for my kimono, pillow, and sword. He never said a word.

The Pleasure Was Ours

One of Maestro's most fascinating characteristics was the difference in the way he conducted at rehearsals and at performances. He conducted every rehearsal as if it were a performance, with great energy and painstaking attention to every detail.

"This is when we are playing for ourselves," he would say. When the time came for the performance itself, he would conduct in a more laid-back manner, as if he were saying to us, "We've done it all in rehearsal. You know what to do. Now just do it." (Stokowski 's rehearsal behavior was just the reverse. At these sessions he would do practically nothing but read through the music and say very little – just sort of go through the motions. But then at the broadcast he would come to life and produce the kind of exciting performance for which he was justly famous.)

At rehearsals, Toscanini never repeated a passage or a movement merely for the sake of repetition. There had to be a reason. However, on a number of occasions when we were nearing the end of a lengthy work and Maestro felt the need to go back, he would latch on to any pretext to enable him to say, "Da capo! Da capo tutto!" (which meant "go back to the beginning").

On one occasion, we were nearing the end of a rather long symphony (I believe it was the Schubert "C Major" symphony), when the "Old Man" called for a return to the beginning. One of the violinists reacted involuntarily by snorting, perhaps better described as a flatulence of the lips. Toscanini turned quickly in the direction of the insulting sound and screamed, "Who make like a horse?" Dead silence greeted his question.

The two words used most often by Maestro were cantare (sing) and vita (life). It was supremely important that every instrument sing and for the music to throb with life. An enormous amount of kinetic energy propelled his music to its inevitable conclusion. I'm sure that Toscanini had each composition he conducted visualized completely in his mind from beginning to end, not unlike an entire scene that is disclosed to the eye for a couple of seconds by a bolt of lightning during a summer storm.

Some musicians have been critical of Maestro's fast tempos, particularly in his later years. I played with him during those years and I never felt that his tempos were too fast. It was always possible to play every note. With one exception — Wagner's "Ride of the Valkyries." Maestro's tempo did give me some problems. I like the comment made by Oscar Shumsky, one of our great violinists. His definition of a professional violinist is "one who can play the "Ride of the Valkyries" with a straight face."

Another canard is the assertion that Toscanini conducted everything strictly in time, as if with a metronome. Wrong. He conducted with a rubato that was as subtle and natural as breathing. Once when I was discussing a score with him he said of a certain passage, "This must be assolutamente preciso (absolutely precise) like with a metronome. Here, I show you." He reached over, selected the appropriate tempo on his electric metronome, and, after switching it on, began to play the phrase on the piano. But after only a few beats he was no longer with the metronome. He shut it off, exclaiming, "Bah, but you cannot be a machine."

When I began to conduct the NBC Symphony, I had the rare privilege of going over scores with Maestro in the study of his home in Riverdale. On one of my visits I asked him, "After you have carefully examined all of the tangible evidence the composer **has** left you on the printed page, how then do you determine the true tempo, **the tr**ue character of that music?"

"My dear Katims," he replied, "you must rely on your good taste and your musical instinct. If you have, you find. If not, don't make music. Mend shoes!"

Toscanini was very fond of telling me about one of his experiences with Puccini when he was preparing to conduct the world premiere of "Turandot." (If he told me this story once, he must have told it to me a dozen times — but it does bear repeating!) Maestro told me that he had a few questions about some of the passages in the score. He went to the composer's home to get the answers. When he arrived he found that Puccini was not immediately available. While he waited he sat down at the piano **and** played the passages in question. As he finished them he felt Puccini's hand on his shoulder, and the composer said, "Bene, Bene – that is just the way I intended those passages." Toscanini then protested, "But Maestro, there is no crescendo here, no diminuendo there – no ritard here, no accelerando there." "Of course not," retorted Puccini, "if I put all those markings in the score, every damn fool would exaggerate!"

Toscanini attended my rehearsals in NBC's Studio 8H. I had no need of a rearview mirror to let me know when he walked into the hall. Every player in the orchestra sat up a bit straighter and was suddenly a bit more attentive. Can you imagine what it felt like to know that the legendary conductor was there watching and listening to what I was doing with his orchestra? To this day I marvel at my having been able to survive the experience! After one of my rehearsals, Maestro questioned me about the way I had handled a certain passage in Mendelssohn's "Scotch Symphony."

"Maestro," I confessed, "I had some doubts about that section so I listened to an aircheck of your performance of a few years ago."

He interrupted me quickly, obviously way ahead of me. "And I did that?" I nodded.

"If I did that," he said, shaking his head, "I was stupido. Stupido!"

There was one aspect of Maestro's character which lessened his enormous stature for me. He very seldom had any words of praise for any of his colleagues. In fact, he was quite critical of them. (Conductor Guido Cantelli was one notable exception.) Toscanini's fabulous memory served him not only with his music, but enabled him to retain grudges and to remember negative criticism. He was also given to rather vulgar expressions. Fortunately, they were usually in Italian and only a handful of musicians in the orchestra understood them.

Maestro rarely, if ever, had a pleasant word to say about certain other conductors. Very often he referred to them as "Dr. Koussevitzky, Dr. Reiner, Dr. Rodzinski, they are all doctors – I'm a conductor."

Milton and Virginia Katims

One day I received a phone call from a group of New York musicians who had presented the great Spanish cellist, Pablo Casals, with a 16-millimeter movie projector. Toscanini was the first person Casals wanted to see on his screen The group of musicians knew that I not only was close to Maestro, but that I fancied myself as an amateur moviemaker. I was delighted to agree to take movies of Maestro when we visited him the following weekend.

It was a beautifully clear day and I was sure to get some good footage of Toscanini. As usual, Virginia and Maestro were busy comparing memories about the cello. He was recalling and singing music, studies and student concertos that he hadn't seen nor heard in 70 years. As soon as there was a lull in the conversation, I told Maestro about the gift Casals had received and the request he had made. Toscanini acted as if he hadn't heard a word I had said. He went right on with his conversation with Virginia. An hour later I tried again with the same result. This happened once more and I made no further attempt to film him because the afternoon light had faded and it was too late for moviemaking. As we were leaving Maestro was helping Virginia into her coat. Quietly, he said to her, "Casals always said that my Brahms was too fast. No pictures!"

After more than ten glorious years with Maestro Toscanini, I felt that I really knew him rather well. That is, until I read his recently published *The Letters of Arturo Toscanini* (Alfred A. Knopf – 2002). The letters were collected, excellently edited, and translated by Harvey Sachs. What a revelation! I did not realize how well-rounded Maestro was. With few exceptions, we always talked about music, but his letters reveal how familiar he was with so many authors of prose and poetry. His knowledge of painters was extraordinary.

Tocanini's extra-marital activities were well known, but not his prowess at writing wonderfully poetic, love letters. (I would recommend that every young, and ever young, love-filled swains read Maestro's love letters and borrow portions for their own use.)

The Pleasure Was Ours

Although I have already mentioned Maestro's fondness for playing practical jokes on his friends, his letters reveal a delicious sense of humor. One example: At a performance of Wagner's "Tristan & Isolde," after the lengthy passionate love duet, Toscanini turned to his neighbor and said, "If those singers were Italian, they'd have seven children by now."

When he gave this to Milton, Steinberg assured him the cartoon was not of him!
(This particular reprint from the *New Yorker*)

Chapter 6
Virginia's View of the Maestro

Virginia: March 25th, 1947 will remain in my memory as long as I live. I was very much aware that it was Toscanini's birthday, his 80th. That day I was in Woman's Hospital in New York City awaiting the birth of our second child. I hoped with all my heart that this would be the day of her (his?) entry into our world. I decided to phone Maestro and congratulate him.

"Happy birthday," I said, delighted that he had answered the phone himself.

"Ah, Vergeenia," he said, with his totally charming Italian accent that never failed to send shivers down my back. "I'm getting very, very old."

"Nonsense, Maestro. For me and for everyone in the music world you are in the prime of life."

Early that evening my wish was granted and my baby was born. A girl. We had already chosen a name and as soon as I recovered enough, I again phoned.

"Guess what, Maestro. I just had a baby girl and we are going to name her Pamela Artura."

Milton and Virginia Katims

"Cara Vergeenia, why not Arturo?"

"But my dear Maestro, she's a little girl."

He responded quickly, "What's the difference?" Ah, the male ego!

Perhaps with the proliferation of gender-confusing names, Toscanini was ahead of his time, as usual. He agreed happily to become Pamela Artura's godfather. A short time later we received a silver cup inscribed: To the wonderful Pamela Artura, from her loving godfather, Arturo Toscanini. And not long after that he sent the baby a beautiful Alexandra doll, swathed in pink satin and enclosed in a glass case. (A few years earlier he had sent our son, Peter, a miniature Coca Cola machine. How American!)

I had long admired Toscanini, but from a distance. When Milton began playing viola in the NBC Symphony with Maestro that distance shortened considerably. At first my association with the "Old Man" was through my husband. But that changed very quickly as I developed a direct line of communication with Toscanini, whom I worshipped as a conductor and adored as a man. It was a two way street!

Buying a Christmas gift for Maestro Toscanini was always a tremendous challenge. We knew that the attic of his home, Villa Pauline in Riverdale, was filled with gifts. It took all of our most creative thinking to pick things that would not land in that attic. One year we sent him a very large cake with a miniature orchestra of Italian hand-carved musicians set on the top. We knew that gift would not land in the attic because it would have been food for the mice. Another year we managed to get a half dozen positive negatives of photo-portraits of our very photogenic old friend. I laced them on the outside of a large lampshade so that when the lamp was lit, Maestro's photos would spring to life six-fold in all their glory. Since it was a desk lamp, Toscanini had it lit night and day even as sunlight streamed through the windows. How he loved that gift!

The Christmas present for Maestro that we remember with the greatest affection resulted from a newspaper column about Toscanini. It was written by a sports writer. After attending an NBC Symphony rehearsal, the columnist reviewed it in sporting event terms. He ended the column with the comment "And Toscanini is still The Champ!" It triggered our idea to give Maestro a beautiful, pearl-gray, terry cloth, half-robe with large mother-of-pearl buttons. On the little tab buttoned to the breast pocket (intended for initials), we had a friend embroider "The Champ!" It was perfect for use after a rehearsal or concert.

We thought Maestro would get a big kick out of the breast-pocket tab bearing his new title and then discard it as he had so many other gifts. But no! He kept it, and while wearing it in his dressing room after a concert, he would point to it and ask his guests, "What means The Champ?" He knew darned well what it meant.

I'll never forget the first time Milton appeared as guest-conductor of the NBC Symphony. I hadn't slept a wink the night before because of worry that something might go wrong, with an entire nation watching and listening to the telecast. The night of the concert I dressed carefully and with a purpose. I chose a rather décolleté gown because I had the naive idea that if the broadcast didn't go well it might somehow distract Toscanini and take his mind off any glitches that might occur.

I sprayed myself with Ma Griffe cologne and, with my heart beating wildly, I went backstage to be with Milton before the concert. Soon Maestro Toscanini arrived, clucking over my husband like a mother hen, brushing him off, and straightening his tie. Now the entire backstage area reeked of Maestro's ultrastrong Italian cologne. Whenever my mind takes me back to that thrilling evening, my sense of smell does a double-take as the overpowering fragrance of Maestro's cologne returns in full force. And that despite the fact that I myself had on what I thought was pretty potent.

I was amused at the way Toscanini kept hovering over Milton, fussing over him as if he were about to send him off for his first day at school. It was obvious that Milton was enjoying all the attention. He asked, "Maestro, where are you going to sit?"

"I don't have a ticket," he answered guilelessly. I wanted to say, with a chuckle, "Are you kidding?"

I quickly took over. With barely a glance and a nod, I took Toscanini by the arm and led him to front seats in the balcony, explaining to him that these seats were set aside for NBC executives. No problem. However, I wondered if the mixture of our two powerful scents would empty that section in short order. Needless to say, I didn't mention that possibility to Arturo. The broadcast began. After each work, Toscanini would poke the executive sitting next to him and shout so that everyone in the balcony could hear, "Apploud! Apploud!" And they did, too. What a cheerleader! In the dressing room afterwards, he embraced my husband and bravoed him with paternal pride. Milton was thrilled but said, "But Maestro, so many little things happened."

"Ah, caro Milton, something always happens. With me, too."

I wanted to hug him for saying that. So I did. It was a wonderful comment from an artist who was hardest of all on himself, always. Out of the corner of my eye I was delighted to see a friend of ours with a camera shooting pictures of Maestro and Milton. What wonderful mementos these photos would be, I thought. As soon as Maestro left someone tapped our friend on his shoulder and asked,

"Do you always take pictures with the lens cap on?" The response has been censored.

The Toscanini I saw that day backstage and in the concert hall was the Toscanini I knew. I thought of him lovingly, passionately, and with unreserved admiration for almost everything he did as a musician and as a man. I'm sure quite a few other women thought of him passionately, as well. Some let themselves become too emotionally and sometimes physically involved with him. His sexual exploits were no secret. I adored his volatility, his unpredictability, and his penetrating eyes, which when fastened upon me or any other woman made us feel very vulnerable. (It was common knowledge that when his driver Guido dropped him off at the 50th St. entrance to the RCA building, Maestro would walk straight past the elevators to the 49th St. side and take a taxi to the home of his current mistress.)

Of course he could freeze any of his musicians with a glance and create tremendous stress in them, but he honestly believed it was all in the cause of producing perfect performances – or as close to perfection as his critical ear would accept. Toscanini was a supreme actor, bringing his innate sense of drama to each score he touched. I worshipped at his shrine.

Because Maestro and I had built such a strong friendship, he thought nothing of phoning me as early as 4 or 5 in the morning and complaining, "Cara Vergeenia, I cannot szleep. Eeez eempossible for me to szleep." He seemed to be oblivious of the fact that he had roused me from a deep sleep. But instead of protesting or sounding grumpy, I was deeply flattered that he would think of calling me at all. I could well imagine the storm of thoughts churning in his ever active, ingenious mind as he tried to sleep. I'm sure that he had so many notes bouncing around in his brain that there was no way he could find rest.

Toscanini always conducted without a score, at rehearsals and concerts, because he was extremely near-sighted and much too vain to wear his thick-lensed eyeglasses. Fortunately, he had a fantastic photographic memory and didn't need a score, but ironically, he couldn't understand why other conductors felt the need to dispense with a score.

We always enjoyed visiting Maestro's beautiful home in Riverdale, New York. Villa Pauline, named in honor of his wife, boasted a breathtaking view of the Hudson River. It was a three-story Tudor, the lower half faced with brick and the upper half a stucco-and-wood combination. A long impressive circular driveway gave the whole setting a majestic look. The gardens were so beautifully manicured that I was certain Toscanini had an Italian gardener.

The mansion's 28 rooms exuded the aura of an artistic genius like Toscanini, who was always a warm, generous host. He gave many parties in his home for members of his orchestra and for visiting artists. When we dined alone with him in the formal, decidedly Italianate, dining room, we usually had a very Spartan diet of a thick minestrone soup, bread, and cheese, with an occasional glass of wine. It was hardly the hearty menu one might associate with a flamboyant personality like the Maestro of all Maestros.

Surprisingly, Toscanini often answered the door himself when we arrived at Villa Pauline. He was always immaculately dressed, his white hair gleaming and perfectly coiffed. As he embraced me, he invariably included a little pat on my derriere. Ah, let's not forget that ever-present cologne! I was his for the asking. Sheer hero-worship my husband called it. What's a little pat on the rear between friends?

Toscanini and Milton would sit at the piano for hours going over scores, Maestro singing all the while in his cracked voice but always on pitch. He would often motion for me to sit next to him on the piano bench while he played portions of Italian operas, again singing at the top of his voice with all the aplomb, if not the quality of a Pavarotti.

On one occasion we brought our daughter, four year old Pamela Artura, with us to visit her famous godfather. As soon as he learned that she had started playing the piano, he asked her to play for him. Without the slightest hesitation Pam climbed up on the piano bench next to Maestro and started to play "Twinkle, Twinkle, Little Star." Toscanini joined right in playing an accompaniment. Pam immediately stopped playing, pushed his hands off the keyboard, and announced,

"I play alone!" He roared with laughter, gave his godchild a big hug, and said, "Ees necessary to have coraggio to play solo!"

After his performances, especially when the NBC Symphony broadcasts were moved to Carnegie Hall, I would rush back to Maestro's dressing room, often in tears, emotionally choked up. I recall vividly a concert performance of Verdi's "Otello." My eyes were streaming as I waited my turn to congratulate him.

The Pleasure Was Ours

"Maestro, I can't find the words to tell you..." That's as far as I got. He grabbed me and shouted, "Finda them, Cara! Finda them!"

Even the fabulous Toscanini needed recognition and acclaim. And perhaps most important of all, he needed continuing confirmation of his musical gifts. He seemed to adore looking into the tearful, admiring eyes of swooning females – like me.

His rehearsals were never dull, never routine. At times, however, I was embarrassed for him and for the musicians and soloists who were the targets of his fiery temper. At one rehearsal I attended, a rather well-endowed soprano was negotiating a difficult aria. Displeased with the way she sang a phrase, Toscanini stopped the orchestra, rapped on his stand for silence, and said to the hapless singer,

"No! No! No! Tu non capisco? Don't you understand? Ahhhhh." He pointed to his head and said, "If only you had here what you have here!" as he moved his hand to his chest.

The soprano turned beet red, and I blushed for her.

At another rehearsal one of the percussionists made a wrong entrance not once, but three times. Maestro flew into a rage.

"You think I enjoy to conduct? No! I suffer molto troppo. Thees ees 'orreeble day. I hate to conduct!" He paused for a moment, as if waiting for reactions, or perhaps to catch his breath. He then continued, as if to confirm his belief in reincarnation and at the same time punish the musicians with the nastiest thought he could summon, and said, "When I come back in my next-a life, I weel not be condottore. Oh, no! I weel be the concierge of a bordello – and I weel not letta any one of you in!"

I couldn't look at the musicians, for fear of adding to their embarrassment. They dared not breathe during the outburst. In my opinion they didn't deserve the tirade; they had been playing their hearts out and it sounded very good to me. But then, nobody ever hired me to conduct an orchestra. Perhaps, I tried reasoning, Maestro had actually been planning this episode long before the rehearsal and was simply trying it out to keep the players on their toes. I have a hunch the old saying applied to him every day of his life: He was crazy like a fox.

In another telltale incident, Toscanini had gathered together an excellent group of singers for a concert performance of Verdi's "Aida." Everything seemed to be going extremely well and the voices were beautifully matched. Suddenly Toscanini slammed down his baton and stopped the orchestra. He directed a blistering oral assault at the gorgeous prima donna. She tried to interrupt him with, "But Arturo! Arturo!"

"Arturo?" he exploded! "Maestro here! Arturo in bed!"

I wondered if I dared go backstage afterwards. But I dared, and I was careful to sneak into his dressing room very quietly to find out if it was safe. In a couple of minutes Toscanini, doused with his inevitable cologne, came out of his small dressing room in which he had changed, looking cheerful and smiling as if nothing had happened. He was ruddy-cheeked, his eyes sparkling with a completely innocent expression. When he saw me, he extended his arms toward me.

"Ah, Cara Vergeenia. Was good rehearsal, yes?"

Had he forgotten so soon? Of course not. What a superb actor he was!

When watching Maestro Toscanini conduct a concert, one could not fully appreciate the amount of work and sweat that had gone into rehearsals. At concert time he walked slowly from the wings, his myopic eyes fixed on the floor ahead of him, lest he stumble. He was invariably sucking on a hard lemon candy that he'd popped into his mouth just before leaving his dressing room. At times, when there was need for a second candy during the broadcast, Toscanini would wait for the pause between selections and hurriedly sneak the candy from his pocket and pop it into his mouth. It usually happened while Ben Grauer was announcing the next work. In his hurry, sometimes Maestro was not able to take all the paper off the candy. He would not permit that to delay the performance. The result was that he would gradually spit out bits of the wrapping paper while never missing a beat.

The Pleasure Was Ours

Toscanini would mount the podium slowly and carefully, wearing a completely modest and humble expression. He would acknowledge the hysterical applause that always greeted him with a quick brusque bow to the audience. Then, anxious to get started, he would quickly turn to face his orchestra and get down to the business of making music.

Maestro always planted his feet on one spot on the podium and seldom moved during the entire broadcast.. From the waist up, his body language was the language of the music. Unlike many other conductors, he did not go through unnecessary physical contortions. He preferred to let the music speak for itself – or perhaps better phrased, speak through him! He was like a glass prism through whom the light of the composer was refracted.

During the last few years of Toscanini's active career, at the end of each rehearsal and each concert, his personal physician was on hand to check his blood pressure. (That was the doctor whose hobby was making the handsome batons used by the Maestro. Milton treasures the one the "Old Man" gave him.) The amazing aspect of the checking of his blood pressure was that Toscanini could always tell within a point or two, exactly what it was.

One summer, after Milton had performed and recorded at the Casals Festival in the south of France, Toscanini had invited us to visit him on his island in Lago Maggiori in Italy. We drove frantically from the Riviera through the Alps in our wheezing Hillman-Minx. At Pallanza, we were met and taken aboard Maestro's boat for the short trip across the lake to his dock. The heat was oppressive and I wore a strapless pink cotton dress. Our celebrated host, silver hair waving in the gentle breeze, stood on the shore, a welcoming committee of one. He helped us out of the boat, put his arm around me and led me through the magnificent gardens. Extraordinarily colorful blooms were everywhere.

As we moved toward the villa, Maestro nuzzled my shoulder. Oh, that Italian cologne! He positively exuded vitality and vigor. I again wondered how many women must have had sexual fantasies about this man – and I was not exempt. He was truly ageless. For one wild moment I toyed with the notion of smothering him in a passionate embrace, covering his face (that incredible wrinkle-free face even in his 80s) with kisses. But my instinctive behavioral alarm rang out, as it usually did in such moments, and my sense of decorum returned. After all, how could Maestro Toscanini appear before his other guests with lipstick on his smooth face and on that carefully combed and waxed mustache? My enormous respect and admiration for him curbed my momentary ardor.

Maestro guided me up the stairs to a large spacious deck overlooking the lake and was quickly surrounded by the many guests awaiting him. Milton and I began to greet some of the people we knew. Toscanini came over to me and asked, "Cara, you like to have drink?"

"Yes, please," I answered. "May I have a bit of Scotch? I'm so tired of Campari and Cinzano, the only drinks I've had in Europe."

"Ah, Vergeenia, you are like my great friend, Frances Alda. She was a wonderful prima donna. She, too, was alcoholic!"

All I could do was giggle. A correction or explanation would have been useless.

Toscanini was 86 years old when Milton and I sat in the third row in Carnegie Hall, knowing that on this very special night we were to hear his last concert with the NBC Symphony. He had been conducting that incomparable orchestra 17 years. What the eager audience did not know was that the remarkable conductor had already turned in his letter of resignation to the executives at NBC. This was indeed to be his final appearance.

As usual, Carnegie Hall was jammed to the rafters. Maestro Toscanini entered slowly from the wings, head bowed once more, mounted the podium, and barely acknowledged the audience's wild applause before turning to the orchestra. He stood motionless for what seemed an eternity. My heart raced. Was he ill? What thoughts were running through his mind at that moment? Finally, he raised his baton. It was an all-Wagner program and his performance was divine and divinely perfect, at least for me.

However, in the performance of the final work on the program, the "Overture to Tannhauser" and the "Venusberg Music." a slight mishap occurred. Not knowing what had happened, I held my breath. Later, one of the players told us that Toscanini, in a brief memory lapse that was remarkable for him, had beat a three-quarter measure in four/four time. The orchestra, accustomed to absolute perfection from its Maestro, faltered momentarily. Toscanini's hands dropped to his side, his head bowed. But the flow of the music continued as the players took over, the head of each section (particularly Frank Miller, head of the cello section) indicating the beat with his instrument or with some body motion. Almost immediately, Toscanini recovered his composure and resumed conducting.

Had he had a loss of memory, or was he emotionally traumatized by the realization that this was his farewell to his beloved orchestra and to so many years of conducting? The concert ended brilliantly, with a tumultuous ovation from the huge audience. Milton and I felt too depressed by the finality of the concert and did not go backstage. I believe that no one was permitted to enter Toscanini's dressing room that night, in view of what had happened in the concert's finale.

I couldn't get the incident out of my mind. Had he, in fact, had a memory slip, however momentary? After all, at his age, he surely was entitled to forget a measure or two. I finally had to dismiss the "memory lapse" explanation because a week later Maestro conducted a recording session with the orchestra. He was remaking portions of previous recordings and he was in excellent form. Our friends in the orchestra said he was his old ebullient self.

A few weeks later we left for the Pacific Northwest where Milton was to guest-conduct a pair of concerts prior to accepting the post of conductor of the Seattle Symphony. Toscanini remained very much on my mind. Since we were in the Northwest, I thought it would be appropriate to send him one of the region's trademarks, a large salmon. After placing a wing collar and white bow tie around the salmon's "neck" – or whatever passes for a salmon's neck – and a baton under a fin, we had it packed in dry ice. Northwest Airlines was delighted to fly the fish to New York and deliver it to the celebrated Maestro in Riverdale. Then we waited for a response.

It wasn't long in coming. We received a telegram from Maestro's son, Walter. It read: Virginia, you idiot don't you remember? Papa hates fish!

I kicked myself for not remembering. Had we wounded Maestro's feelings at a time when he was so emotionally vulnerable? Had I insulted him by dressing a fish in the accoutrements of a conductor? It was a question that was never answered, and probably didn't need one.

With Milton's position in Seattle finalized, we flew back to New York to bid our beloved friend farewell. This time a maid answered the door and signaled toward the study. We hurried past her to the study where we found the "Old Man" sitting at his desk, his head in his hands. He had never seemed old to us, but now he suddenly was.

"Maestro!" I cried, my arms outstretched to hug him. He stood slowly.

"Cara, do not call me Maestro. I am no longer a Maestro. I am nothing!"

We wept silently. There was no scent of cologne. That was the last time we saw him. He died three years later.

My Favorite Cowboy –
Maestro – 1950

Virginia with The
Maestro on
Isolino, his island
in Lago Maggiori

With Henryk Szeryng and the Royal Philharmonic in London's Albert Hall

Chapter 7
Go West Young Man

Milton: In the early years of my career I made two major decisions. The first was to switch from the violin to the viola because of my ambition to become a conductor. The second was to move from New York to Seattle in the Pacific Northwest.

I needed no coin-toss to make the first decision. Although I had been studying the violin from the age eight until I finished college at age twenty, I didn't consider music as a full-time profession until I became a violist and began pursuing in earnest my dream of being a conductor. As a violist I would learn the alto clef (one of the C clefs) which I would need to read the transposing instruments of the orchestra, like the clarinet and the trumpet. At the same time I would sit almost in the center of the orchestra, with the best view of the conductor and play a part in the middle of the score, allowing me to be more aware of the lines played by the instruments above and below me. (These were the basis of the thinking that motivated my change to the viola) My major as an undergraduate at Columbia University had been psychology. (I've asked my friends never to mention that in front of my wife Virginia, because she would most likely collapse with laughter: Milton, a psychologist?) Without a doubt it was my ability as a violist that opened the doors to my career as a conductor. I never had a moment of doubt about that "big sister" of the string family. It was a case of love at first sound!

My decision to move my little family 3,000 miles across the country was more difficult to make. In New York I was leading an enviably exciting musical life – as principal guest conductor of the incomparable NBC Symphony, as first desk violist with the awe-inspiring Toscanini, and as his assistant, as a member of the New York Piano Quartet (with violinist Alexander Schneider, cellist Frank Miller and pianist Miecio Horszowski), and as the regular guest violist with the Budapest String Quartet. Did I really wish to give up this extraordinary musical life?

These questions kept tormenting me, keeping me awake nights. Should I move from the security of being a staff conductor at NBC to the unknown responsibilities and challenges of guiding the destiny of a regional orchestra in a much smaller city? Should I give up the relative ease of programming for an unseen audience (although the NBC Symphony did have an invited audience) for a situation in which programming had to be crafted with a careful eye on the box-office? Should I give up a situation in which I had no responsibility for the personnel of the orchestra to one in which I would have to act in many diverse capacities – including (as I was to discover later) serving as a marriage counselor?

These and countless other thoughts coursed through my mind as I pondered the prospects. Was I being fair to my wife, a gifted cellist, asking her to give up a busy touring career with Columbia Artists Community Concerts? And what effect might the move have on our two young children, Peter and Pamela?

In the midst of all these whirling questions I recalled the challenge tossed at me by my manager, Arthur Judson, head of Columbia Artists Management. He said, "Milton, anyone can stand on the podium in front of the NBC Symphony, wave a stick at all those wonderful musicians and know that whatever you do they'd

Go West!
To new
musical adventures

Arriving in Seattle–
Peter (11), Pam (7),
Virginia (?), Milton (who's counting?)

sound great! But can you stand before a much lesser group and make them sound good? (I had reason to recall this conversation later on, when Toscanini told me" that "there are no bad orchestras, just bad conductors.") That did it! I decided to accept the challenge!

Of course there were other factors which helped me to decide to accept the Seattle Symphony's offer of a contract. Maestro Toscanini had announced his retirement, and the NBC Symphony was about to be dismantled. I also believed that radio stations would not continue to sustain a large staff orchestra much longer because of the tremendous expense. According to NBC's figures the symphony cost them one million dollars a year (17 million dollars from 1937 to 1954). But, they said nothing about the 32 million dollars earned by Toscanini recordings for RCA, the parent company during the same period. I also feared that the days of serious music live on the air were numbered.

The time was ripe for me to take the leadership of a symphony orchestra of my own.

My guest-conducting so many coast-to-coast broadcasts of the NBC Symphony (52) had brought me to the attention of many cities with orchestras. At least four of them expressed interest in engaging me as their conductor. I chose Seattle because I sensed that it held the most potential for growth. A few guest-conducting visits confirmed my conviction that it would be an ideal city in which to live and an ideal community in which to bring up our children.

Seattle's scenic beauty is hard to beat. It is a heaven-anointed city surrounded by mountains (the Olympics to the west, the Cascades to the east, and glorious Mount Rainier to the south) and blessed by two large bodies of water (Puget Sound to the west and Lake Washington to the east) and beautiful forests, small lakes, and rivers everywhere. If any region in America deserves to be called God's Country, this certainly is it.

A few friends in New York warned me that the Seattle area's legendary rainfall would soon cause us to grow webbed feet. But others assured me that Seattle had fewer inches of rain each year than New York. I checked it, and they were right. Seattleites with or without webbed feet refer to the moisture as "dry rain" and pay no attention to it. I'd say, after years of living and working there, that the Seattle rain is about as dry as a dry martini. No matter. Virginia and I soon joined the natives in disregarding the weather. Actually, I came to prefer it. The cooler, comfortable weather caused me to be much more content to sit on my backside for hours, studying scores and keeping my viola alive. And when the sun came out, which it often did, I was tempted to play hooky in the parks, at the beaches, or on the tennis courts.

When Virginia and I announced to Peter, then eleven, and Pamela, seven, that we were moving from Long Island across the country to Seattle, Pam asked with a worried frown, "Are there children out there?" She would soon find out that she had no cause to worry. Pam slipped naturally and quickly into friendships with her new playmates in Seattle's Laurelhurst District. They were so intrigued with her accent (which she soon lost) that they constantly urged her, "C'mon, Pam, tawk New Yawk."

One highlight of our trip came with our stop in Chicago, where I had been engaged to conduct a pair of concerts at Grant Park. One of the concerts fell on my birthday, June 24. When I walked on-stage to start the performance, I was surprised to see a large group of young people gathered just below the stage. They led the large audience in singing "Happy Birthday" and the members of the orchestra joined in. Needless to say, it was thrilling and I tried to be at my best with the baton that night.

Although Virginia and I had flown back and forth across our country many times, this was our first opportunity to experience America and all its enormous beauty at ground level. Driving every mile of the way was considerably different than the 500-mile an hour bird's eye view we had had from airliners.

After oohing and ahing our way through the South Dakota Bad Lands and marveling at our four presidents on Mount Rushmore, we stopped for lunch one day at a typical Western ranch. No sooner were we seated at our table than Pam was at my side whispering to me that she had to go. I pointed back to where I had seen the rest room signs and she left. Within a half-minute she was back whispering, "What am I Daddy, a setter or a pointer?"

When we arrived in Seattle, we drove straight to the house that I had rented the previous June, when I was in Seattle to conduct a special Seattle Symphony concert for a Rotary convention. I had absolutely no hesitation in renting the Laurelhurst district house after I saw the living-room view of Lake Washington just below and the Cascade Mountain Range and Mount Rainier in the distance, like a giant calendar picture on the wall. The view had sold me. But I had no idea how many baths or bedrooms were in the house! When I had hurriedly leased the house, I hadn't bothered to look past the overwhelming living-room view. We were all thrilled with the choice!

We had barely finished unpacking when Gordon Scott, president of the symphony board whisked us off to Vancouver, B.C. There we boarded the motor yacht, Thea Foss, which had once been John Barrymore's "Infanta," for a ten-day cruise of Canada's San Juan Islands. It was so beautiful that I thought this must be what heaven is like. The trip was not only our introduction to the glamorous side of the Northwest, it was also Gordon's way of having us meet some very important friends, potential symphony supporters.

I found out later that when Gordon invited his friends to cruise with the new conductor they had said, "What on earth are we going to talk about with a symphony conductor?" Unwittingly, I soon answered that question. The first night out I played gin rummy with Howard Wright (an important builder), who, I learned, had quite an enviable reputation as a master of the game. When I wound up the winner, thanks to an incredible run of the cards, Howard accused Gordon of hosting a card shark, not a symphony conductor.

The Seattle Symphony almost lost its new conductor before his first downbeat. When we moored off Stewart Island, Gordon and Henry Isaacson decided to go fish-ing. There was just enough room in the launch for me to tag along so that I could record the event with my new movie camera. No one had warned me about the Yuclata Rapids. I made the mistake of standing up to get shots of their landing a big one, and a sudden whirlpool tossed me overboard. The swirling water must have been the freezing temperature of Glacier Bay. They shouted at me to drop the camera, but I insisted on clutching it with my right hand and keeping my head above the surface by beating the water furiously with my left hand. Fortunately for me, the young engineer piloting the launch was an expert at it . He brought it alongside me quickly and hauled me out of the water before I became a block of ice.

Gordon's face was white with shock. He told me later that he could already see the headlines in the Seattle newspapers: Symphony president drowns new conductor! My unscheduled bath in the Yuclata Rapids was the first of two mishaps that threatened to scuttle the start of my first season in Seattle. A short time later I was challenged to a game of squash by Dr. Hans Lehmann, the enthusiastic Seattle music lover whom I had met in New York and one of the Seattle Symphony's greatest champions. As I twisted my body to make a shot, I slipped a disc and fell to the floor in pain. The accident landed me in traction in Seattle's Swedish Hospital.

One of the first duties I had to forgo was a series of speaking engagements that had been arranged for the symphony's new conductor. Virginia, like the great trouper she is, took over and fulfilled all of the dates with remarkable success. The audiences loved her. Her Seattle career had been launched before mine! I couldn't have been happier.

Meanwhile, doctors surrounded my hospital bed. Hans Lehmann, shaking his head nervously, was at the foot of the bed. At my right was neurosurgeon Wolf Klemperer and at my left orthopedic surgeon Ernest Stewart. It was as if the two of them had scalpels at the ready, itching to get at me. But I wasn't about to let either surgeon put a knife in my back.

Milton and Virginia Katims

Fortune smiled again. Hans introduced me to Millie Mayer, a German angel of a physical therapist, in whose capable arms I spent much of the following year. She counseled me to be patient and advised me that most of her patients were "post"-operative, not "pre"-operative. Along with almost daily treatments of deepest massage, instant traction, wet heat, and a variety of exercises, Millie took full advantage of having me at her mercy, squeezing in a well-calculated campaign to persuade me to program the music of Gustav Mahler. She had many accomplices, including other Mahler afficionados, Leonard Bernstein, a long time friend, and lawyer Carl Pruzan, a new friend and Mahler champion in Seattle. My early programming of Mahler in Seattle was a surprise to no one, least of all Millie.

Conducting the entire first season with a brace around my middle wasn't too bad. Anyway I had more important things to think about. The previous 18 years I had been conducting many radio and television programs for an unseen audience with whom I had a distant impersonal relationship. Mostly, even with the NBC Symphony audiences, I had to avoid extremely far-out repertoire to keep from ruffling the feathers of the broadcasting executives.

But now I had to think about my responsibility to guide the musical taste of Northwest music lovers, to attract potential subscribers to the concerts, to compete with the water and mountain sports for attendance, to devise creative programming while keeping an eye on the box office, and to cultivate my relationship with the members of the orchestra, to say nothing of my dealings with the symphony's board. And although I would not be directly involved with the fund-raising, I had to be fully aware of the need.

One of the greatest challenges facing me was the need to raise the orchestra's level of quality. In the seven preceding years I had been the principal guest conductor of what could be called the greatest virtuoso orchestra that has ever been formed, Toscanini's NBC Symphony. After more than 50 broadcasts conducting the most distinguished musicians gathered on one stage, how would I react to the musicians of the Seattle Symphony? With the sound of the NBC Symphony ringing clearly in my ears, I set that sound as my goal for what was now my orchestra. I would make no concessions to the fact that the orchestra was comprised of a mixture of experienced professionals, schoolteachers, and housewives.

Furthermore, the orchestra was still a cooperative in one of the most pro-labor-cities in America. Because of their dissatisfaction with the previous conductor, about whom the symphony board would do nothing, the musicians had withdrawn from the Symphony Society. They became an independent group that chose its own conductor and who were engaged as a complete orchestral entity by the Symphony Society. Before I left New York, I had decided I would give the arrangement a fair trial. But before the first season reached the halfway mark, I knew I couldn't live with the situation, nor begin to reach the goals I had set for myself and the orchestra. Neither the orchestra nor I could succeed unless I could make all artistic decisions. (We were still in the era before the advent of powerful orchestra committees.)

I requested a meeting with all the players. With determination and the strongest argument I could muster, I put before them my blueprint for turning the Seattle Symphony into one of America's major orchestras. The plan included enlarging the orchestra's size, extending the season, increasing the size of the geographic area we reached, hastening the day we would have a proper hall for our concerts, and making sure that the hall would be ideal for opera and ballet, as well (added income for the players). However, my main goal was to raise the performance level of the orchestra.

To reach these goals I told the musicians that I had to assume the complete and unchallenged role of music director, as well as conductor, and that they would have to dissolve their cooperative. If they did so, I was prepared to stay and work my head off for them and the city of Seattle. If not, I would head back to New York to resume my career there as a conductor and violist.

Despite the determined effort of a small hard core to retain the cooperative, the overwhelming majority of musicians voted to dissolve the cooperative and accept my proposed blueprint for the future. The Seattle Symphony proceeded to a much higher level and within a few years became one of the nation's major orchestras. I believe I kept my promise!

During the period of the "Katims' SSO crisis," there was a meeting of the symphony board, many concerned symphony subscribers and supporters. The president of the board, rather active in supporting the crisis, was asked about his credentials as a critic of the conductor. He replied, "I studied piano as a boy." No one thought to ask the audiences what they thought.

There were memos and notes flying back and forth. Emmett Watson, a columnist in one of the local newspapers, was reporting all in his column. This greatly displeased the board president. He summoned Watson and me to his home, where he proceeded to harangue both of us for almost two hours. Finally, Emmett stood up and announced that he had to leave. We left together. When we were out on the sidewalk, he turned to me and said, "My God, is this what you've had to contend with?"

I didn't bother to tell Emmett about the society matron (held in the pocket of the symphony president). She accosted me one evening, right before a performance, with, "How long do you intend to stay I Seattle?' I did not ask about a her musical credentials.

There were more of these characters, but I have intentionally omitted them. They know who they are!

Chapter 8
Meeting the Greats

Virginia: For more than two decades Milton and I were totally immersed in the cultural life of Seattle and the Pacific Northwest. It was a glorious experience for both of us. Under Milton's direction, aided by the infusion of fresh talent into the orchestra's ranks, his blueprint took wing. The symphony made enormous progress in a relatively short time. The proof came with more and more sold-out performances, an extended season, a mounting number of contributors for the sustaining fund, a recording contract, and finally the fulfillment of the dream of touring the orchestra in the entire Northwest region, as well as California and Alaska.

One of our fears before moving to Seattle had been that the distance from New York and other important cultural centers would remove us from associations with the great names in music, in particular, and the arts, in general. To our delight, just the opposite occurred. Milton's establishment as one of the first American born conductors to head a major orchestra brought ever greater opportunities to work with the world's supreme artists and to be invited to guest-conduct and perform in cities throughout the world. His status also gave us the opportunity to renew associations with the gifted artists we had met in our earlier years.

When Milton and I reminisce about the great artists whom we have been privileged to know and join in performance, we're reminded of the American show tune which typifies the great majority of those super-talents. It's "People," the wonderful Jule Styne song from the Broadway hit "Funny Girl" of the early 1960s. Bob Merrill's emotionally gripping lyrics wind up with the line, "People who need people are the luckiest people in the world." That line applies to most of the artists we have known. Sometimes they may have seemed to have been self-centered and arrogant, but Milton and I know that they seem to have been "people who need people," perhaps more than others who are constantly in the limelight – such as politicians, actors, actresses, and athletes. Musical artists need people because the audience completes the triad of composer, performer and listener to make up the musical experience. They are also inspired and sustained by the response of an audience, to say nothing about being nourished with applause and bravos.

We treasure our recollections of these singular artists. Memories of Claudio Arrau come immediately to mind. When Milton invited him to appear as piano soloist with the orchestra, he also asked him if he would join us in a performance of the "Dvorak Piano Quintet" at a benefit for the orchestra. His immediate and charming response was, "Of course. Chamber music is my complete joy!"

We played the first of several Candlelight Musicales before an overflow crowd in the Spanish Ballroom in Seattle's Olympic Hotel. Joining Claudio in the performance were Henry Siegl, the orchestra's concert-master; his assistant Heimo Haitto, playing second violin; Milton as violist; and I with my cello. Nobody was more anxious to start the concert than Arrau, himself. As we prepared to follow him on to the stage, he said, with a twinkle in his eye,

"Come on, let's go. We have a date with Dvorak and I just can't wait to sit on my piano bench. It makes me feel so sexy!" The audience never knew why we were all laughing as we walked on-stage.

The Pleasure Was Ours

Arrau, one of the world's great pianists, was one of the most nervous performers before going on stage that we have ever known. On the evening of his first performance with the orchestra, he and I were in the wings as Milton opened the concert with a Bach orchestral suite. Claudio paced back and forth, wringing his hands constantly as if trying to stretch his fingers another inch. He would stop in front of me every now and then and bemoan the fact that his mother had encouraged him to practice the piano instead of urging him to become a typist. A few cruel critics have accused him of treating the piano like a typewriter, of producing a dry sound, or of failing to reach out emotionally to his audience. We knew better. No pianist could match his extensive grasp of the piano literature and few could match his success.

*M*ilton: Our move to Seattle actually enhanced our future relationships with old friends and luminaries in the world of music. I think that getting established in a permanent position as conductor of a fine orchestra proved to be providential. The invitations to perform and guest-conduct elsewhere around the world increased substantially.

One such invitation drew me even closer to the incomparable cellist Pablo Casals and all the superb musicians and singers he attracted to the world-famous Casals Festival. I'll always remember our first trip to perform at the festival. It was June, 1952, and Virginia and I found ourselves in Paris, where driving an automobile is an experience no first-time visitor in that fabled city ever forgets. Before leaving the States, we had ordered and paid for a new Hillman-Minx convertible to be delivered in France. In Paris I took the Metro from the Place de la Concorde, near our hotel, to Neuilly, where I picked up the car. With absolutely no knowledge of French (I thought "tout droit" meant "always right") and with a map of Paris on my lap, I succeeded somehow in getting back to our hotel, although I was trapped for a time in the maelstrom around the Etoile, which threatened to foil that objective.

Milton and Virginia Katims

With Virginia in tow and Prades, the festival site, as our target, I pointed the car in the direction my friend Sasha Schneider had suggested as the best route from Paris to Prades, south through the Loire Valley. However, in studying the map I found what looked to me like a much more direct route between the two cities and I took it. Not long into the trip I realized we were climbing ever higher and higher through the Massifs Centrals Mountains. I apologized to Virginia, but like the real trouper she always was she said it was a great opportunity to see colorful villages and landscapes we might never have experienced otherwise.

We were among the last arrivals at our hotel in Molitg-les-Bains, two kilometers from Prades. Most of the other festival performers had been there for hours. Among them were Myra Hess, Eugene Istomin, and Mieco Horszowski (pianists), Isaac Stern and Joseph Szigeti (violinists), Jenny Tourel (singer), and Paul Tortelier (cellist). Because our room was still being prepared, Virginia and I decided to go to lunch. When we returned to our room I found a note under the door. As closely as I can remember, it read as follows:

"Dear Mr. Katims, Welcome to Molitg-les-Bains. I am looking forward to playing chamber music with you. Would you please note that from 11:30 in the morning to 1pm and from 4:30 to 6 pm, I would appreciate your not practicing. My room is right next to yours. I nap during those periods. (signed) Joseph Szigeti."

I sat down immediately to pen my response:

"Dear Mr. Szigeti, Thanks very much for your warm words of welcome. I, too, am looking forward to making music with you. May I say that you don't seem to know much about violists. We never practice! Sincerely, Milton Katims."

I was looking forward eagerly to playing and recording the "Brahms C Minor Piano Quartet" with Szigeti. Many years earlier Virginia and I had heard him play a magnificent sonata recital at the Library of Congress with the brilliant Hungarian composer/pianist Bela Bartok. I still remember the program – "Beethovan Kreutzer Sonata," "Debussy Sonata," and two compositions by Bartok. (It was recorded and is available on a CD.) Despite differences in our playing styles, I admired Szigeti's musicianship.

(I recall the contrast of these differences playing viola quintets with the Hungarian String Quartet to my experiences with the four Russians in the Budapest String Quartet. From the moment I first sat down to play with the Budapesters, I felt as if I had been making music with them for years. My schooling as a violinist and violist had been very similar to theirs.)

The atmosphere was wonderfully cordial as we began rehearsals that day in Prades. With Myra Hess at the piano and Paul Tortelier playing the cello, the differences between Szigeti and me were considerably softened. Myra was a delight to know and even more of a delight to join in making music. Her warm personality was reflected in the sound she produced, and her clear thinking was evident in the crystalline quality of her mastery at the keyboard. At that first rehearsal I was very much aware that she had just recently been knighted by the British crown. After calling her "Dame Myra" a few times, she stood up and said, "Milton, for Gawd's sake! Not Dame Myra! Plain Myra."

Paul's prowess as one of the foremost cellists of our time was well known, and I gloried in the sounds he made. What may not have been known, however, was his phenomenal ability at solfeggio, the vocal do-re-mi used to articulate a musical phrase. For example, he could solfege Paganini's "Moto Perpetuo" at an unbelievably fast tempo. I don't think I could have played it at that speed on the violin or viola! It's unfortunate that we American musicians are not all trained in the art of solfeggio as an integral part of our studies. I'm convinced it would make better musicians of us all.

On the morning we were scheduled to record the Brahms, Szigeti threw a tantrum. He came up with such a case of nerves that he threatened to leave town, rather than appear for the recording session. It was startling behavior for such a distinguished, experienced virtuoso. While we were trying to figure out what to do, Virginia stepped into the breach and used all of her feminine charm to coax him into doing the recording. "You're so wonderful. I want to hear you on this recording!" The world is waiting to hear you!" It worked. Why shouldn't it have? She had practiced on me for years!

Just before leaving Prades, Joseph sent her a photograph of himself, which he autographed: "To lovely Virginia, who mothered us on the battlefield."

As Virginia and I drove to our first meeting with Maitre Pablo Casals, my mind did a fast rewind to that day so many years earlier when I was introduced to the exquisite artistry of the great cellist. I was about eight or nine when my parents took me to the Brooklyn Academy of Music for a Casals recital. We sat high up in the balcony, and throughout the recital I felt that he was talking directly to me with his cello. Years later I was to hear both Casals and Toscanini express the identical thought – "that music should have the same logic as speech."

By the time I first took part in a Casals Festival, I had been playing, teaching, and giving considerable thought to the "Bach Six Solo Suites" for almost fifteen years. However, the manuscript of my edition of the suites transcribed for the viola had undergone so many changes, because I played them a bit differently each time, that I decided I couldn't possibly let International Music publish them. When I discussed this with Casals, however, he persuaded me to let them publish my edition. In a letter from Puerto Rico, he wrote:

"I think it is good that you publish your own edition of the "Bach Solo Suites for Viola." I think that the idea of your preface is an excellent one, because it is natural that you can never play the same way twice. The basic ideas are the same, but it is not possible to play this music – or, in fact, any music – the same way every time. This is the main reason for my not having ever agreed to publish an edition of the Bach Suites, in spite of the many requests I have received. (signed) P. Casals"

When we arrived at Maitre Casals' house that day in Prades, Virginia realized she had forgotten Sasha's warning that she shouldn't wear shorts when visiting the cel-

With pianist Claudio Arrau, talking over Dvorak quintet for a benefit concert

The Istomin, Stern, Rose Trio with volist Katims (Playhouse opening in Seattle)

list. She decided to wait by the gate while I went up to greet him. Almost before I had introduced myself he wanted to know where my wife was. When I told him, he immediately went to the window to see for himself. He took one look and insisted that Virginia come up so he could meet her. So much for Sasha's advice.

The orchestra rehearsals began in earnest and proceeded that way till we were ready to start the festival. I discovered quickly that playing chamber music with that great artist or responding to his conducting was constantly inspiring, stimulating, and alive with excitement. I recalled one of Toscanini's favorite admonitions, "The greatest crime in performance is to be boring." No crimes were ever committed at a Casals Festival.

I was intrigued by the almost agonized sound that accompanied the start of each down bow Casals drew. It was like a groan. At that point in the Maitre's long life as a cellist, he may not have been the consummate virtuoso of his earlier years, but he was still a great teacher, with ever fresh ideas. At a rehearsal of the "Trio of the Scherzo" movement of the "Schubert C Major Quintet," Casals urged Tortelier and me to play the duet between us with the precision of a march. At the end of the short descending passage, the two violins and first cello joined us in a very soft passage with a barely recognizable beat. We all simultaneously asked, "Where's the beat?"

Casals stood up and, shaking his finger at us, exclaimed, "You bad boys – you bad boys! Here you must count with your soul!"

I was tempted to suggest that it might be better to count with our heart, because at least it has a beat. But, I resisted the temptation. Our recording (Columbia and now SONY)) of the Schubert remains at the very top of my favorites.

The Casals Festival was by no means all-serious sessions of practice, rehearsals and concerts. There were many lighter moments as well – moments when we would get together at the National Hotel to relax, have a drink and swap favorite stories about other musicians. I don't recall when the National Hotel was built, but I do know that it was very old. One night after a concert in which I had played and we were trying hard to relax, Virginia asked for directions to the ladies room. Bernie Goldberg, first flutist of the Pittsburg Symphony, offered to guide her to the second floor location of the single unisex rest room in the hotel. Virginia soon discovered that this old hotel did not have modern plumbing. Typical of most French rural villages, it had a hole in the floor. She had just put herself in the appropriate position when Bernie suddenly reopened the door and said, "By the way, Milton played beautifully this evening!"

Before leaving Prades for my first trip to Israel to guest conduct the Israel Philharmonic, I asked Isaac Stern to teach me a few words in Hebrew. His response was that it would be quite unnecessary because most of the members of the orchestra understood English. When I insisted, I was given the words "sheket b'vakesha," appropriate to use at any time during a rehearsal of the Israel Philharmonic. The translation? "Shut-up, please."

About five or six years later, when I had the pleasure (and privilege) of taking part in the first Casals Festival in Puerto Rico, Maitre Casals suffered a mild heart attack during the first rehearsal. He was instantly put to bed and a cardiologist was called. At that time the most famous heart doctor in the country was Paul Dudley White, who attended President Dwight Eisenhower. Fortunately, Dr. White was in Miami at the time and he was able to fly right over to San Juan.

As he walked into Casals' bedroom the old man recognized him immediately and said, "You're a very famous man."

With a modest shrug, Dr. White replied, "Yes, that may be so, but I'm not nearly as famous as you are."

Casals' responded, "Yes, that's right."

Virginia and Milton's first Atlantic crossing (on the Liberte) sharing a table with soon to be famous photographer Richard Avedon and his lovely wife Evelyn

Chapter 9
The Pianists in Our Lives

Arthur Rubinstein

Virginia: When Virginia met Arthur at Sea-Tac Airport the last time he came to play with the Seattle Symphony, he asked, "Why are you growing a mustache?" She was surprised and puzzled, but said nothing. Later, he explained that he was suffering from an attack of shingles in his eye, which affected his eyesight and caused him to say that. By a cruel coincidence, Virginia suffered from the same virus in her left eye some years later. But if that incident at the airport was not enough to burn that visit of Arthur's into my memory, what happened at the first night performance certainly would have.

I had finished the rather lengthy opening orchestral tutti of the "Mozart D Minor Piano Concerto" and Arthur started playing the solo part. With nothing to do for several measures, I began to enjoy the usual Rubinstein magic while following the score. But after only two or three phrases I realized, to my horror, that he was not playing what I was looking at in the score. Thinking that he might have had a memory slip and inadvertently skipped to a similar passage later in the movement, I began leafing frantically through the score, searching for what he was playing so that I could alert the orchestra and bring them in at the proper spot.

My heart was beating wildly and my gray hairs were multiplying rapidly. But before I could locate anything resembling what Arthur was playing, he suddenly stopped. I turned to him and he said very quietly, "We begin again."

In order to give him plenty of time to recover, because I had no idea whether he had had a memory lapse, or something worse, I signaled the orchestra to start again at the very beginning. This time everything went beautifully and Rubinstein received a well-deserved standing ovation. He drew a second ovation later for his vibrant reading of the Beethoven "Emperor Concerto," which closed the concert.

In his dressing room afterwards he explained that because of the shingles in his eye, the keyboard started waving like a banner in the breeze. It disconcerted him so much that it's a wonder that he was able to continue. That evening, at the small reception in our home, I asked Arthur to autograph his recording of the Mozart concerto. He wrote: "To Milton, with love, Arthur." Then I handed him his recording of the "Emperor Concerto" for another autograph. Without a moment's hesitation he wrote: "To the same Milton, with the same love, from the same Arthur."

A few weeks later I received a phone call from Annabelle Whitestone (Rubinstein's manager in Barcelona). She wanted to know if I would be free to fly to Spain two months later? Arthur wanted me to conduct two concertos, the "Mozart D Minor Concerto" and the Schumann, for him in Barcelona. I didn't bother to look at my schedule. My answer was an immediate, "Yes!" Nothing was going to stop me. In Barcelona there were no problems and the audience went wild. That concert proved to be Rubinstein's final orchestral appearance in Europe, just as the Seattle concerts were his last in the states.

I have long felt that if I were a pianist, I would wish to play like Rubinstein, with a

Rubenstein "the Great"
in a last minute
exchange with Katims

Concert manager Arthur Judson, with Erika Morrini, violinist and Milton Katims in Seattle

*A jocular moment
with "King" Arthur*

*Rubeinstein
with his harem*

beautiful singing sound and a warm romantic approach to the music. Technical facility was not an end in itself, but a means of exploring and discovering the voice of the composer. He cared little about the notes he scattered under the piano along the way. Details, details. His playing, larger than life, was a very accurate reflection of the man.

He was more than a mere piano virtuoso. Much more! He was a virtuoso interpreter of life itself. Just as it was always a joy to share his music making, it was our great good fortune to share his contagious affair with life. He would hold us enthralled for hours as he talked about many subjects – history, science, politics and, of course, the arts. Nothing seemed to be outside of his quick mind. He also had unlimited energy that put ours to shame. After sitting in our car for hours after a concert and the inevitable post-concert party, I would be exhausted and he didn't know how to say "dubranets" (goodnight in Polish). In desperation, I would say, "Arthur, we love you dearly, but please go to bed! Please!!"

Arthur was most interested in my having spent more than ten years with Toscanini. (In my pantheon of musical geniuses, these two artists share top billing.) I reminded Arthur that I had been playing in the NBC Symphony when he appeared with Maestro in that memorable performance of the "Beethoven C Minor Concerto" (the 3rd).

That performance had pleased Maestro so much that he gave permission for its release by RCA. I treasure my copy. (Although he made three later recordings of the concerto, this war time performance is uniquely still incandescent.)

At a late supper with Arthur one night in Seattle, the subject of children came up. We knew that Arthur's son, John, at that time was in the Army at Fort Lewis, about 40 miles south of Seattle. Virginia asked if John were a pianist. Rubinstein exploded, "Good God, no!"

Taken aback, Virginia asked, "Why so vehement?"

"Because if John were not as good a pianist as I am, he'd be very unhappy. And if he were a better pianist than I am, I'd be miserable!"

Milton and Virginia Katims

On another occasion we asked Arthur what to say to a colleague backstage after a less than memorable performance when there was no way to escape going backstage after the concert. Arthur recommended, "Just shake hands with your colleague and say, very sincerely, "Fantastic, is not the word!"

I've long wondered whether another of my favorite anecdotes about Arthur is apocryphal or if it really happened: A large, elegant group, in which Arthur Rubinstein was the guest of honor, had just finished dinner and moved into the living room. Arthur settled into a comfortable chair and lit one of his favorite cigars. The hostess turned to him and asked, "Maestro, would you please play something for us. I just had the piano tuned."

Arthur nodded assent, much to the surprised delight of all the guests, put down his cigar, headed for the Steinway, and adjusted the height of the piano bench. He then played an arpeggio at great speed from the bottom to the top of the keyboard, closed the piano lid, went back to his seat and resumed smoking his cigar.

The nervous hostess asked anxiously, "Is anything wrong?"

"Oh no, nothing at all. That's all I ate."

*V*irginia: Many years ago Arthur Rubinstein invited us to visit him during one of our trips to Paris. The summer sun was still shining as we arrived at Arthur's home on Avenue Foch, next door to where Claude Debussy had once lived. Rubinstein, himself, opened the door and greeted us with hugs.

He led us into his elegant studio where the walls seemed to silently echo the myriad of memorable sounds that must have come from his grand piano during his many hours of practice. His maid brought us glasses of vodka and crackers with some very black caviar. As we sipped the vodka Arthur sat at the piano, which was in a bay window overlooking park Monceau. His fingers idly caressed the keys. Suddenly he asked, "Do you know this charming little piece by Schumann?"

He began to play, one piece led to another. After the Schumann he went on with several pieces by Chopin, Schubert and Liszt. We love impromptu recitals and this one was turning out to be one of the best. His rebellious white hair shined in the rays of the still bright sun. He played with warmth, poetry, great suavity, and above all with affection, exactly the contemplative way he always performed in the concert hall. Finally he stopped playing and faced us.

"When I die, do you know what music I wish to be played at my funeral? The 'Adagio from the C Major Quintet' by Schubert." (I wonder whether his wish was fulfilled?) "Well now, that's enough music. Come, let me show you my house."

His rooms were full of paintings and sculptures. Among them were several pieces of sculpture that had been given to him by Picasso, including one of Arthur's derriere! (Now there's a collector's item if I've ever seen one!) In about three hours we had been treated to a private recital by one of the world's great pianists and then a museum tour of his fabulous collection. When we returned to his studio he said we should be thinking about dinner.

"My beautiful Nella (Mrs. Rubinstein) is away from Paris. That is really too bad. She's a gourmet cook." He paused, looking up at the ceiling in deep thought. "Ah, I know," Arthur said, clapping his hands. "We shall go to Maxim's for dinner."

Whenever we think of Arthur, the memory of that unforgettable afternoon and the dinner that followed comes to mind in glorious detail. Following Rubinstein into one of the world's most famous restaurants, with the maitre'd, the wine stewards and the waiters bowing and backing, gave us the fantastic feeling that we were following Moses through the parting waters of the Red Sea. It was a never-to-be-forgotten experience. All of the diners received Arthur like a conquering hero. How they loved him! It had to be called a super-royal treatment. Needless to say the food and wines were exquisite and the service extra special. We're grateful that we were able to experience Maxim's as guests of that unique artist – his wit and charm, to say nothing of his knowledge of wine – a constant delight.

Milton and Virginia Katims

A few years later, after we had coaxed him a number of times and succeeded in having him return to perform in Seattle, I impulsively wrote him this letter:

"Dear Arthur, how I miss you – not only for your artistry but because you are a true citizen of the world. You are a consummate observer of the world scene. How many evenings we have spent talking with you after your performances with the Seattle Symphony – talking 'til two and three in the morning. We would be exhausted, but you seemed ever fresh and ready to keep going. I remember a party we gave in your honor at our home. You had said to me, 'Virginia, please, not more than 30 guests.' I began getting calls from almost everyone in Seattle when they heard, via the grapevine, that we'd be entertaining you. We ended up with 75 or 80 guests! But you were so gracious as you entered our home saying, 'I'm not shy!' as you were enveloped by excited "Bravos!" I had arranged for you to have supper in our red bedroom surrounded by five of our most gorgeous young women as your dinner companions. Each time I entered the room, you had a different girl on your lap – Arthur and his harem."

In a response dated March 7, 1961, Arthur replied:

"My Dear Virginia, You were an angel to send me those wonderful photographs of my 'harem.' I like your personal contribution the best, but what touched me more than the photographs was what you wrote about the concert. You and your husband are quite wonderful people, and I enjoyed every moment I was with you. Tell Milton of my admiration for his conducting. I hope that in the near future, we will be able again to do something together. Affectionately, Arthur Rubinstein."

The only bitter disappointment he gave me was when he was terminally ill. We learned that he had left his lovely wife Nella, and his beautiful Avenue Foch home to take an apartment in Geneva with glamorous Annabelle (Whitestone), who had been his manager in Spain (she was also Milton's manager). I regretted that it was no longer possible to let him know how I felt. "What can I say, Arthur? I guess you just had an over-powering love of women. ALL women!"

*Milton bearing a gift for
Greek pianis
Gina Bachauer
after SSO concert*

*Princess Irene (of Greece) with the Katims and Rob't . Denny Watt after pianist Irene's
performance with Gina Bachauer and the Seattle Symphony*

Milton and Virginia Katims

Gina Bachauer

Virginia: She walked on-stage like a Greek goddess. Milton was guest conducting the New York Philharmonic in Avery Fisher Hall and Gina Bachauer was his soloist in "Prokofieff's Third Piano Concerto." The Prokofieff is full of high drama, requiring a huge amount of sheer strength because of its technical demands. Who better than a Greek goddess to project it forcefully out into the hall?

Later, in her dressing room she and Milton embraced heartily in a victory hug.

"Gina," Milton said, "you play like a man!"

Her quick response was, "Which man?"

With her very white skin and her jet-black hair drawn into a bun, the Greek pianist always commanded attention. On another program in which she appeared as soloist, with Milton conducting the National Symphony of Washington, D.C., Gina played the lovely, lyrical "Grieg Piano Concerto" and a thoroughly classical Mozart concerto. On that occasion, I asked her where she got all the energy she displayed in her constant world tours and the widely varied piano fare she performed.

"I take this wonderful vitamin you can buy only in Europe," she said and presented me with an unopened bottle. It did nothing for me. Speed walking on the beautiful Burke-Gilman Trail that lies just below our Seattle condo does more for me than any vitamin.

One year when we were in London for Milton's guest-conducting dates with the London Philharmonic, Gina was also in town. She invited us to the stunning apartment of Fleur Cowles, the internationally noted painter, whose trademark scenes are of exquisite jungle foliage and animals. I thought we had entered one of the world's finest art museums. The walls were hung with gorgeous tapestries and art works of the great masters, as well as with her own paintings.

The Pleasure Was Ours

Among the guests was the distinguished British actor Sir John Gielgud, who promptly invited us to the play in which he was performing. We accepted, of course. At the theater we watched Elizabeth Taylor and Richard Burton stroll down the aisle at intermission time. I overheard her say, "Now people can see how really fat I am" (she wasn't, at least not at that time).

After the performance Gielgud had invited us to visit in his dressing room, where Milton and I shared champagne and bon mots with John, Liz, Richard, and others. Liz's eyes were everything we had heard. Marvelous eyes. But what species of genes produces lavender eyes? I was impressed, as always, by Burton's commanding, musical voice, but I must confess I was taken aback at seeing his pockmarked face up close.

Later on, Fleur Cowles accepted our invitation to bring a collection of her paintings to one of Seattle's Symphoneve Balls, the huge annual fund-raising party for the orchestra's sustaining fund. She was the hit of the ball in more ways than one. Thanks to her presence every painting quickly sold – $25,000 worth in 30 minutes! She gave half the profit to the symphony. The next time we were in England, Fleur invited us to visit her at her country home in Surrey, which has been designated a national monument by the British government.

We owed all these delightful experiences to our Greek friend, Gina Bachauer, who had still one more bit of good fortune to offer. The next time she traveled to Seattle for an appearance with the symphony, she brought a student of hers, Princess Irene of Greece, to join her in the "Bach Concerto No. 2" for two pianos and orchestra. Irene played quite well and was a worthy partner to her famous tutor. The princess was a smash hit as she swept on-stage in a glittering, white gown, with a little diamond tiara atop her dark brown hair. She looked and played as a princess should. The Royal Evening arranged afterward in their honor was also a smash hit.

When the British conductor Alec Sherman, married Gina, he gave up his career in order to cater to her needs and help further her career. Alec catered to all of Gina's needs. Often before she was aware of them. He wanted her to devote all of her energy and attention to those piano keys. In one unique instance he had to devote his time to those keys – well, actually only one of them.

Here's what happened: On the first evening of a pair of concerts at which Gina was appearing as soloist with the Houston Symphony, the fairly new concertmaster, young Ronald Patterson (who recently joined the faculty of the School of Music at the University of Washington after two decades as concertmaster of the Monte Carlo Philharmonic) made his entrance on-stage before the concerto and headed for the piano to give the orchestra the customary "A." Much to the amused surprise of his colleagues in the orchestra, Ron struck the wrong note! He immediately corrected his mistake. At the repeat performance the following evening it was Patterson's turn to be surprised (if not amused). Taped to the "A" was a large black X, Alec Sherman's doing. I decided that Alec was in a perfect position to understand and appreciate my complaints about the trials of being a maestro's wife.

One evening he told us an unforgettable story about a conductor whom he refused to name, and with good reason: "This very famous conductor had just conducted 'Brahms First Symphony' to close his program. He was accorded an ovation, which lasted through four or five curtain calls. Finally, he took reluctant leave of his admiring audience and retreated to his dressing room, where his wife patiently awaited him. He tore off his very wet, concert clothing, tossed them aside, and slipped into his terry cloth robe just in time to greet the adoring females who soon surrounded him. While he drank in every flattering word (and believed all of them) his dutiful wife went about the task of picking up all his sweaty clothing, folding everything carefully into a small suitcase.

"Then came the inevitable, after-concert party. The conductor and his wife were no sooner inside the party home when he was again surrounded by still more adoring females telling him how wonderful he was. Still performing dutifully, his wife provided him with tall drinks and food from the buffet table. Her chores done, she was able to fill a plate for herself and find a quiet seat among the dull members of the symphony board.

"Finally, the conductor and his patient and weary wife were whisked away and taken home. In pregnant silence they prepared for bed and slipped under the covers of their separate beds. As he reached for the night-light on the small table between them and heaved one more sigh of satisfaction over how wonderful he had been that evening, his wife asked in a very quiet voice,

'Darling, what was wrong with the tempo of the slow movement tonight?' Not waiting for a reply, she had taken her revenge, quickly turned over, and closed her eyes in restful sleep. And the conductor? He tossed and turned the entire night, wondering, 'Now, what was wrong with the tempo of the slow movement?'"

Eugene Istomin

Milton: I was conducting the Buffalo Philharmonic in a performance of "Chopin's Second Piano Concerto," with Eugene Istomin as soloist. We were in the middle of the opening orchestral tutti when I found myself quite confused. I had just turned to cue the first violins, but they didn't play! The woodwinds played instead. Out of the corner of my eye, I saw Eugene peering up at me in a very peculiar manner.

Later he wrote his own version of the incident: "One of the most amusing moments in my career came at a time in 1950, when I connived with members of the Buffalo Philharmonic to play a prank on our conductor, a certain Milton Katims, during a performance of the "Chopin Second Piano Concerto." We had performed the work at subscription concerts in Kleinhans Hall in Buffalo and were now on a short runout tour with the same program.

"It was quite the conventional habit to make a cut in the opening orchestral tutti, so that the solo piano's dramatic and glamorous entrance would not be delayed too long. Many recordings of this beautiful work by artists like Arthur Rubinstein, Giomar Novaes, and even myself, with Eugene Ormandy, were made with the cut. But for the Buffalo performances we were not making the usual cut, because Milton felt there was already too little for the orchestra to play.

"At the final concert on the tour (at Colgate University in Hamilton, NY), I conspired with the players to make the cut without telling Maestro Katims. At the performance, the spectacle of Milton's horrified expression of stunned surprise – head nodding back and forth as if he were denying the reality of what we had done, while he tried to catch up with the score, was a choice moment, yet one of which I am not at all proud, since I was no longer a twelve-year-old schoolboy at the time. However, apart from having to reimburse Milton for his cardiologist's bill, no serious damage was done by the incident."

Although I was momentarily upset by Eugene's prank, I said very little about it. I waited patiently for the right moment to return the favor. It came about ten years later when Eugene came to Seattle to play the "Schumann Piano Concerto" with the Seattle Symphony. The concerto is in A minor. I had our librarian put out the parts for both the Schumann and the "Grieg Piano Concerto," which is in the same key.

At the first rehearsal after Eugene played the opening of the Schumann, I conducted the orchestra in the opening of the Grieg. He may have been laughing or crying inside, but Eugene didn't bat an eye. He shook his head and said with a wry grin, "Very funny. Very funny."

I pointed to him and said in a whispered, "Gotcha." To be truthful, practical jokes like these are sort of common among musicians. (Even Toscanini was very fond of playing practical jokes on his friends.)

In the half century since winning the Leventritt Competition, which included a solo appearance with the New York Philharmonic, Eugene Istomin achieved an enviable reputation as one of the world's leading pianists. However, I would venture to say that his name is much better known among his fellow artists than by the general public. The reason is that he is a musician's pianist. His powerful virtuosity, tempered by a rare poetic intellect and style, has brought him triple acclaim – as a recitalist, a chamber musician, and a soloist with the world's greatest orchestras and conductors.

For a number of years he was a member of what New York musicians called the "Half-Million-Dollar Trio." Violinist Isaac Stern and cellist Leonard Rose were the two other members. (Violinist Jascha Heifetz, cellist Gregor Piatigorsky, and pianist Arthur Rubinstein made up the "Million-Dollar Trio.") While I was active in New York, I frequently had the great pleasure of making music with Eugene and getting to know his Russian parents, both of whom were musicians.

As a violist, I have always appreciated how much better off I am than pianists in one very important respect. I always have the comfort of playing on my own instrument. Pianists, on the other hand, are constantly faced with the challenge of playing an instrument with which they are unfamiliar. Eugene Istomin solved that problem neatly for a time, but at quite an expense. He was accompanied on his tours by his own piano technician and, using a specially equipped G.M. medium duty truck, by two Steinway concert-grand pianos, plus a small upright. Eugene had the luxury of playing pianos he knew well and also the pleasure of bringing the pianistic standards of New York and London to whatever size city in which he performed.

Eugene was fond of telling us about the time the Stern-Rose-Istomin Trio performed for the Kennedys in the White House. After playing for a distinguished group of invited guests in the East Room, the three musicians were invited to dine with the Kennedys in their private quarters. Also invited were conductor Leonard Bernstein and composer Aaron Copland. At one point before dinner Eugene was part of a small group, which included the president, Lenny, and Isaac Stern.

"There was a big Democratic Party event going on in Madison Square Garden in

New York. All the bigwigs in the party were there. To start the proceedings, Metropolitan Opera tenor Jan Peerce sang our national anthem. Then Lenny Bernstein came out and explained it. President Kennedy roared with laughter. Bernstein just stood there straight faced and asked, 'Is that the end of the story?'"

Eugene punctuated his account by telling us that, although his dinner companion was charming and very attractive, she wasn't the greatest conversationalist. He had been sitting next to Jackie Kennedy!

Eugene's parents must have started his piano lessons when he was very young because his prodigious musical gifts were discovered at age six by Alexander Siloti (a famous Ukranian pianist-conductor, a student of Liszt and teacher of Rachmaninoff). At the age of twelve Eugene went to the Curtis Institute to study with Rudolf Serkin and Mieczyslaw Horszowski. Eugene is married to Marta (widow of) Pablo Casals. She was for a number of years Director of the Kennedy Center for the Performing Arts and is now president of the Manhattan School of Music in New York.

Eugene recalls the most meaningful and poignant moment of his career: "It was my first meeting with Pablo Casals in March 1950, before the first Prades Festival. His warmth and unpretentious humanity made an everlasting impression on me. After I played a short Bach piece for him he brought out his cello and, sitting down right in front of me, this legendary figure proceeded to play an entire Bach solo suite. To use revival-meeting language, 'I thought that I had died and gone to heaven!' But, I was right here on earth and had just received a lesson in simple grace with which the truly great conduct themselves."

Pianist Eugene Istomin and Marta Casals Istomin (President of Manhattan School of Music)

Composer Wm. Bolcom with mezzo Joan Morris

"One moment, Maestro!" (A most unusual moment during a Rubinstein-Katims orchestra rehearsal)

Chapter 10
Pianists, Opus 2

Byron Janis

Milton: I saw a marked similarity in the hands of Byron Janis and the sculptured hand of the great Polish composer, Frederick Chopin, which sits on the piano in Byron's Park Avenue apartment in New York. The similarity lends some credence to the belief that Byron is the reincarnation of the famous pianist, who composed a major portion of the vast literature for the piano. This belief, supported and encouraged by Janis himself, is held by many musicians.

In a brilliant career that reached its 50th anniversary in 1998, Byron insured his reputation as one of the world's great pianists. It's not surprising that he was one of the few young pianists Vladimir Horowitz agreed to coach. The many honors and awards Byron has earned, among them the French Legion d'Honneur and the Grande Prix des Disques, confirm Horowitz's judgment.

Milton and Virginia Katims

In the early '70s Byron asked me to fly with him to Paris to conduct the entire Rachmaninoff piano-orchestra repertoire with him and the Padesloupe Orchestra on two successive evenings. My previous experiences with Byron had been so rewarding that I was delighted to accept the invitation. The Paris performances were no less exciting.

My collaborations with Arthur Rubinstein came to mind. As with Arthur, I had the strong feeling that if I were a pianist instead of a violist, I'd want to play the piano the way Byron did. His musical ideas coincided with mine so consistently that we rarely had to resort to words to achieve our common goal. It was almost uncanny. When we did talk Byron didn't simply turn his head toward me, he would turn his entire body in my direction. Only later did I learn that he had to do so because of the onset of arthritis, which gradually became so widespread and severe that it would curtail his career.

I believe the advancing arthritis had much to do with his decision to turn his talents to composing. He wrote the musical theme for the Global Forum on Human Survival, and for a PBS television special. His composing talent was also manifested in the score he wrote for a major TV special about his father-in-law, the celebrated actor Gary Cooper. Although arthritis forced him to cut back on his recital tours Byron has continued to play many fund-raising concerts for the Arthritis Foundation, for which he serves as Ambassador. He is one of the foundation's leading national spokesmen. Without question, he is an American hero in more ways than one.

Sharing the artist's room with Byron wherever we have performed together was a great deal of fun for a number of reasons. One was that he has a marvelous sense of humor (I know he has because he always laughs at my jokes). Another is that he exhibited none of the debilitating nervousness many performers display just before a performance. A third reason, and perhaps the best of them all, was the presence of his lovely wife Maria, Gary Cooper's daughter, an extremely gifted and successful painter. We have one of her paintings on a wall in our home.

The Pleasure Was Ours

Maria is also talented as a barber. It was always fun watching her snip superfluous locks from her husband's head, arranging his coiffeur expertly just before he walked on stage. Who else gets such loving and creative service from a spouse just before the big moment?

The Paris adventure with Byron was marred briefly by one very negative experience for which I was totally unprepared and in which Byron was not involved. One of the two all-Rachmaninoff programs included the "Rhapsodie on a Theme" of Paganini and two of the concertos, while the other was to have featured the "Symphonic Dances" to fill out the musical fare. Unfortunately, the orchestra parts for the "Dances" did not arrive in time for the rehearsals, and so I was forced to substitute Tchaikovsky's "Romeo & Juliet." The unavoidable program change was announced just before I walked toward the podium to conduct the Tchaikovsky.

When they saw me, the audience greeted me with a round of boos – an experience that jolted me as I had never been before, and hope never to be again. It was a shock I cannot forget; I finished the program, with jaws clenched and sweaty palms.

Tchaikovsky fared far better than I did. I learned something else I shall never forget: Everything I had read and heard about Parisian audiences is true. They demand what they pay for and accept no substitutes.

One of the many indications of Byron's marvelous sense of humor is his ready willingness to laugh at himself. During one of our many conversations trading performance experiences, Byron told me, "I was giving a recital in Pittsburgh, at the Carnegie Hall there, which is part of the Carnegie Mellon Institute. I went to the hall to practice on the piano, as I usually do the morning of a concert. The doors leading into the auditorium from the foyer have small panes of glass. As I was working I noticed a gentleman outside looking through one of the panes into the Hall, obviously listening and watching me as I practiced. Nothing annoys me more than this sort of intrusion on my working privacy, but I thought the best thing would be to ignore him and eventually he would go away. As time passed he still remained, listening and watching."

"Finally, my temper got the best of me and I stormed off the stage to open the door and ask him to please leave. To my amazement, what confronted me was a portrait of a charming 19th century gentleman hanging on the wall opposite the door, his eyes and head positioned in such a manner that he was always forced to watch everything that went on in the Hall. Perhaps he was listening, too!"

Recently Janis made his first recording in many years – an all-Chopin recital which was greeted with critical acclaim.

Van Cliburn

Virginia: Van Cliburn has managed the incredibly difficult task of living up to his own legend. Three decades after achieving world renown by winning the Tchaikovsky Prize in Moscow, his pianism and musicianship are still constantly changing and constantly growing. And through the years of fame, the tall (6 foot 4), rangy fellow with the great mop of curly hair has kept his boyish charm and impeccably gracious Southern manner.

Van has an honesty and intensity as a performer and as a human being that will not permit him to rest, to be satisfied with yesterday's plaudits. His extreme sensitivity has always created an additional challenge to his storied concert career.

One night after a Seattle appearance that could only be described as sensational, he told me thoughtfully, "Each performance is a new test, Virginia. All I can think about is the terrifying responsibility that never ends and that never grows any easier – the utter loneliness of a pianist as he walks on-stage, the isolation, and the expectations of each audience. And I ask myself each time, "Have I done enough work? Will I touch someone with my musical ideas and with my own feelings, as well as with the technique that everyone seems to take for granted these days?'

"I pray each time – pray for the strength and for that wonderful, and so often elusive, freedom in my performance."

Van was born in Shreveport, Louisiana. His New York debut with the Philharmonic came after he won the important Leventritt Award. But it was not until he won the Moscow prize in 1958 that his name became a household word. The almost hysterical acclaim given Van by the Russians succeeded in waking up the rest of the world, particularly his own countrymen, to his gifts. When he returned to the United States, he was given a ticker-tape parade by the people of New York, the first and only time (as far as we know) an American musician has been so honored.

I have always found Van Cliburn to be a beautiful person, filled with honesty and compassion. He inspired the founding of the Cliburn Foundation and the Cliburn Piano Competition in Fort Worth, Texas. That, plus the encouragement he has given so many gifted young pianists, are excellent examples of his caring nature.

Van has two idiosyncrasies. He says he never reads his concert reviews and he usually arrives at the concert hall so late that he gives both conductor and manager high blood pressure. I was backstage once, with Milton nervously pacing in the wings and awaiting his arrival as soloist of the evening. The orchestra was tuned, a hush had come over the audience, and Milton was poised to go on-stage. At the last moment, Van dashed in, nonchalantly grinned, embraced Milton and said, mischievously, "Let's go!"

Leon Fleisher

Milton: "If you beat me I'll never engage you again!" It was my threat to pianist Leon Fleisher just before our ping-pong match in the Spanish Ballroom of Seattle's old Olympic Hotel. The match was the highly publicized encore at the Candlelight Musicale, the annual benefit Virginia and I staged for the Seattle Symphony. We had just performed for a very responsive audience of chamber-music enthusiasts.

The musical portion of the event had concluded with Schubert's "Trout Quintet" (in the Pacific Northwest, we call it the Salmon Quintet). Our players, in addition to Leon at the Steinway, were violinist Henry Siegl, the orchestra's concertmaster; Virginia, straddling her Grancino cello; Jim Harnett, head of the orchestra's double bass section, with his "bull fiddle," and me, with my Testore viola.

With so many in attendance in the ballroom, our quintet barely had bowing room on the small space allotted us for a stage. The informal chamber-music concert followed the tradition Virginia and I had initiated soon after our arrival in Seattle. It always featured the symphony soloist, usually a long time friend who was appearing with the orchestra at the same time. Our aim was to recreate, in the much larger setting of the Spanish Ballroom, the informal music-making ambience we frequently enjoyed in our home. Some of the other good friends who had joined us for a benefit were Isaac Stern, Henryk Szeryng, Leonard Rose, Claudio Arrau, and Eugene Istomin.

When I challenged Leon Fleisher to a ping-pong match as a climax to the musicale, I had no idea that he had been New York State's junior champion! I had my first inkling that I was in trouble when he showed up at the table, paddle in hand, and a spanking-white sweatshirt with the words "Steinway Stealers" emblazoned in black across the front and a huge number "88" on the back. And he didn't sport just the single paddle in his right hand. He also had a large assortment of very special paddles in a bag. Talk about psychological intimidation. But I fancied myself as a pretty fair player, and I thought I had a chance to win.

Forget it! He beat me handily. And, worst of all, he drew an ovation from the very happy crowd. Another ovation! As if he needed one.

The Pleasure Was Ours

Despite my faux threat, of course, I invited Leon to return as soloist with the orchestra. The circumstances, however, were quite different. At the time of the Candlelight Musicale, it could be said Leon was very much a two-fisted pianist. I had had the joy of conducting his tremendous performance of "Brahms' Piano Concerto No. 2 in B-Flat," a monumental work that duplicates on a grand scale the chamber-music-like collaboration of soloist, conductor, and orchestra. The orchestra's role is much more than a mere accompaniment.

Leon deserved the tumultuous accolades audiences always gave him. But shortly afterwards misfortune struck. His right wrist was afflicted with carpal tunnel syndrome. He could not play with his right hand for any extended period of time. One critic referred to him sympathetically, as "probably the most debilitated musician of our time." His inability to use his right hand was caused, most likely, by his intense eight or ten hours of daily practice – or, as Leon himself expressed it – by "pumping ivory" that damaged his muscles. His attempt to work through the problem by practicing even harder resulted in a severe case of repetitive stress injury.

Although he sought medical help from doctors who specialized in instrumentalists' injuries, Leon decided his problem might be better understood by doctors specializing in sports injuries. He believed there was a need for better understanding of the physiology of muscles, as, for example, the way ballet dancers approach their art and their muscular problems. Perhaps we instrumentalists should study ballet – and learn by doing. Leon recommended that course to his students; and to set an example, he himself enrolled in a ballet class.

As he was forced to cut down on his own playing, Leon threw himself almost completely into his teaching at Peabody in Baltimore. Following the path set by his world-famous teacher, pianist Artur Schnabel, he chose class teaching rather than individual lessons. "It is, in part, a question of efficiency," he says. "The students learn ten to twelve times more repertoire and they also gain the valuable experience of performing for critical listeners."

127

Milton and Virginia Katims

His concert touring with the usual two-handed literature curtailed, Leon turned to the repertoire of piano music written for the left hand alone. He also bought himself a baton, like so many other virtuoso instrumentalists. It was in both these modes, but at different times, that he returned to Seattle to play the "Ravel Piano Concerto for Left Hand" and Benjamin Britten's "Diversions" for Left Hand Op.21." Whether with one or two hands, Leon's very special qualities always shone through. He, too, is one of those gifted talents who is a musician's pianist. Leon toured the West Coast with us as our soloist, alternating the Ravel and Britten works each evening.

I have two added reasons for remembering that tour with Leon. One was that for the entire trip, Leon and I traveled in the car of then symphony manager Alan Watrous, and we played gin rummy in the back seat as Alan drove. We kept score on paper. I was extraordinarily lucky as the cards fell my way time after time. I couldn't lose. At the end of the tour, he owed me about $800. I never collected! But at least I had evened the score with the ping-pong star of the "Steinway Stealers."

The other reason was our experience in Los Angeles. The orchestra members and I had checked into a very luxurious motel on Olympic Drive. Being the conductor, I had been given the Presidential Suite, and a quite elegant one at that. On the second morning of our stay I was almost thrown out of bed by a very large earthquake at 6 a.m. (in 1973). My TV set and the lights were blinking on and off like a theater marquee. I'd be lying if I said I wasn't frightened as never before. I forgot that I should have stood in one of the doorways. Instead, I clung to the mattress. I can't remember how long my panic lasted, but gradually I began to relax, no longer really caring what happened.

When it was over, I discovered the reason why I had relaxed. My bedroom was immediately above the motel liquor store. The fumes emanating from all the broken bottles of whiskey were coming up through the cracks in the floor of my room. It was Fate's odd version of a cheap drunk! And an intoxicating finale to an earth-shaking experience.

*The Katims
with pianist
Van Cliburn
in Fort Worth,
Texas*

*At the Casals Festival in Puerto Rito, the Katims with pianists Rudi Serkin and Eugene Istomin
and cellist Mischa Schneider (of the Budapest String Quartet)*

Byron Janis signing photos

Maria (Cooper) and Byron Janis in Seattle

The Pleasure Was Ours

The first time Virginia and I saw Leon with baton in hand was at Round Top in Texas. He seemed to be quite at home at the podium, so I invited him to guest-conduct a pair of Seattle Symphony concerts. When he asked for a high stool for rehearsals I thought nothing of it. Many conductors prefer sitting during rehearsals (Toscanini, a notable exception, never sat down). But when Leon requested the stool for the concerts, too, I did think it strange. My questioning look drew the explanation from him that he felt very self-conscious standing with his back to the audience and "exposing my wide derriere." (He would have disdained Picasso's sculpture of Rubinstein's seat!)

Today Leon's right hand has recovered enough to permit him to return to the keyboard with both hands. Knowing what a serious and thoughtful musician he is, I'm sure he must take great comfort in being able to return to the rich, vast repertoire that two-handed pianists enjoy. Leon has much to give.

Traveling with him, aside from unpaid gin rummy debts and earthquakes, was always a lot of fun. Next to his great talent as a pianist, his sense of humor is his most appealing characteristic. While we were on tour with the Seattle Symphony, which has a large number of women in it, Leon asked me if I knew when we had been on tour too long? I had no reply, but he went on to say, "When the women in the orchestra began to look attractive to you, you've been away from home too long!" Does Leon dare to play Seattle again?

The Serkins (Rudolf and Peter)

*V*irginia: Music has its share of famous father-son virtuosi, but none surpasses the name Serkin. First, I must talk about Papa, Rudolf Serkin, one of the most remarkable pianists of our time. I will never forget his performance of the "Brahms' B-Flat Piano Concerto" with Milton and the Seattle Symphony. The manager of the orchestra, Ruth McCreery, suggested that Rudi play an encore after his fourth bow.

Milton and Virginia Katims

"Madame," he said, "the only encore I can play after the 'Brahms' 2nd Piano Concerto' is Beethoven's 'Hammerklavier Sonata,' and that would take 55 minutes."Needless to say, Ruth beat a hasty retreat. There was no encore.

We first met Rudi at a Casals Festival. He was a modest, quiet, hard-working perfectionist, whose approach to music was well balanced between his heart and his head. His international career had started with his debut with the Vienna Symphony when he was twelve years old. An important part of his musical life was spent in collaboration with famed violinist, Adolf Busch, who was also his father-in-law. They played violin and piano recitals and also appeared together with the Busch Chamber Players.

He made his American debut at a Coolidge Festival in Washington, D.C. Soon thereafter, he made an auspicious appearance with Toscanini and the New York Philharmonic. He solidified his reputation with a series of "Mozart" and "Beethoven Concertos," with the National Orchestral Association conducted by Leon Barzin, and a "Beethoven Sonata" series with Busch. But Rudi was interested in more than a career as a concert pianist. His deep interest in young artists led him to accept the directorship of the Curtis Institute, and then to create the Marlboro Festival in Vermont. He became an inspiration for all the gifted, young musicians who flocked to his side. Just imagine what it meant for those young people with whom he played chamber music.

On one of our trips to the East Coast, Milton and I rented a car to drive up to Marlboro to renew acquaintances with old friends — among them the Schneider brothers (Mischa and Sasha), Felix Galamir, Isadore Cohen, and, of course, Rudi Serkin. All of them and many more friends would be there eventually.

At the entrance to the colony's grounds we passed a large sign reading: "Drive with care. Musicians at play." Lunch was about to be served so we went into the large dining hall and found Mischa there. Soon after we sat down, I felt a pair of hands gently cover my eyes. I guessed, "Felix!"

"No," said a familiar voice, as he removed his hands. "It's only me, Rudi."

The day after his performance of the Brahms in Seattle, I attended a ladies' luncheon at which his playing was the chief subject of conversation. One lady was wondering how Serkin kept from falling off the bench, because he went through such strenuous physical motions when he played.

Trying to be facetious to match the silly question, I said, "Oh, he uses Christian Science." "Oh, no, Mrs. Katims. Didn't you see the way he screwed himself to the bench when he first sat down?"

I didn't have the heart to embarrass the lady by explaining that Rudi was simply adjusting the height of the piano bench.

Peter Serkin

Virginia: Many years later I had my first opportunity to hear Peter Serkin, the already famous son of the long-famous father. Peter had been invited to play a recital on the President's Series at the University of Washington's Meany Hall. I admit I was anxious to compare pere et fils. Which one was better and why? I had hoped that it would be a draw. All I knew about young Peter was the stunning publicity I had read after his New York concerts and the rather wild tales I had heard about him when he was younger. I also had some personal information from our own son, Peter, who had "hung out" with young Serkin in his early New York days when both were rebels. The word was that "Young Serkin was trying to cut himself adrift from his authoritarian father."

After hearing Peter play I knew that the acorn had not fallen far from the oak, despite the talk about his reported desire to "cut himself adrift." Instead of a rebel, I heard a wonderfully polished, young pianist with gifts similar to those that had marked his great roots. He strode on-stage tall and slender, his eyeglasses giving him a rather scholarly appearance. No full dress for Peter. He wore a gray suit and a non-descript tie – and he carried his music in his hand. Carried his music?

I wondered why he hadn't memorized the music he was to play. Was he imitating the great Dame Myra Hess, who always used the score when she played? When I looked at my program I had my answer. Serkin was opening his concert with a piece written by Takemitsu, whose music is extremely complicated and harmonically eclectic. But what a strange choice for an opening number. No Scarlatti, not even a bit of Mozart? No Schubert "Moments Musicales," nor anything Papa Serkin might have chosen. Peter explained to the audience that this was to be dedicated to the Japanese composer, who had died recently and with whom he had enjoyed a warm and very personal relationship.

I have to acknowledge I found the piece fascinating. Peter was just warming up. His "Variations and Fugue on a Theme of Bach" by Reger was a stunning work stunningly played. So was the rest of the program, including Beethoven's "Les Adieus Sonata." Milton and I were amazed by his talent and maturity. Like father like son. An authoritarian father? I doubt it.

Peter is a committed champion of new music. I asked him why. "It comes from my intense curiosity about new ideas in everything, music, books, whatever. My curiosity seems to come naturally to me, even touching my interpretations of all the music I play, new or old. Sometimes, I suppose, my search for new musical ideas may alienate some people in the calcified, conservative audiences."

I remembered the stories about the young Peter Serkin, touring almost exclusively with Tashi, a group which for years devoted itself to nothing but contemporary music, and of the young Serkin clad in a dashiki. At that time he had "dropped out and turned on," like so many baby boomers. When I reminded him of his early days, he said, "Yes, but now I'm even playing the famous music with which my Dad was always associated – the "Appassionata" and 'Moonlight Sonatas' of Beethoven. Great stuff, but, of course, that's why they have survived and why audiences relate to them. Yes, I've changed. Probably less of an attitude on my part, I guess. I think I'm in a good place emotionally.

"My personal life is great with my wife, Regina. As the father of four, very interesting kids, I love to sit down at the piano with our youngest Elena, but I don't want to push her. Me, of all people. And now, this summer, Tanglewood is coming up, and it's galvanizing for me to work with young musicians. How stimulating it is to put all these elements together and play music. If only the whole world could pursue this musical togetherness."

I wrote two notes to Peter, asking him to tell me the most inspirational, traumatic, or amusing experience of his career, but I received no reply. When I asked my own son Peter why he thought I had received no response, he said, "Mom, did it ever occur to you that perhaps all of a musician's feelings and experiences are embodied in his or her performances?" Hmmm. "Right on," I said to myself.

In retrospect, what has impressed me most about Peter Serkin's playing has been the feeling of improvisation in almost every phrase, whether the music is old or new. I recall the letter I once wrote to Arthur Rubinstein, complimenting him for the "sense of improvisation" he had brought to an old warhorse. His response was that I could not have paid him a greater compliment. I knew exactly what he meant, and now my own son was reminding me of what I already knew.

We musicians practice our hearts out, striving to perfect our playing of the music at hand and sometimes the result is a lack of spontaneity in the performance. The great challenge, no matter how many times we perform a piece, is to achieve the performer's most important goal: To re-create, with accent on the "create." Each performance must have the freshness of a first performance.

Katims rehearsing the Japan Philharmonic in Tokyo wearing the gift from the orchestra

Chapter 11
Pianists, Opus 3

Gary Graffman

Milton: As director of the prestigious Curtis Institute of Music, pianist Gary Graffman follows a distinguished trio of performing artists who directed that famous conservatory: pianists Josef Hoffman and Rudolf Serkin and violinist Ephrem Zimbalist. Gary, however, differs from his famous predecessors in that he himself is a product of the Institute and is making significant contributions to it and to the world of music.

Gary comes by his musical talent quite naturally. His father, Vladimir, was a professional violinist. Gary would be tucking a violin under his chin today if his father had had his way. Papa Volodya decided it was time for his son to start learning to play the violin when Gary was three. After a number of months of putting up with the scratching and the errant intonation, Papa decided that the problem was the father-son relationship. He took the boy to play for one of Vladimir's colleagues who, after hearing little Gary play, said, "It's too late. You should have brought him to me a year ago."

It was then decided that Gary should learn an easier instrument. Enter, the piano. It is generally acknowledged that in the very early stages learning to play the piano is easier than learning a string instrument. The piano becomes more difficult later on. At the age of seven, Gary was taken to audition for entrance to Curtis, and he evidently impressed the jury. His studies were to continue there under the sympathetic eyes and ears of Isabelle Vengerova, whom Gary describes as "an imposing figure, not very tall but extremely wide, who sailed about the studio like an overstuffed battleship in search of the enemy, cannons loaded and ready for action."

That quote is from Gary's fascinating autobiography, *I Really Should Be Practicing (Reflections on the Pleasures and Perils of Playing the Piano in Public)*. I recommend the book to anyone who can read, musician or not. The musicians will relate and react to the delicious humor that fills the book, and the non-musicians will encounter a delightful introduction to our world, without equal.

A story Gary likes to repeat took place when he was about to rehearse the Tschaikowsky "1st Piano Concerto," with Andre Previn conducting the Los Angeles Philharmonic. Gary had just flown from the South Seas to Los Angeles and greeted Andre with, "And to think, only yesterday I was driving in Papeete!"

Without missing a beat Andre retorted, "You must have made all the lights!"

Gary served as a charter member of the OYAPs (Outstanding Young American Pianists), whose members include Leon Fleisher, Eugene Istomin, Julius Katchen, Seymour Lipkin, Van Cliburn, and Jacob Lateiner. Perhaps by this time the name of the group has been changed to OMAP (Outstanding Middle-aged American Pianists). Leon and Gary have been particularly close colleagues, to such an extent that both were afflicted with carpal tunnel syndrome at almost the same time. That's the debilitating ailment in which the wrists of their right hands are incapacitated enough to force them to restrict their repertoire to works for the left hand alone. William Bolcom, the dynamic American composer, has written a concerto for two left hands for Gary and Leon.

Gary's pianistic prowess has taken him all over the world with his charming wife Naomi, his severest, but most sympathetic, critic. Like Eugene Istomin, Gary hated facing a different piano wherever he performed, so he too paid the cost of shipping his favorite Steinway grand from New York to each concert destination. The OYAPs adopted this practice for all members, often sharing the costs when touring dates were scheduled.

In his book, Gary describes the fascinating process in detail. A very special lot of concert grands were kept for Steinway artists in the basement of the Steinway Building on West 57th Street in New York. Each of the OYAP members tried them all and selected the one he liked best. That piano was given the number assigned to the soloist (in Gary's case it was #199) and was subsequently shipped to the appropriate concert destinations. At one time Gary's piano, #199, which he had dubbed his "mistress," had to be returned to the Steinway shop for repairs. Temporarily he used another piano, which he christened Christine and felt that he was being unfaithful to #199.

A glittering celebration was staged at Carnegie Hall on the 100th birthday of the Steinway Company. Twenty well known pianists, including the OYAP members, of course, were seated at 20 Steinway grands. At the 21st piano, conducting the group, was Dimitri Mitropoulos, (the Greek maestro who was quite bald), causing one New York wit to comment, "This is the first time 20 Steinways were conducted by a Baldwin!"

Graffman's successful career took off after he won the prizes of the short-lived Rachmaninoff Foundation and the ongoing important Leventritt Award. These led to engagements to solo with Eugene Ormandy and the Philadelphia Orchestra. Gary astutely realized how important playing chamber music would be in his preparations for performing with an orchestra. He would be given the same chamber-music advice a few years later by conductor-pianist George Szell of the Cleveland Orchestra.

Sol Hurok, the internationally noted impresario, was impressed by the awards Gary had won and brought him under his management. However, that association didn't last very long. When the Hurok office failed to carry through its contractual obligation to Gary's satisfaction, he scrapped the affiliation. Imagine firing Sol Hurok!

We were most interested when Gary told us about his playing not only for the legendary Vladimir Horowitz but also, a few months later, for Rudolf Serkin, and the difference in their approaches. While Horowitz wanted to re-create the sound of the human voice on the piano, Serkin thought in terms of the sounds of different orchestral instruments. Each conviction was valid, of course, but I must say-that if I were a pianist, I would strive to achieve both goals.

Gary's comparison of a performing musician with the role of an actor is quite intriguing. A composer, he says, includes many performance clues like phrasing, pedaling, dynamics, and even fingering in his score, while an author like Shakespeare, for example, provides very few. From that Graffman concludes that it should be easier for a musician to realize Beethoven's intentions than for an actor to discern Shakespeare's. I disagree! Despite the absence of instructions from the playwright, the actor must be more successful than the musician because he has the meaning and the logic of the words to assist him. For the performing musician, the notes on the printed page, no matter how many added directions, are but the bare beginning of making music.

The Pleasure Was Ours

Ingrate

One unbelievable, but unfortunately true, story is about an extremely temperamental and irritating pianist, whose name I won't reveal for obvious reasons. He was recording the Beethoven "Hammerklavier Sonata" and kept going over different sections of each movement until he felt that the engineer had more than enough tape to piece together a complete performance. The pianist left the studio after instructing the technical staff to notify him when the edited proof was ready. About three weeks later he was called to listen to the finished tape.

The engineer had made 41 insertions (!) and finally had come up with a finished proof that was absolutely seamless. The pianist listened to two run-throughs and then said airily, "That's OK." He failed to utter at least a "thank you" as he headed for the exit.

But before he reached the door, the work-weary engineer called out, "Don't you wish you played that way?"

Murray Perahia

Virginia: One of my favorite brilliant young stars of the keyboard is Murray Perahia, one of Milton's original "Stars of the Future." The first time I saw him, Murray walked on-stage to rehearse a concerto with the Seattle Symphony. Milton was conducting. I was sitting in the hall with a few musicians and some curious souls who had sneaked into the rehearsal to hear a pianist about whom we had heard or read very little. (His performance in Seattle came before he won the prestigious, very demanding Leeds International Piano Competition in England.)

As he walked to the piano I thought, "My Lord, this young man may never make it through the rehearsal, let alone the concert!" I had never seen a performer so skinny and pale. How would he survive the stresses and strains of the concert circuit, which deals severe physical and mental punishment to artists? The rehearsal began and I was immediately in awe. Murray played beautifully and emotionally, his frail body swaying with the music. I was most impressed, but I still wondered how this bare wisp of a young man could continue getting such wonderful music out of a concert grand for very long.

I went backstage, introduced myself, and without thinking asked Murray, "When did you have your last square meal? You can't survive in this profession unless you have a lot of strength, physical strength."

"I've always looked this way," he said. "I do eat, but I don't have much of an appetite."

I took things into my own hands. "Please, come home with us now. I have a great homemade soup, and I'll broil a steak for you."

He seemed embarrassed, but because I was the conductor's wife what could he do? We drove home and I sat him down at the table and actually tied a towel around his neck, as if he were one of my own children. I put a steaming bowl of vegetable soup before him.

"I really don't like vegetables," he said meekly.

"I don't care," I said in a tone that surprised me as much as it must have shocked him. "You'll learn to like them. You have to build a strong body."

I toasted a couple of slices of wheat bread for him to dunk in the soup.

"I don't like this kind of bread," he said weakly. "I like white bread."

"You learn to like it," I said, sounding more and more like a bonafide Jewish Mother. "It's good for you and builds muscle." Murray's concerts in Seattle were a triumph for him, Milton, and the orchestra. I was sure it was my hearty meal that did it!

We heard Murray play in London a few years ago. He looked fantastic! Lots of wheat bread and veggie soup later, he has a beautiful wife and three lovely children. Of course, he is still relatively slim, but also strong and muscular. He no longer looks as if he is on a hunger strike.

In the intervening years he has gone on to a stunning, extremely busy career that has taken him virtually everywhere. Early on he played a concert at the Aldeburgh Festival where he met composer Benjamin Britten and tenor Peter Pears. Later, he became co-director of the festival (1981 to 1989). Along the way he developed a close friendship with Vladimir Horowitz, whose musical perception and personality have been an abiding inspiration to the young pianist.

Murray has made many first-rate recordings, including the complete cycle of "Mozart Piano Concertos." Music lovers who want to hear Mozart played as they dream of hearing it should get Perahia's recordings - all of them.

When asked to name his major sources of inspiration, Murray named a most interesting trio of artists: watching Pablo Casals' performance of the "Bach St. Matthew Passion," playing two piano works with Rudi Serkin at Marlboro, and accompanying Peter Pears in a cycle of Benjamin Britten songs.

Murray's association with Benjamin Britten has already been noted, but I cannot resist adding the following very revealing incident: Perahia was accompanying Peter Pears in a cycle of Britten's songs. Britten was weak and quite ill as he was recovering from heart surgery. During the rehearsal he asked Murray to play some chords in a certain way, but he didn't quite understand the direction. Britten got up, walked over to the piano, sat down, and beautifully played with Pears to illustrate what he had meant. Inspirational! Ah, the power of music to help one rise above physical infirmities. Britten died a short time later.

Lorin Hollander

Milton: Another one-time, boy wonder who has grown into one of the most mature and thoughtful pianists of the day is Lorin Hollander. His career has been most unusual. He gave his first concert in his kindergarten class, playing a two-part Bach invention. Alas! He also had his first encounter with music critics at the same time, although I must say it was somewhat less abstract than one normally finds music criticism: He was beaten up in the school yard by members of his audience. His fellow classmates!

A short time before that experience we had received a phone call from his mother, Mary, inviting us to come over to hear the Hollander's four year-old play the piano. Normally we would have shied away from this kind of chore, another look at still another wunderkind? But Lorin's father, Max, was a good friend, the associate concertmaster of Toscanini's NBC Symphony. Virginia and I decided the youngster must have some talent.

After we heard Lorin play some Bach quite creditably, Virginia, always concerned about the "slavery" of being a professional musician, asked the boy if he really wanted a career as a concert pianist. With great seriousness and the demeanor of a much older person, Lorin told her, "Of course I plan to be a pianist. Not only that, but I plan to be the best in the world."

It was a startlingly, bold statement from a little, four-year old redhead, whose feet dangled from the piano stool because they couldn't reach the pedals. That serious, precocious little boy certainly knew what he wanted to do and what he wanted to be. Throughout the years of our friendship with Mary and Max, we watched Lorin develop, never once relinquishing his life plan, which extended beyond merely becoming a master of the keyboard. Today he is called an influential philosopher and educator, who has lectured on a variety of subjects relating to music, the arts, science, creativity, and psychology. He also followed in the footsteps of Leonard Bernstein, Mstislav Rostropovich, and Marian Anderson, in becoming national chairman of "Young Audiences" in 1981.

Lorin's career began with a Carnegie Hall debut at the age of eleven. In subsequent years he has played countless recitals in most of the world's principal music centers and soloed with virtually every major orchestra in the U.S. and abroad. He was one of the many young artists I invited to play with the orchestra when I became conductor of the Seattle Symphony. Each time I was on the podium and looked down at Lorin at the piano, I had to smile at the memory of the little, red-haired boy whose feet could not reach the pedals.

But when I had conversations later with the now thinning-haired, young man, I was impressed with his profound thinking on a variety of subjects, most notably his views on arts in education. I agree strongly with him when he says, "The arts for me are the emotions. Why is it that when funds are low in our schools, the first to lose them are the arts? Why not take some from the arts, some from sports, some from languages, and some from other disciplines? But, no, funding is taken only from the arts. This is criminal. If you remove arts education from the schools, the result is to invite mental chaos.

"When you take the arts out of the school curriculum, you take away the chance for children to express emotion in a creative way. You take away their learning to work with the concept of quality, elegance, beauty, passion, artistic structure, and a peaceful sense of contemplation. It is to weep!!"

These are the thoughts of an ever-probing, profound mind.

We weren't always in town when Lorin returned to play in Seattle, but we did hear his performance with the Seattle Symphony when he played the St. Saens "Egyptian Piano Concerto, the Fifth," which he had played with me in one of his earliest appearances in Seattle. He played brilliantly and the audience took him to its heart as usual, with a rousing ovation.

Afterwards we went backstage to his dressing room. He didn't know we were in the audience. In the rush, he sailed right past us, looking like an American guru, bearded like the Bard, and reached for a glass of Evian water. The sweat was still pouring from his face, proof of the toll of a challenging performance. Belatedly he recognized us, and hugs were exchanged. He flopped onto a couch and began to speak in a voice that wasn't much above a whisper. In minutes he brought us up to date on his grown children and showed us a photo of his three-month-old.

With obvious passion in his voice, he said, "Every child has the potential to be a genius. The genes alone will not determine the newborn's destiny. Much will depend upon the parents' input."

Virginia and I had the same thought. It sounded as if we could reliably expect that another Lorin had been born. Considering the precocity and nervous energy of the original, we could only say, "Heaven help them all — the new child and the parents."

Chapter 12
Pianists, Opus 4

Milton: We can't take leave of extraordinary pianists with whom I have made music without including Bela Siki, William Bolcom, and Abbey Simon.

Bela Siki

Hungarian-born Bela Siki, is without a doubt one of the most modest musicians I have ever met. That statement should come as no surprise to those who spend any time among professional musicians. Bela prefers talking (and most lovingly!) about every pianist but himself. One would never guess that he is a successful, well-traveled, keyboard artist, who has performed worldwide and is also known everywhere, not only as a teacher, but as a jurist in international piano competitions.

I have always found it difficult to separate this stellar artist from the affable, helpful neighbor he has been. For many years Bela and his lovely wife Yolande, a

Milton and Virginia Katims

French-speaking Swiss from Geneva, lived across the street from us in the quiet Laurelhurst section of Seattle. (Bela was teaching at the University of Washington.) We watched their two fine children, Muriel and Francois, grow up, just as they watched our Peter and Pamela. (Muriel is now a top-rated, anchor woman on Swiss television in Geneva and Francois is an executive with the Boeing Co. Our Peter is in radio and doing meditative research in Australia and Pamela is communications director of the North Shore School District in Seattle.) The neighborly growing-up years brought all eight of us very close together.

Bela, Virginia, and I also have had a professional relationship. He appeared as soloist with the Seattle Symphony a number of times when I was its conductor. Also, he, Virginia, and I have joined to play chamber music. One of the final things I did before leaving Seattle for Houston was to record, with Bela as soloist, the Dohnanyi "Variations on a Nursery Rhyme" for Vox and Robert Suderburg's Piano Concerto, "The Mirror of Time," for Columbia. One of the first things I did upon our return to Seattle was to record the Bach "Gamba Sonatas" with Bela for Pantheon Legends and to co-edit the sonatas for International Music Company.

But Bela should be permitted to speak for himself (just imagine his words spoken with a delightful Hungarian accent), "During the long years of my performing career I have had the opportunity to meet and exchange ideas with many of my exceptionally gifted colleagues. Those meetings and conversations gave me a great many rewarding and happy moments. I grew up in a music-loving family in Budapest, where I was born. My parents took me to concerts and to the opera when I was very young. In live performances and through recordings, I heard artists like Dohnanyi, Cortot, Gieseking, Backhaus, Fischer, and Rubinstein.

"When I was barely 20 years old, I became a student of Dohnanyi at the Franz Liszt Academy. It was a great honor because he accepted no more than three students in his master course. Dohnanyi was a born genius, blessed with hands that produced the most beautiful sound on the piano. He had a vast repertoire, thanks to what would be called a computer memory today. One reading of any work was enough to imprint it indelibly in his memory, and he could play it years later with little or no practice. This incredible gift made it very difficult for those of us who were studying with him. He expected the same from us and believed we should learn a new work for each lesson, no matter what else we had to do. As a teacher, he was most interested in the long line and seldom paid attention to detail.

"One day I asked Dohnanyi how he managed to be so even-tempered, so friendly and polite with everyone, and so much at peace with himself. After all, weren't artists expected to be temperamental and demanding? He smiled and answered, 'That's because I instantly forget hatred attacks, or anything unpleasant.'

"I had asked the question because an exceptionally malevolent and nasty review of a Dohnanyi recital had appeared just that morning in a Budapest newspaper. He had a right to blow off steam and to castigate the reviewer, but instead all he said about the notice was, 'I believe the audience is better served when I play and the reviewer writes, rather than the other way around.' I have always kept those words in mind, as well as his admonition to remember only the pleasant things and forget the unpleasant. Artistic expression grows best in a pleasant, harmonious atmosphere."

"Two years after my final lesson with Dohnanyi," Bela continued, "I had the good fortune to meet another genius in the person of Dino Lipatti, a young man with aristocratic features, jet black hair, and expressive black eyes. When I heard Lipatti's piano recording, I was speechless. I had never heard such perfection. As a result, I canceled my plans to study with Edwin Fischer, who had accepted me and was expecting me in Lucerne. After a hastily arranged audition, Lipatti took me on as a student. The fact that he spoke only Romanian and French and I spoke only Hungarian and German presented a temporary problem, which I quickly solved by taking a crash course in basic French, just enough to understand him."

"I soon discovered the reason for the perfection of his playing: He never played anything in public until he was confident that it was ready to be performed. In the

1930s and 1940s, we had two types of pianists, generally speaking – those who sought technical perfection, like Backhaus, and those for whom the personal and emotional content was most important, like Cortot. For me, Lipatti combined both of these approaches, playing with the highest technical perfection, but only as a means toward the highest musical demands. Lipatti believed that to know the style of a composer you had to know his whole output. To know a Beethoven sonata you should know the composer's string quartets and symphonies."

"As a teacher, Lipatti was thorough and conscientious – and always serious. His entire pedagogic career lasted only five years, with only a handful of students around him. I was most fortunate to have been one of them. His death at an early age because of leukemia was a tragedy for us and for all pianists. It was a great tragedy for the world. Even today, many years after his death, I still feel his influence."

I asked Bela about other legendary figures he had known intimately, particularly Walter Gieseking, one of the most celebrated interpreters of Beethoven and the French Impressionists. Bela said it was generally believed that Gieseking was born in Lyon, France, because his father was the German consul there. The truth, however, is far more interesting.

Gieseking's parents were not married. To make certain that their expected child would not be considered a bastard, they moved to Lyon, where, if the father had been present at birth and acknowledged being the father, the newborn would be registered in his name, even though the parents were unable to produce a marriage certificate.

Bela discovered that historic bit from sketches for Walter Gieseking's autobiography, which accidentally fell into his hands for a short time. Because Gieseking spent the first ten years of his life in France, he absorbed French culture thoroughly and gained an exceptional understanding of French music. The music lover who needs proof of this need only listen to one of his Debussy recordings.

It is very little known that Gieseking played the violin quite well, well enough to play in the second-violin section, if not the first, in a symphony orchestra. That ability saved him from front-line service in the First World War and may very well have saved his life!

"What I remember most about Gieseking," Bela said, "is the piano tone that nobody else could imitate. The sound of each note would jump from the piano like a little ping-pong ball. His huge hands were capable of incredible delicacies on the keyboard. His recordings of Ravel, especially, will remain landmarks of perfection for a long time."

Bela often reminisced about his encounters with other distinguished colleagues. Alfred Cortot, who had been Lipatti's teacher, was able to offer interpretive, emotional analyses that were striking and convincing at the same time. His suggestions were seldom technical in nature. For him, each note had to have a meaning of its own. His recordings of Chopin's "24 Preludes" stand unchallenged in the repertoire.

Another remarkable French pianist was Robert Casadesus, with whom I had the joy of making music in Seattle in a symphony program that included his gifted wife, Gaby, and their equally gifted son, Jean. Siki was so impressed with the cadenza to the "C-Minor Mozart, K-491," which Robert played in a recording, that he wrote to him requesting a copy. Casadesus responded immediately, "The cadenza is not mine. I wish it were. It is by St. Saens. You can buy it anywhere for $1.25."

Bela and I were fond of swapping stories about many other pianists, but the discussion seemed always to come back time and again to Arthur Rubinstein. There was only one Arthur Rubinstein. I am reminded of President Kennedy's famous comment that the White House hosted its most scintillating dinner party when Thomas Jefferson dined alone. I could easily think of Rubinstein in Jefferson's chair. He was that great a human being and mental giant.

One of my favorite Bela Siki experiences took place on a concert tour of South America. My impresario, Jose Perez, decided to accompany me when I went to play a concert in Colonia Suiza, Uruguay, a city that is just a few hours' drive from Montevideo. I was looking forward to seeing the city that had been founded by Swiss immigrants in the 19th century. We arrived in time for an afternoon reception and Jose dismissed the car and driver. It was not until it was time to dress for the concert that we realized, with horror, that my concert clothing was in the trunk of the car - now nowhere to be seen. I had on a sports jacket, slacks, and sports shoes, most inappropriate for a concert. Jose was wearing a dark business suit, and although he was at least three sizes larger than I was, we decided that the only solution was not only to exchange clothing, but shoes as well, since he was wearing a black pair.

I looked like Charlie Chaplin without the bowler and cane. Jose didn't fare much better; although, at least he could stay out of sight. We got through the concert ordeal and, despite the discomfort we both suffered, the audience demanded encore after encore. Offstage I could see Jose's alternating happiness and despair over the encores. My shoes were killing him! Both of us needed several hours to recuperate afterward. All he could say, over and over again, was, "I will never let my car and driver out of my sight again. I will never let my car and driver out of my sight again. I will never...."

William Bolcom, Composer, Pianist

*M*ilton: As we walked off the Carnegie Hall stage my piano soloist muttered, more to himself than to me, "My Gawd! My fingers felt like ten frankfurters!" Composer-pianist William Bolcom had just played the New York premiere of his piano concerto with the National Orchestral Association, which I was guest-conducting.

I assured him that this reaction to his performance was very much in the minority, that the audience, the orchestra, and I had enjoyed his exciting reading of his own demanding concerto. But I wasn't at all surprised at Bill's self-deprecating comment. It was so typical of his modesty and of his love for flippant quips, which could never camouflage his very real depth of mind and heart.

Bill had first played his piano concerto with the Seattle Symphony after we had had a number of meetings at his Greenwich Village pied-a-terre, where I not only absorbed his ideas and feelings about his concerto, but also renewed my many years of friendship with this fascinating young musician. I thought back to my early professional association with Bill Bolcom, long before he won a Pulitzer Prize and before he became a full professor at the University of Michigan at Ann Arbor – and long before he became one of America's most sought-after composers.

Back in the '60s I was music director of the La Jolla Musical Arts Society in California, where I presented a series of summer concerts in Sherwood Hall with a crackerjack chamber orchestra made up of first-rate musicians from the Los Angeles movie studios. Each program included the premiere of a work by an American composer, commissioned with the financial help of the association's men's committee. I had already conducted new works by William Bergsma, David del Tredeci, Benjamin Lees, and others. Friends had raved about a young Seattle phenomenon named William Bolcom, so I asked him to write a piece for us.

The result, the first of many collaborative efforts, was called "Fives." It was so impressive a work that, after conducting its first performance in La Jolla, I programmed it in Seattle. I have always enjoyed the role of musical mid-wife, bringing to life the brainchild of a composer.

How can I best describe the pleasure of being part of the creative process? It has been my experience that composers generally fall into two categories – those who are flexible, who are quite willing to listen to suggested changes and those whose reaction is, "No, I want it the way I wrote it!" My unspoken reaction to the latter has always been, "OK, Bub, that's the way you're going to get it."

Milton and Virginia Katims

Bill Bolcom belongs to the first group – always eagerly listening to different ideas, then deciding whether his Muse accepts the change. That may have a lot to do with the tremendous success he has enjoyed.

I recall the experience composer Don Gillis had with Maestro Toscanini, who was planning to program Gillis's "Symphony 5 1/2" as soon as it was completed. At the piano Maestro read through the fourth and final movement of the short symphony and said to Don,

"Ma, no, Geelis. In this movement you are a bad boy at the beginning, a very bad boy in the middle, and then, suddenly, for no reason at all near the end, you are a good boy. Perque? Why?"

Gillis retrieved his score and promised to rewrite the entire ending. About ten days later, when Don brought in the revised movement, Maestro Toscanini approved the new version. Then he reached across the piano, picked up two large pages of orchestral manuscript , tore them in half and tossed them into his waste basket, saying with a smile, "Now we do not need these."

Don retrieved those two torn pages later and discovered that Toscanini had also written a new ending to "Symphony 5 1/2"!

Early in the morning after the premiere of "Fives," Bill Bolcom and Virginia were walking along the beach in La Jolla when Bill, in a very contemplative mood, said, "You know, Virginia, I'm a lousy sleeper the night one of my works has been performed. But last night after that wonderful concert, I slept like a brand-new baby. I had taken a couple of Tylenol pills to calm myself after that exciting ovation, and you know what? I had the most fabulous dream. I saw my whole future stretched out before me, as clear as a summer's day. I saw exactly the road I should pursue in my professional career."

I have no way of knowing the precise contents of his fabulous dream, but a glance at his accomplishments indicates it must have been right on target. His awards and honors have been numerous. The list of artists for whom he has written compositions reads like a Who's Who of the best of the crop. His output has covered a wide variety of music, from song cycles, chamber music, and symphonic works to opera. His very latest has been the triumphant premiere (October 1999), by the Lyric Opera Company of Chicago, of his operatic setting of Arthur Miller's "A View from the Bridge." Along with his very serious classical course, Bolcom has carried on a parallel career in lighter American fare partnering the very gifted and personable mezzo-soprano

Joan Morris, Mezzo

Milton: A mutual friend decided that Joan should meet Bill. In Joan's words, "My friend picked me up in a cab after I failed my Julliard audition, took me down to Bill's apartment in Greenwich Village, literally delivering me to him. She sat and talked with us for a while, and then left us to be alone. I stayed and stayed and stayed. We talked and talked. Finally, we ordered some Chinese food and talked some more. In our talk Bill told me that he was never going to get married again because marriage hadn't worked for him. I remember thinking that it was OK by me, since we'd only stay together as long as we were happy anyway. And we are. Still happy anyway!" Now, quite a few years later, Joan and Bill are the happiest couple we know.

They have been performing as a duo everywhere in the world. Their extensive repertoire includes American popular songs from the end of the 19th century through the 1920s and 1930s and cabaret songs by Bill. Virginia and I have enjoyed the fun of hearing them do their charming stuff in our own living room. When they're on-stage, they bring the same intimacy and living room feeling to their performance.

Joan Morris, also a native of the Northwest – Portland, Oregon, to be exact – was trained privately in speech and voice prior to her scholarship studies in acting at the American Academy of Dramatic Arts in New York. She also has had perform-ance experience in some of Manhattan's choicest nightspots, like the Waldorf Astoria's Peacock Alley and the Café Carlyle. No wonder she is so much at ease on stage wooing an audience.

Bill moves effortlessly between the classical and popular repertoires. It's impos-sible to pin a particular label on him. Unless it's "genius," of course. He seems to be perfectly at home in whichever type of music he's into at the moment.

Abbey Simon

Milton: I picked up the phone and heard, "How's your backhand?" I knew instantly that it was our good friend, pianist Abbey Simon. When he and I played viola-piano sonatas, we were as congenial and cooperative as can be imagined in producing quality ensemble music. However, across the net from each other on the tennis court, it was quite another matter! We were fierce combatants. Most of the time, the familiar call of "Love" in tennis had to take a backseat. Abbey was con-stantly shouting, "Kill! Kill!" That is, as much kill as could be allowed between two, very close friends.

Long before I took on the responsibilities of guiding the University of Houston School of Music, I had been convinced that a music school is only as good as its fac-ulty, that it is essential to have faculty members who are performing artists with great visibility so they can attract gifted students to the school. That was the philos-ophy of William Schuman when he was president of the Julliard School of Music and invited me to join the faculty to teach viola. (At the time I was one of the most active violists in New York.)

That was precisely the way our friendship with Abbey Simon started. I lured him away from the School of Music at the University of Indiana. I had heard raves about Abbey from Patti Farbman, who was studying with him in Bloomington. (Patti is the daughter of two of our closest friends, Edith and Harry Farbman, both fine musicians.)

As soon as I succeeded in getting the necessary funds for a distinguished professorship (the Cullen Professorship), I decided to try for Abbey. He was very receptive. When he arrived in Houston to meet with me and the dean of the School of Fine Arts, he immediately laid down one hurdle to his acceptance: He would take the position if he did not have to attend any faculty meetings! Because I felt the same way he did about those meetings, I agreed. So did the dean. I also told him I wanted him to continue his affiliation with Julliard when the question came up, because his being a member of the Julliard faculty added to his value to us. At about the same time we were able to add the wonderful Greek mezzo, Elena Nikolaidi, to our faculty. Now we were definitely on our way.

There is a quiet strength about Abbey Simon. He may be below average height physically, but in the world of virtuoso pianists he has enormous stature. I find it difficult to understand why he isn't much more of a household word. At the keyboard he looks as if he is about to drive forward into the piano, hunching over the keys on a piano stool that is specially tilted forward by legs of uneven length. It's called total concentration.

Although Abbey has amassed an enormous list of successful recordings, he insists he prefers live concert performances. Unlike the recording studio, where everything is done in bits and pieces, a recital engenders a high level of energy on both sides of the footlights. The audience and the artist are in a give-and-take situation. For the touring performer, the air is always different, the piano is always different, and the acoustics are always different. Therefore, the dynamics of a live performance have a unique quality all their own. The repertoire may be the same, but it's a totally new experience every time. And that is what I love.

157

Milton and Virginia Katims

In my final year at the University of Houston, Abbey and I created an annual Piano Festival that takes place late in January. Two pianists are invited to join Abbey in playing a recital and giving a master class on a weekend (Friday, Saturday, and Sunday). Pianists, teachers, students and the general public are invited to attend both the recitals and the master classes. At the first festival, a young pianist scheduled to play for Abbey failed to appear. Claude Frank, one of the other two artists participating in the festival, was sitting with me in the audience. He offered to replace the student and play for Abbey, who looked askance at this turn of events.

"What would you like to play?" Abbey asked.

"'The Chopin 'F-Minor Fantasie.'"

"OK." Here endeth a beautiful friendship!

After Claude had played about 15 minutes, Abbey stopped him and proceeded to take the performance apart, phrase by phrase. It was a devastating critique, much to the amazement, shock, surprise, and/or delight of the audience, depending upon their point of view. Of course, Abbey and Claude were simply doing in public what we musicians do in private much of the time – being constructively (?) critical of each other. But in public? (Coda: They are still friends!!)

Abbey has a quick mind, with a tongue to match, but he can laugh at himself. I particularly like the incident that took place in San Antonio, Texas: On the day before his concert, he told us, a young lady journalist appeared at his hotel to interview him. He answered all her questions and gave her the usual information, plus printed material about his career. Imagine his consternation when he opened the newspaper the next morning and saw a large photo of himself under the following headline: "Simon Will Sing Tonight"

Chapter 13
Violinists

Jascha Heifetz

Milton: Like all the pianists who have graced our lives, the scintillating violinists we have known well, as colleagues and friends, also are "people who need people." Any discussion of the great violinists of the world must begin with the incomparable Jascha Heifetz.

I picked up the phone one day many years ago and it took only a few moments for me to recognize the voice at the other end. It was authoritative and slightly accented, and the fact that he did not identify himself made it a bit less difficult to realize who was calling. Jascha Heifetz never identified himself, because he expected everybody to recognize his voice. Not that he called me that often. This time it was to ask if I were free to come to Los Angeles to play chamber music with him and Gregor Piatigorsky. Of course, I was thrilled to accept the invitation.

Milton and Virginia Katims

Emanuel Feuermann, the virtuoso cellist who played in the "Million Dollar Trio" with Heifetz and Arthur Rubinstein (prior to Piatigorsky), so admired Heifetz's spectacular left hand on the fingerboard that he was determined to emulate it on the much longer fingerboard of his cello. That he succeeded so brilliantly is the stuff of music history.

Virginia and I feel so fortunate to have lived in the time of these truly greats. They were two kings of music – Heifetz, who (we believe) will never be surpassed as a violinist, and Feuermann, who holds the same unique place among cellists. To have played chamber music with both of these wonderful artists are musical memories I treasure.

Jascha, whose playing was often criticized by some people as being cold, was just the opposite for me. His playing had warmth and passion. He may have given the visual impression of coldness to audiences because of his appearance. Jascha rarely smiled and his face almost never reflected the emotion that poured from the sheer perfection of his playing. It all seemed so easy and natural; he never appeared to have any difficulty with anything.

The last time I heard Heifetz play in public was at a recital in Seattle in the old Civic Auditorium, which was a big barn of a hall. After the concert impresaria, Cecelia Schultz, whom we called the Sol Hurok of the Northwest, took Virginia and me to supper with Heifetz. Jascha announced that he had hated playing in the Civic Auditorium and would never return to Seattle to perform until we had a proper hall. I told him that I would get to work on having an acoustically great new hall so that I could invite him to play with the Seattle Symphony. He told me to concentrate on my conducting and not get mixed up with political or architectural activities, but I paid no attention to his advice.

Virginia and I worked vigorously to help get the bond issue passed that resulted in construction of the beautiful new Opera House within the shell of the old Civic Auditorium. (It was at the insistence of Mrs. Schultz that it was named the Opera

House, despite the insistence of the two architects, Benny Priteca and Jim Chiarelli, that it was really just a multi-purpose auditorium.) To think that it cost just six million dollars!

During the transformation of the old Civic Auditorium into the Opera House, the Seattle Symphony performed for a couple of seasons in the Moore Theater on 2nd Avenue. We had to play each program three nights because of the limited number of seats. Each program was advertised on the marquee at the front of the theater. The one that I liked best was when I programmed Berlioz' "Damnation of Faust," with Alfred Frankenstein giving a few talks about that great score. The marquee? Double Feature – The Damnation of Faust and Frankenstein!

As soon as we were assured of having the hall built, I wrote to Jascha inviting him to come out of semi-retirement and appear as soloist with the Seattle Symphony, playing one or two concertos and, I'd hoped, performing Mozart's "Sinfonie Concertante for Violin and Viola," with me as viola soloist. It was the most flattering and unabashed fan letter I have ever written. I couldn't see how he could fail to respond. Sure enough, after a few weeks I received one of those unidentified phone calls from the great man. He thanked me warmly for the glowing fan letter, but said he could not accept my invitation to play because he would then have to deal with all of the other invitations he had been receiving.

I suggested that I would keep his appearance very quiet, that I would tell no one. His response? "In that case, I couldn't play at all!"

Heifetz was a dual personality, a very complicated one I could never fathom. At times his behavior was impossible to understand or to condone. When he tired of Frances, his second wife (his first wife was the beautiful actress Florence Vidor), he kept her out of his house by having all the locks changed.

Another instance of his aberrant behavior came at lunchtime during the rehearsals of the "Million Dollar Trio" at his home. He would leave Rubinstein and Piatigorsky in the studio to eat the sandwiches they had brought with them while he repaired to his dining room where his man served him a hot lunch.

Heifetz was also a very good pianist. As a hobby he wrote fugues for the piano in the style of Bach. However, I must confess that I did not admire him as a teacher. He was such a natural as a violinist that he did not have to analyze what he was doing. As a result, he never analyzed or explained what a student was doing incorrectly. Instead, he played the passage to illustrate how it should be performed and expected the student to imitate him.

There's a fascinating sidelight relating to his appointment as a distinguished professor of violin at the University of Southern California. Dean Grant Beglarian was out of town when he arrived at the U.S.C. School of Music for his first meeting. The dean's assistant as much as told Heifetz, "Don't call us. We'll call you." The assistant felt that Heifetz did not have the required academic credits and experience. Mercifully, I don't recall the assistant's name.

Heifetz had other formidable skills. His athletic prowess was well known. He was a first-rate tennis player and with his incredible eye-hand coordination, he was unbeatable at table tennis. Unfortunately, I never had the opportunity to test my ability as a ping-pong player against him; I know from mutual friends who had faced him that his reputation was well deserved. He was a perfectionist, not only in playing his instrument, but also in many other aspects of his life. One of these was the use of language. He hated platitudes. Whenever anyone said to him, "Have a nice day," his response, handed down imperiously and with disdain in his voice was, "I've made other plans."

Because of his celebrity status, Heifetz was a natural target of humorous stories, some of them true. In the 1930s, a popular name on radio was Jay Rubinoff, who played middle-brow music on the violin. According to very reliable witnesses Heifetz arrived at NBC one afternoon carrying his violin. The security guard turned him away from the passenger elevators, directing him to the freight elevator.

Jascha Heifetz giving his son Jay a few
tennis tips (courtesy of L.A. Archives)

Longtime friend and colleague Lord Yehudi Menuhin
in the lotus position

Looks may be deceptive –
Isaac and Milton are quite
serious about their Mozart

Princess Grace greeting artists Jean Pierre Rampal (flute), Isaac Stern (violin), and Katims (conductor)
backstage after Menton Festival

The Pleasure Was Ours

The great violinist protested, "You don't understand! I'm Jascha Heifetz and I'm here to rehearse with Maestro Toscanini and the NBC Symphony." The security guard refused to be intimidated, persisting, "I don't care if you're Rubinoff. You still have to use the freight elevator!"

As a result of the aforementioned phone call, Virginia and I did fly down to Los Angeles and I had the thrill of playing chamber music with Jascha. But I must confess I found it difficult to play with him. The problem was not fitting in, matching his tone, or keeping up with him. Not at all. My problem with him was at the beginning of each movement. Having played a great deal of chamber music with many violinists, I was accustomed to a slight lift of the first violinist's bow or violin as an indication of when to start. Heifetz gave no such indication; he just put his bow down on the string and began to play. I found myself actually guessing when he was going to start. and I'm sure the other players also did the same.

We must have become adept at guessing his intentions because we played straight through a number of quartets, both string and piano quartets, with Piatigorsky at the cello, Isadore Cohen on second violin, and Leonard Pennario at the piano.

All of this took place in the spacious living room of a music lover's home. About 50 invited guests were present. Virginia, who had worshipped at the Heifetz shrine almost all of her young life, was ecstatic at finding herself in the same room with her idol.

*V*irginia: That afternoon and evening with Jascha and the other musicians was unforgettable. The music was so exciting. They all played marvelously. After a couple of hours a gourmet buffet dinner was served. I chatted with the musicians while the guests queued up for the food. Once I filled my plate, I looked around the room to find every seat taken. Every one, that was, except the chair right next to Heifetz. He looked at me, smiled, and beckoned me to join him.

Milton and Virginia Katims

Virginia Peterson Katims join the greatest violinist in the world? I prayed that I wouldn't drop my plate as I walked toward him. I settled down. Jascha looked at me expectantly. I was absolutely tongue-tied. Paralyzed, I looked away at the other guests, but I could feel Heifetz's eyes boring in on me. Finally, I blurted out in the dumbest, most insipid, childlike voice, "You're wonderful!"

He gave me an utterly disgusted look and went to sit on the staircase. How I hated myself at that moment. Later Jascha told Milton that he was planning to play a recital at U.S.C. in a few weeks. "Oh," I gushed, "I'd like to fly down from Seattle to hear you. What are you going to play?" He gave me that Jack Benny, deadpan look and said, "The violin!"

Yehudi Menuhin

Milton: The phone in Yehudi Menuhin's hotel suite rang more than a half-dozen times and Virginia was about to hang up when she heard the violinist's "Yes" in a very tight, strained voice. She apologized for phoning him at a most inopportune time, thinking that he might just have been sitting in the smallest room of his suite. "I'll call back later. please forgive me." "No, no, no," said Yehudi. "My voice always sounds choked like this when I'm standing on my head doing my yoga exercises."

A blizzard was raging outside our hotel in Buffalo, New York that midwinter, Saturday afternoon. Yehudi had been my soloist in the "Beethoven Violin Concerto" with the Buffalo Philharmonic the previous evening in the first of a pair of subscription concerts. The second performance was scheduled the next afternoon – if the blizzard didn't intervene. I had suggested to Virginia that she call Yehudi and invite him to have dinner with us. After concerts there was always much to talk about and, of course, we would chat about the possibility of a cancellation of the Sunday matinee.

The Pleasure Was Ours

Yehudi promptly accepted the invitation. We did meet for dinner and the Sunday afternoon concert did take place. The fact that Yehudi, the members of the orchestra, and Virginia and I outnumbered the hardy music lovers who braved the blizzard for Beethoven, Menuhin, and Katims has always been a strong deposit in my memory bank.

The name Yehudi has long been synonymous with the word "wunderkind," or prodigy. Like a meteor, little Yehudi flashed upon the world's music stage and very soon became a name everyone knew, music lover or not. Virginia's association with him goes back to those early years. Although he was born in New York City of Russian-Jewish parents, the Menuhin family soon moved to San Francisco, Virginia's hometown. Her older brother, Harvey Peterson, was a gifted violinist who had been a student of the famous Eugene Ysaye. Harvey, a few years older than Yehudi, was engaged to play violin duets with the wunderkind to introduce him not only to duet literature, but other chamber music as well.

As you can readily imagine, the Menuhin household schedule and daily planning revolved around little Yehudi. He was put to bed with the recorded sounds of Bach in his ears, and he awoke to the sounds of Beethoven and Brahms filling his bedroom. Yehudi's parents were enormously ambitious for him.

At the age of seven he made his debut with the San Francisco Symphony, playing the Lalo "Symphonie Espagnole." Dressed in short velvet pants that caressed his already chubby little legs, the boy wonder received his first tremendous ovation. Four years later he had already made historic debuts at New York's Carnegie Hall and in London, Paris, and Berlin. Before he entered his teens, Yehudi was well launched on a career that in the ensuing decades was to take him everywhere in the world, playing and recording with all the leading conductors and orchestras. The word "phenomenal" followed him wherever he went.

Yehudi's wide-ranging interests spread far beyond the confines of the violin and classical music. He worshipped the great French jazz fiddler, Stephane Grappelli, with whom he made a number of best-selling records. He also admired the music of India and Ravi Shankar, the sitarist with whom he also made many successful recordings. To his great credit, Yehudi used his renown as a musician to advance his inherent humanism, to help young musicians, promote international understanding and peace, and for many other causes that coincided with his role as a humanist.

Virginia and I would not have been surprised when her phone call interrupted his head stand in Buffalo if we had read his book, *Life Class, a Collection of Exercises for Mind and Body*, which we did read later. The book was prompted by his first visit to India at the invitation of Prime Minister Pandit Nehru in 1952. One of the most rewarding ways to understand the mind of Yehudi Menuhin is to read his autobiography, *Unfinished Journey*, which has achieved wide success. I enjoyed it very much, enhanced because we had the added luxury of our close association with him for so many years.

Those memories include so many recollections – Diana, his charming wife, a fugitive from the world of ballet, feeding him tablespoonfuls of honey for quick energy before a concert; his gentle but intense eyes gazing up at me as I conducted the orchestral accompaniment; the warm hospitality he and Diana offered whenever we visited them in London; and the fun of receiving letters from the couple, who signed themselves, "YehuDiana." It was a wonderful marriage because she provided him with the most compassionate support and understanding, the two personalities dovetailing just as neatly as "YehuDiana."

One of the Menuhin achievements we musicians appreciate about him during his long and productive life has been his creation of a boarding school for promising young musicians, who start at age seven. The school, inspired by a similar one in Moscow, makes it possible for children to receive their academic and musical education under one roof. I have long thought that Yehudi's concept should have been adopted years ago by American schools, public and private. In

1977 Yehudi founded the International Academy of Graduate String Players in Gstaad, Switzerland, the site of the annual Menuhin Music Festival, for which he was awarded Swiss citizenship.

Like many other musicians who have achieved greatness as instrumentalists, Yehudi also had a conductor's baton tucked away in his sleeve. Each year he guest-conducted the Berlin Philharmonic in a special series of concerts. He was president and associate conductor of London's Royal Philharmonic Orchestra and of the Halle Orchestra, and also principal guest-conductor of the English String Orchestra, the Warsaw Sinfonia, and the Philharmonia Hungarica. I wonder what he did in his spare time!?

The list of awards and other honors for Yehudi goes on and on. It's worth mentioning a few of them to show the remarkable scope of the man. In 1960 he was awarded the Nehru Peace Prize for International Understanding, and in 1992, he was honored with the title of Ambassador of Goodwill by U.N.E.S.C.O. In England, where he lived, he was given the Royal Philharmonic Society's Gold Medal, and in 1993, Queen Elizabeth II bestowed knighthood on him and presented him with a Life Peerage.

France gave him the Legion d'Honneur, Belgium the Ordre Leopold, Spain the Gran Cruz del Merito Civil, Germany the Order of Merit, and China an honorary professorship at the Beijing Conservatory of Music. He received gold medals in music from organizations in New York, Paris, and Jerusalem, as well as honorary doctorates from 27 universities, including Oxford, Cambridge, and the Sorbonne.

It was with a profound sense of personal loss that we learned (March 12, 1999) that Yehudi had died in Berlin, where he was no doubt, conducting. He must surely have enjoyed a tumultuous welcome by the angels in heaven.

Milton and Virginia Katims

Isaac Stern

Virginia: One evening violinist Isaac Stern, artist Marc Chagall, Milton, and I were seated on the terrace of a small hotel on the French Riviera overlooking the Mediterranean. Isaac had just performed at the Menton Music Festival with my husband conducting. Chagall, a close friend of Stern's and an avid music lover, had attended the concert. It was late when we arrived at the cafe, the night was luminous, and the moon provided glittering cascades of light on the sea. The conversation was engaging, too. We talked about the concert, art in general, and the beauty of the evening. We also ate couscous, one of Isaac's favorite dishes, and talked about the "Brahms Violin Concerto."

Isaac spoke about the urgency of the music and of performing it ideally with a conductor who understood its chamber-music quality and, to quote him precisely, "a conductor who can give the massive base from which the soloist can take wing."

Marc observed, "Ah, I think my art is more ephemeral than yours."

"Not at all," Isaac responded. "A painting hangs on the wall for all to see and to ponder. A piece of music is heard for a moment, hopefully felt for a moment, and then disappears into the air."

The conversation, which dug deeply into the subject of the true affinity of music and art was mind-boggling, as Isaac, Marc, and Milton exchanged, tested, disputed, and honed their ideas far into the night. If only I had had a recorder handy!

I recalled an incident that took place after Isaac and Milton had performed Mozart's "Sinfonie Concertante for Violin and Viola" at this very same Menton Festival a few years earlier. The end of the last movement is marked by a tricky arpeggio which the viola plays first and then the violin. The passage starts at the very bottom of the instrument and ends on a very high E-flat. At every rehearsal Milton missed the high top note as Isaac laughed and hit his perfectly each time. However, at the performance, Milton hit the final note right on the nose, but Isaac missed his.

The Pleasure Was Ours

The applause and the shouts of "Bravo!" refused to stop! Offstage, just before the final bow, Milton said to Isaac, "How about playing the final movement over again?"

Isaac's quick response was, "... you!" He smiled as he said it.

When I considered the gigantic scope of Isaac's interests and activities, I wondered when he has time to practice his violin. He was forever involving himself in provocative projects, as saving New York's Carnegie Hall. On January 30, 1997, New York paid tribute to Isaac, as well it should have, for being the principal force behind the drive that saved Carnegie Hall from the wrecking ball and prevented yet another skyscraper that was scheduled to replace it. His role in the rescue was so great that the refurbished historic concert hall now bears the name: The Isaac Stern Auditorium. Now president of the corporation that manages the hall, Isaac has performed there an amazing total of 175 times! Little wonder that he wanted so much to save it.

And that's not all. Isaac has given much of his time to guiding gifted young musicians, while shuttling around the world as a much-in-demand soloist and chamber music player.

A man of amazing diversity, broad interests, and boundless enthusiasm, Isaac traces his beginning to the little town of Kreminiecz, Russia, where he was born. His family brought him to the U.S. when he was a year old, eventually moving to San Francisco, where he studied the violin and debuted with the San Francisco Symphony at the age of eleven.

I was studying at the San Francisco Conservatory of Music when Isaac was there. Like Yehudi, he was a "wunderkind" and the most exciting talent the school had ever had. I was just beginning to saw away on the cello.

An adolescent crush that I had for Isaac's teacher Nathan Abbas and the admiration I had for young Isaac's enormous gifts inspired me to sprinkle rose petals all over the floor of Abbas's studio just before Isaac's lesson one day. Abbas was so furious that he forced me to pick up every single petal. I don't believe I ever confessed this to Isaac.

Milton and Virginia Katims

He would arrive for his lessons with his mother and was always accompanied by a large collie. It seemed to me that the dog listened to his master play the violin not only with rapt attention, but with respect. Since that time Isaac's career has skyrocketed throughout the world. Now at the pinnacle of his solo career, he continues to play with symphony orchestras around the globe and is also deeply involved in playing chamber music with the finest artists.

Milton just finished reading Isaac's memoir, *My First 79 Years*. I have rarely seen my husband so absorbed in a book. And when he reached the final pages he said, "Isaac, as usual, has so many important words of wisdom to offer young, and not so young, musicians, particularly string players. His warmth, as a man and as a great musical artist, leaps from every page." Without reservation, Milton recommends the book not only to musicians, but to all who would enjoy going backstage with Isaac and having a vivid look at the life of a wonderful artist.

I remember one occasion when Isaac, collaborating with pianist Yefim Bronfman, played a recital at the Seattle Opera House. After, a string player who had been in the audience said, "We always learn something very special when Stern plays – phrasing, tone production, vibrato, all the things we thought we knew. Each time we find a wealth of new ideas in the playing of Isaac Stern." What better accolade could an artist receive?

Oscar Shumsky

Milton: After hearing Fritz Kreisler play his cadenzas to the Beethoven "Violin Concerto" just twice, Oscar could play them. Early on when Kreisler heard Oscar play, he predicted that Oscar Shumsky would become one of the finest violinists of the century. Evidently Kreisler was not only a wonderful musician and violinist, but also a very good prophet. More recently, the equally gifted Russian violinist, David Oistrakh, called Oscar "one of the world's greatest violinists."

These opinions are shared by many musicians. Why is his name not the house-hold name it deserves to be? Some critics say that he does not bring to the public platform the fantastic personality to match the perfection of playing that he exhibits in the privacy of his own studio. I disagree! Having had the joy of making music with Oscar (as both violist and conductor) and having been his friend and colleague for about 60 years, I, too, believe his reputation with the general public should equal what musicians think of him – one of the most extraordinary violinists of his generation – of any generation!

But Shumsky dislikes publicity. He balks at the idea of having someone handle public relations for him. He also would rather avoid touring, playing an enormous number of concerts. A wonderful teacher, he taught his son Eric, now a very gifted violist. But Oscar resigned from the faculty of the Julliard School of Music because he felt that it took too much time from his own practicing. What a pity – he has so much to give!

With a vibrant sound, immaculate intonation, and a limitless command of the technical challenges of the violin, Oscar is a joy to hear – a joy to join in playing chamber music. His musicianship is superb! Withal, there is an utter simplicity about Oscar Shumsky – as a man and as a musician, he puts on no airs.

A graduate of the Curtis Institute of Music in Philadelphia, Shumsky enjoys a fruitful career in which chamber music has played a most important part. He was first violinist of the Primrose String Quartet during the years he was a member of the NBC Symphony with Toscanini. And, although I have never seen him conduct, I have been told on impeccable authority that he brings to the baton the very same qualities that go into his own playing and teaching.

As a violist I am quite critical of violinists who casually pick up and play the viola. I don't believe that they produce a real viola sound. But Oscar is one of a few violinists who can sound like a violist. (Pinchus Zukerman is another.) In the 1950s he was co-director with Glenn Gould of the Stratford Festival in Canada. They frequently performed in duo sonatas and were often joined by cellist Leonard Rose in piano trios.

Oscar Shumsky's gifts do not stop with the violin, viola and baton. He is an excellent photographer and also very handy with the tools of carpentry. When he bought a very old house in Rye, New York, he decided to do all of the remodeling himself. He made many trips to the local lumber yard to buy lumber, window frames and new doors. At the same time he was concertmaster of the Firestone Orchestra, a popular weekly television program. Periodically, he appeared as soloist on the program.

One day after one of the clerks at the lumber yard happened to hear one of Oscar's solo appearances on the program, he was very excited when he reported for work. He exclaimed to all his co-workers, "You know that carpenter up on Rockledge Road? He plays the violin, too!"

Itzhak Perlman

Milton: It was concert time at Tel Aviv's Mann Auditorium. As Itzhak Perlman, my soloist and a good friend, and I walked on-stage, the capacity audience erupted in a tumultuous cheer for its favorite son, in expectation of his performance of a Paganini concerto.

We entered from the side of the stage and worked our way through the aisle between string sections of the Israel Philharmonic. I followed Itzhak, carrying his Stradivarius. Despite my constant pleading with him to slow down, Itzhak, whose legs were paralyzed by polio in childhood, was racing ahead, his two metal crutches flashing in the bright stage lights.

Suddenly, his crutches skidded on two metal strips in the stage floor and he fell. The audience gasped and became pin-drop silent. Itzhak immediately sat up and members of the orchestra helped him stand and retrieved his crutches. As soon as he had them, he was up and off again, this time almost twice as fast, as if to show he was unhurt!

The audience's collective sigh of relief was clearly audible as it watched Itzhak reach his chair on the riser next to the podium and sit down. Then they resumed their noisy, deafening welcome. As I handed him his Strad and he was brushing himself off, he said, with a very broad smile, "I hope the morning newspapers don't report that Perlman fell flat on his face last evening."

He needn't have worried. His performance of the Paganini was sensational. Perhaps his accident added a slight thrill of danger to his extraordinary virtuosity. The audience stood as one and cheered when I gave the final beat. I've never heard such a unified shout like that one. In minutes, audience members rushed the stage, like breakers crashing on a beach. Later backstage I overheard a music lover mumbling awkward condolences to Itzhak about his fall. With a bright smile, he said, "Oh, that! That's showbiz, baby."

Itzhak is able to communicate his irrepressible joy in making music to his listeners more than most artists I know. In spite of the early blow dealt him by polio, he exudes the joy of living. He loves life and life obviously loves him. It has bestowed so much talent on him, as well as the enormous capacity to work hard to develop his gifts to their fullest.

Itzhak's popularity has made him a constant world traveler. Awards have followed him everywhere, as well they should. He has accomplished virtually everything he's put his mind to, even singing the role of the jailer in a special TV performance of Puccini's "Tosca!"

His remarkable versatility has captivated audiences in many forms of music in every nation. He has shown an amazing feel for playing Kentucky Blue Grass fiddle with country-music performers. And like his marvelous colleague cellist, Yo Yo Ma, he has sat in often on sessions with pianist Oscar Peterson and other jazz greats. He could have made a fortune in any musical category he chose.

Milton and Virginia Katims

Virginia and I love Itzhak and his very attractive wife Toby, who gave up the study of the violin to marry him. We love them for who they are and because of their limitless devotion to family. They have five brilliant offspring, all of them involved in serious pursuits. Unlike so many busy fathers, Itzhak always finds time to sit down with his children, communicate with them, and spur them on emotionally and intellectually. Mom takes over for both of them when he is off "doing his thing," but when he's home, he is Pop, pure and simple.

Henryk Szeryng

Virginia: We think fondly of Henryk Szeryng, the Polish-born violinist, for many reasons, all of which contributed to our delight in enjoying his company as a close colleague for many years. First and foremost, he was a perfectionist as a violinist, which carried him to worldwide acclaim. And second, he was a perfectionist without peer in his living habits. Those who visited him in his spanking clean, shiny, and beautiful suite in London's posh Savoy Hotel learn that quickly. He also had a similarly speck-free home for a time in Mexico, where he enjoyed the status of "ambassador at large."

Milton invited him to play the Mozart "Sinfonie Concertante for Violin and Viola" with him on one of his visits to Seattle. In addition to the live performances with the Seattle Symphony, a commission from the Gull Oil Company made it possible for Henryk, Milton, and the orchestra to record the work for a television special entitled "Mozart in Seattle." In fact, the TV cameras rolled from the moment Milton, in his yellow Corvette, picked up Henryk at the airport.

The cameras continued to grind away at our home, where the two men rehearsed the Mozart before rehearsals with the orchestra. Henryk, the clean-living perfectionist, asked to be excused for a few minutes so he could wash his hands. Twenty minutes later we were still waiting for him to return, all of those minutes extremely expensive for the sponsor. Finally, somewhat concerned, I went to the bathroom door and knocked. Receiving no response I turned the doorknob, found the door open, and walked in, fearing the worst.

There was Henryk, soaking happily in a hot tub. As I tried to withdraw in embarrassment, he looked over and said, "Don't worry, Virginia. I'll be out any time now."

I stopped in my tracks, "For Gawdsake, Henryk, you don't have to be clean physically for the cameras. Only your fiddling has to be clean!"

Moments later we laughed off the entire incident and put it away in the broadening file marked "Szeryng, Mr. Clean." Thereafter, everything went beautifully. The video that resulted has been a hit on PBS and worldwide TV, thanks to Gull Oil's expert promotional skills.

A couple of years later, the violinist phoned from London, "Milton, I need you to fly over and conduct three concerti for me two weeks from now."

We made airline and hotel reservations within the hour and in short order found ourselves in London ready for the rehearsals and first concert, which had been scheduled in the vast barn the British call Albert Hall. It was an historic place all right, but I wondered if it could possibly be filled for the program. I needn't have worried. The ticket sales were brisk and the hall was packed.

That evening Henryk and Milton walked on-stage perfectly groomed. After the applause died down, Milton reached for his baton to start the "Bach E Major Concerto for Violin and Orchestra." But Henryk took his violin from under his chin, held up his hand to signify a slight delay, reached over and flicked a bit of lint from Milton's full-dress jacket. Milton was ready to murder him, but when Henryk gave him a beatific smile of innocence, he burst out laughing. So did the audience, which was now in a great mood to enjoy the music that followed.

Milton and Virginia Katims

Jaime Laredo – Sharon Robinson, cello

Milton: How many musicians can boast that they have had conferred on them the status of "National Hero," have had a stadium named after them, and have been honored with a commemorative set of twelve postage stamps issued in their name? Jaime Laredo, violinist supreme, is the only one I know. His native Bolivia. (He was born in Cochabamba, which sounds like a South American dance.) He was appointed cultural attaché to the United States, a position he relinquished when he became a U.S. citizen some years later.

Jaime's studies with Joseph Gingold and Ivan Galamian, as well as his training as a protégé of conductor George Szell, prepared him well for his outstanding career in music. The list of artists, conductors, and orchestras with whom he has performed reads like a music directory. Also attesting to his prowess are the large number of awards he has won, including the prestigious Queen Elizabeth Competition in Brussels at the age of seventeen.

Today, it's customary to speak of both Mr. and Mrs. Laredo because their musical careers have become so dramatically entwined. Sharon Robinson, a magnificent cellist, became the second Mrs. Laredo. (Jaime's first wife, Ruth, is an extremely gifted pianist.)

I had the pleasure of joining Jaime in performances of the Mozart "Sinfonie Concertante" not only in New York's "Mostly Mozart" series at Lincoln Center, but also in Madrid, Spain, with the Orchestra Nacional. But that was before I became aware that he had invaded my two territories, soloing as a violist and conducting. He was extremely easy to work with and his brilliant playing added to my enjoyment of the Mozart, which I have played with so many exceptional violinists over the years.

It was after the Madrid concert that Argentine's foremost composer, Alberto Ginastera, was among the visitors backstage. I was thrilled when he told me that he admired my playing and conducting and that he would like to write a work that I

Delightful and gifted couple
Sharon Robinson, cellist,
and Jaime Laredo, violinist

Violinists Kyung Wa Chung and David Abel discussing Stravinsky concerto
with Katims

Itzhak Perlman (violin) discussing concerto with Katims in Israel

*In London's Royal Albert Hall – Vrginia flanked by volinist Henryk Szeryng
and husband, conductor Katims*

could play and conduct. I was delighted because I admire his music greatly. But destiny was cruel! Ginastera did not live to compose the work.

When Virginia asked Sharon if she would like to add to what we had written about Jaime, she wrote the following: "It was at the height of the Vietnam War. Jaime, already a famous concert violinist, was called to take his physical for the Army. Dreading the whole experience, he trekked from New York to his draft board in Philadelphia. Passing each test with flying colors, he moved to the last line, which led to the Army psychologist.

"As he entered the interview cubicle, he handed in all of his papers and sat down ready to be grilled. Without looking up the doctor said, 'Are you the violinist? I heard you play with the Philadelphia Orchestra last season. I have your recordings. The Army is no place for you.' You can imagine Jaime's relief as the psychologist classified him 1-Y!"

During our years in Houston, I was very much aware of one special family of musicians in that city: The Robinson family. The father was a well known bass player, the mother was a violinist, and each of the children played a string instrument. They must have created quite a Charles Ivesian sound when they all decided to practice. One of Sharon's brothers, Hal, is an excellent doublebass player, who was for a time a member of my faculty at the University of Houston School of Music and is now solo bass with the Philadelphia Orchestra.

There must have been quite a competitive spirit among the Robinson siblings. Sharon is no slouch. She played her first cello concert at age seven and made her orchestral debut with the Houston Symphony at fourteen. All of her early studies were in Houston. Then she went to the Peabody in Baltimore where she met Jaime. Was it love at first sight? "No," says Sharon, but Jaime arranged for Sharon to be invited to the Marlboro Festival in Vermont. It was there in the shadow of the Green Mountains that love bloomed between the violinist and cellist. After a number of pancake breakfasts, they realized that they enjoyed playing duos with each other and should make it a permanent arrangement. Not just making pancakes, that is.

The marriage in no way slowed Sharon's pursuit of a major career. There was no stopping to bake cookies. In addition to becoming an important one-third of the Kalichstein-Laredo-Robinson Piano Trio, Sharon, who has grown from a freckled-faced adolescent into a gorgeous, young woman, has garnered many awards. Among them are the Avery Fisher Recital Award, the Leventritt, and the Piatigorsky Memorial Award of Johns Hopkins University. She has also earned descriptive critical comments like "a breathtaking mastery enhanced by an inner rapture" (*Washington Post*) and "wonderful balance of virtuosity and lyricism" (*New York Times*).

Sharon reminisces, "Quite a few years ago, I was called at the last minute by Columbia Artists to play a recital in a small town in Middle America. I called my pianist, bought three airline tickets (one for my cello), and scurried to the town for the performance. As my pianist and I were waiting in the wings, we heard the concert promoter onstage making an announcement, 'Ladies and gentlemen, we have some bad news. Paula Robison (flutist) has had to cancel this evening's performance due to illness. We tried and tried to get a famous artist to replace her, but everyone we thought of was busy. So we settled on cellist Sharon Robinson. I hope you enjoy the evening.'

"I stood backstage with an open jaw, smoke coming out of my ears. But the show must go on. I decided to take the magnanimous route and just go out and play with all my heart. But I'll never go back to that town! Besides, earlier that evening the president of the Community Concert Series announced the group would try to sign up better artists for the following season – the old, typical C.C. gaffe that so many musicians have had to endure."

The Pleasure Was Ours

Kyung Wha Chung

Milton: During my 22 years as conductor of the Seattle Symphony, I creat ed a special Sunday series, Stars of the Future, to showcase very gifted young instrumentalists. I invited them to solo with the orchestra, playing the same concer-to to be performed the following evenings by an established artist. When I described my idea to my longtime friend and colleague, violinist Sasha Schneider, with whom I had played with the Budapest String Quartet and the New York Piano Quartet, he responded enthusiastically, calling it a great idea. But ten minutes later he called me back – he had changed his mind!

"It's a terrible idea," he said. "What if the kids are better then we are?"

I had good reason to recall that phone conversation when Kyung Wha Chung gave a terrific performance of the "Stravinsky Violin Concerto" one Sunday after-noon shortly thereafter. She played with all the fire and abandon of an inspired Gypsy, projecting all of the provocative ideas of the great Russian composer. Music poured from her violin with the sheer force of a projectile. There was no way the somewhat better known violinist at the two following concerts could compare with the young lady from Korea.

Only fourteen years old at the time, Kyung Wha had come to this country with her six siblings and her parents. Her mother and father were to run the Korean restaurant at the 1962 World's Fair in Seattle. Classical Western music had been introduced in Korea after World War II. Obviously the elder Chungs had filled their home in Seoul with the sounds of our music. Every one of the children became so enamored with it that they all studied an instrument – flute, clarinet, piano, violin and cello. Their home must have sounded like a scene from the play, "You Can't take it with You!"

I soon met the family and invited three of the gifted children to appear as soloists with the Seattle Symphony. The three were Kyung Wha (whom I soon nicknamed "Cookie"), Myung Wha, the cellist, and Myung Whun, the pianist, who was the youngest and so small that his feet could not reach the pedals of the piano. I called him "Billy." Today I would call him Maestro Billy. He is enjoying a successful career as a conductor. Their appearance with the orchestra stands out in my memory for many reasons. Cookie and Billy each played a concerto in the first half of the concert and the two sisters played the Brahms Double (violin and cello) in the second half.

But while their performances were quite remarkable and well received by the enthusiastic audience, a non-musical aspect of that afternoon cemented the concert in my mind. This was back in the early 1960s and the very vocal protests over the Vietnam War invaded the Opera House by way of a group known as the Seattle Seven. They were loud and unruly. I spotted them very quickly in seats near the stage.

Although I don't recall precisely what I said, I tore into them for disrupting the concert. I told them that when they has achieved the discipline and work ethic of the gifted young artists on the stage and had accomplished something in their own lives, I would listen to what they had to say. I added, with obvious anger in my voice, "Until then keep quiet or leave the hall!" It stopped them short and they slunk down in their seats while the entire audience erupted in cheers and applause.

That incident vividly came back to me recently while I sat in the Opera House with Virginia, awaiting the appearance on-stage of the very same Kyung Wha Chung, now a mature, worldly and experienced concert star. She was about to play the "Beethoven Violin Concerto" with the Seattle Symphony under the direction its current conductor Gerard Schwarz. When Cookie walked briskly on stage amid warm and loud applause, she looked sensational in a black strapless, artfully draped evening gown.

Virginia told me later that she had been worried about those bare arms. Would there be shaking flab with all of the left had vibrato and the right bowing arm moving ever faster? She need not have worried. Cookie was firmly in charge, as if she had been working out in some gym or spa. On the other hand, as soon as I saw the strapless gown I couldn't help recalling that very familiar story about singer Mary Garden when she wore a similarly daring, strapless gown. A very old Chauncey Depew asked her, "Mary, what keeps your dress up?" Her demure answer? "Your age, Chauncey, your age!"

During the lengthy, opening orchestral tutti Kyung Wha, violin tucked under her arm, was clearly and completely involved in the music before playing a note. She moved her body with the music in such rapture that she appeared to be conducting along with Schwarz. It was obvious that she knew the score very well – knew when each solo instrument or section of the orchestra was about to add their voices.

When she began to play, exhibiting a full, beautiful tone, immaculate intonation, a flawless technique that served the music, and phrasing that had the logic of speech, her body English became even more pronounced. She crouched for a pianissimo and extended her head and body forward for a fortissimo. We named it the "Cookie crouch." Each and every note received her undivided attention. But her intense attention to every detail by no means deterred her from building long, arching lines. All of her youthful, raw power was still there. But it was no longer raw. The early rough edges had been beautifully rounded by her many years of searching and just hard work. It was most impressive music making.

As Cookie was revealing once again the many wonders of Beethoven, I found myself recalling that at the close of the 1962 Seattle World's Fair, U.S. Immigration was about to refuse to renew the Chung family visas and send them back to Korea. But Joe Gandy, one of the executives of the fair, and I went to the I.M.S. and explained to them that the Chung family was precisely the kind of gifted people we needed to attract to our country.

Fortunately they listened to us.

Katims guest conducting a rehearsal of the Philadelphia Orchestra

Chapter 14
Renowned Cellists

Emanuel "Munio" Feuermann

Milton: Playing chamber music with the great cellist Emanuel Feuermann was one of the most unforgettable experiences of my career as a violist. Munio would play a phrase with his elegant brilliance then, when it was my turn to echo that phrase on my viola, he would stop playing, lean on his cello and look at me quizzically, as if to say, "Well, now let's see what you're going to do with that one."

As he proceeded onto the stage of Carnegie Hall one evening many years ago for a performance of Strauss' "Don Quixote," with Leon Barzin conducting the orchestra of the National Orchestral Association, (in which I played the part of Sancho Panza), Munio tossed admonitory words over his shoulder, "Milton, take it easy with your big tone!" Needless to say, I was so thrilled to be sharing the stage with the "King of Cellists" that I savored every moment.

Milton and Virginia Katims

Knowing him, watching and listening to him play, making music with him, and looking on at the few lessons Virginia had with him, I learned a great deal about playing the viola. Munio was fond of recalling that he had been inspired by watching his inimitable colleague, violinist Jascha Heifetz, play. I have already mentioned one facet of that admiration, but it bears repeating. Munio saw no reason why he shouldn't be able to duplicate, on his much larger fingerboard, the incredible maneuverability Heifetz exhibited on the violin. There are so many aspects of my viola playing that I owe to him.

I think of Feuermann every time I play a long glissando. As my finger slides up (or down) on my fingerboard, I can hear him say, "Slow the motion of your bow almost to a walk. As you reach the note you're heading for, resume the speed of the bow." He was so right. Every time I use a caterpillar fingering (extending my fourth finger to the position above, or my first finger to the position below), or when I play an up-bow staccato, being aware of the pressure-release of the index finger of my right hand, I think of Munio and his pearls of string-playing wisdom. All of the string players who studied or performed with him owe him the same debt, to say nothing of the violists whom I have coached.

When I recall his sudden, tragic, shocking, needless, ill-fated death at the age of 39 of a botched hemorrhoid operation, I become enraged. Without testing Munio for his reaction to the drug, those who were preparing him for surgery gave him morphine, to which he was allergic. Peritonitis set in and caused his death. What an abrupt end to one of the most brilliant careers in the annals of music. The gods must have wept!

*V*irginia: Munio was born in the tiny town of Kolomea in Galicia, once a part of the Austro-Hungarian Empire. The Feuermanns were the musical family in the town. Papa was a triple threat – conductor, violinist and cellist – and full of energy. Munio must have inherited his father's enormous drive and also his constant

Eva Reifenberg, engaged to marry Emanuel Geuermann, "King" of cellists

The King of cellists, Emanuel Feuermann, being admired by his daughter Monica

With very gifted cellist Yo Yo Ma – always expect the unexpected

Gregor Piatigorsky and Katims discuss a fine point during rehearsal of a work especially written for the two instrumentalists by Grant Beglarian, and performed with the SSO in 1973

efforts to improve himself. Brother Sigmund was an excellent violinist and sister Sophie, a fine, professional pianist. At age five Munio was given a discarded violin that had once been Sigmund's. He played it under his chin and also cello style between his legs with great aplomb.

One day a local minister, who had a boy who was Munio's age, visited the Feuermanns to play the cello for Papa. The moment Munio saw the instrument and heard it played, he was transfixed. He shrieked happily and demanded that his father teach him to play it. From the beginning Munio was a perfectionist. He not only practiced for hours, but even at his young age he analyzed everything he did. Destiny ordained that he was to become not only the greatest of all cellists, but also a superb, demanding teacher.

Munio was a fine student at school and a voracious reader. At fifteen he was off to Leipzig to study with the noted Julius Klengel. The entire family went to the railroad station to see him off. As he was about to board the train, his father called out, "Come back a second Casals, Emanuel!"

"No," Munio shouted back, "I'll come back a first Feuermann!"

After tutoring him for close to three years, Klengel said of Munio, "A divinely favored artist and a lovable young man." Lovable? Some might not agree. He had a quick and potent temper, with a sarcastic tongue to match.

His biographer, Seymour Itzkoff, wrote in his superb book, *Emanuel Feuermann, Virtuoso*: "He was never at a loss for words. His sharp tongue acted as a shield, a defense of his immensely sensitive nature. His sarcasm, his wisecracks, and often his clowning around with orchestra musicians (and even with the conductor) were his way of transforming his natural defensiveness into an aggressiveness, which Munio seemed to feel so necessary for a performer."

I had three or four lessons with Feuermann long before I was ready for a teacher of his stature. How I had the nerve to take my cello out of its case and play for him, I'll never know. It was a hot, humid, summer day in Scarsdale, New York when I went for my first lesson. I was wearing very short, hot pink pants. He looked me up and down and said, "You come to play for me in such a costume?"

I giggled self-consciously. Milton, with whom I had begun to go steady, had come with me. At the cellist's bidding, I played the last movement of the "Lalo Concerto" that, after a romantic introduction, charges ahead into a brilliant Spanish section. I thought I had played it fairly well. Feuermann was unimpressed.

"Do me a favor," he said. "Tune your cello."

"But it is in tune," I protested.

"The way you tune is too casual. Take time. Use exactly the same pressure on both strings as you tune."

I felt like an imbecile. He spent the rest of the lesson showing me different bowings to practice, spending much of the time on up-and-down bow staccato. His ideas were significant, but his entire manner was insulting; he was treating me as if I were a child. I soon realized that he was showing off to impress Milton. He was not only sarcastic, but also smirking about it.

I managed to smile pleasantly, thanked him as we said good-bye, and left. I certainly didn't look forward to practicing all those bowings he had given me. I had a few more lessons with him. I played the "Brahms E-Minor Sonata" without being crucified. Then, at the next lesson, I played a simple Corelli sonata. He was absolutely impossible. Although I tried hard to control myself, my eyes filled with tears. He came close to me, looked at the tears and, in a scathing voice, said to Milton, "Look! The mother of your future children!"

I jumped up, steaming. I wanted to stab him with the endpin of my cello, but I resisted, put my cello in its case, and stormed out of the house. Eva, his darling wife, came running after me. "Virginia, he doesn't mean it. That's just his way, especially with girl cellists."

I can't remember if I paid him the $15 for that lesson. I never went back, and I hated him and I hated Milton for agreeing with everything he had said. That was it.

On the spot, I resolved to find myself a different boyfriend, not a string player.

About a week or two later, Munio wrote me a short note: "Virginia, this is a very tough profession. You must learn to be tough." I never have.

In time I have grown to agree with Milton's opinion of Munio as the greatest cellist of the century. Although I still have doubts about his tact as a teacher, I share Milton's grief over his untimely death to this day.

Coda: I strongly recommend Seymour Itzkoff's biography, *Emanuel Feuermann, Virtuoso*. It's a "must read" for cellists. Itzkoff, who also plays the cello, teaches philosophy at Smith College in Northampton, Massachusetts. I guess that if you want to be a cellist, you have to be philosophical!

Gregor "Grischa" Piatigorsky

Virginia: I have a bad (good?) habit. Even though I'm happily married to Milton, I fall in love with every great artist, whether he's fat, short, bald, devastatingly handsome or whatever. Such a great artist was Gregor Piatigorsky, the sensational Russian born cellist, who was "Grischa" to his friends.

He was an enormous man. Boxing fans say he reminded them of Primo Carnera. When Grischa strode on-stage holding his cello high, the instrument looked like a violin.

Our first encounter with him was when he played Strauss' "Don Quixote" with the Seattle Symphony. Henry Siegl, concertmaster, played the Dulcinea violin solos, and the first violist, Vilem Sokol, played the role of Sancho Panza.

Performances of the "Dvorak Concerto" followed. Grischa commissioned Grant Beglarian to write a "Duo Concertante for Viola and Cello," intended for Milton and Grischa, which they performed the last time our Russian friend visited Seattle. We became very good friends of the cellist and his wife Jacqueline, who is a member of the Rothschild family. She is an attractive, gifted woman, a fine sculpture, an expert chess player, and, of all things, a bassoonist. What a combination!

Grischa had a terrific imagination, and, like so many musicians, was a most creative story teller, much of the time with tongue in cheek. One year Milton and I, along with Grischa, were judges at a Young Artists Competition in Los Angeles. An extremely gifted and pretty, fifteen-year-old violinist was among the competitors. When she finished playing, Grischa turned to us and said, "This young lady has everything – a wonderful sound and ample technique. She needs only one thing."

"What's that?" I asked, and I shouldn't have. His mischievous answer, "A love affair!"

We were at a supper party given in honor of Piatigorsky in the beautiful home of Thelma and Dr. Hans Lehmann. Grischa had just performed with the orchestra. Also at the party were Isaac Stern and Sasha Schneider, who were just passing through, en route to engagements elsewhere. During a rare lull in the conversation, I reminded Grischa that he had not sent me one of his personal experiences or a reminiscence for a cookbook that I was writing. "Oh, Vergeenia, let me theenk. Ah yes, I have good experience for you. One night I was playing concert in leetle town of Denvair. You know Denvair?" We all nodded, so he went on.

"Thees was one of best concerts from me. I was happy – I play very well. Back–stage came beauteeful voman. You know Vergeenia, long blonde hair, long meenk coat, dark meenk! She say to me, 'I have fallen in love with your cello playing – I would like to know you better.' You know, Vergeenia – what I going to say? Long blonde hair, long meenk coat, very dark meenk. I say, 'Please to come to my hotel at meednight. First, I must go to very boring reception. You know, peenk punch, leetle sandwiches, very leetle!'

"I go back to hotel before meednight. She weel not come, I tell myself – but I take shower and put on cologne. Now, ees midnight, and I hear leetle knock at door. I open.

194

There she ees. You know Vergeenia, long blonde hair, long meenk coat. I say, "Please to take coat." You know Vergeenia, ees nothing underneath. Only long blonde hair. We spend beauteeful night. Next day, following evening, following day. Suddenly I remember! Tonight I must play Dvorak with Cheecago Symphony. I rush to airport – last plane to Cheecago has gone. I say, 'Please to charter plane.' They say, 'Eempossible.' What I'm going to do?"

At that moment Grischa paused for a breath and looked around the table to see us all smirking a bit. We knew, as well as he, that you cannot play a concerto without showing up for at least one or two rehearsals. He caught our doubting looks. We wondered how he was going to escape from the trap he had set for himself. Finally, he said, with a sheepish grin on his face, "Nevair mind. Ees all beeg lie!"

What an irresistible combination of a great artist and great raconteur. Two years later Milton suggested that I write to ask Grischa to return to Seattle for another appearance with the symphony. But by this time he was quite ill.

He replied:

"Dear Virginia, You made me very happy – but how could I thank you for your wonderful letter and for your wonderful feelings and friendship. Perhaps I could, in return, express my feelings for you and Milton by playing with him, for you, in Seattle. But it is not an easy task to play as beautiful as you deserve. At times I think perhaps I could, and then there is a last minute cancellation. No, dearest Virginia, I can't do that. This is the most difficult 'no' I have ever said. With great affection for you and Milton and love from Jacqueline. Happy New Year."

Grischa died of lung cancer shortly after writing the letter. We miss him profoundly.

Milton and Virginia Katims

Yo Yo Ma

Milton: Many years ago I attended a party given by one of the managers of Columbia Artists in New York. Soon after Virginia and I arrived, I found myself sitting alone, a drink in hand, in a corner of the large living room filled with many well known, easily recognized artists. I was fascinated, listening to a veritable multiple fugue of voices, each musician talking about himself. Virtually all musicians are extremely fond of talking about themselves. One glaring exception is Yo Yo Ma, who is considered the outstanding cellist of his generation. He much prefers to talk about anything but himself. His interests are so far-ranging that he can talk easily about any subject.

Yo Yo has one of the most inquisitive minds I have ever met. He's curious about everything. How many serious musicians can discourse on the origins of American bluegrass music, ancient Chinese instruments, and Dr. Albert Schweitzer? How many are constantly concerned with extending the boundaries of their art, performing and recording "Hush" with vocalist Bobby McFerrin, "Appalachia Waltz" with fiddler–Mark O'Connor and bassist Edgar Meyer, and re-recording the "Bach Six Solo Suites," this time combining audio with creative videos? In addition to his exploratory mind, Yo Yo possesses a delightful sense of humor.

In response to my wanting to know how his view of the Bach solo suites has evolved, Yo Yo pondered his reply, chin in hand, then said in mock seriousness, "Let me see. I play them more out of tune, the rhythm is worse, and there are more memory slips. Other than that, they are about the same." But then he laughs off his reply and immediately becomes serious in answering my question. He says the suites have a timelessness that makes them very special, universality like the plays of Shakespeare. I agree. (The "C Minor 5th Suite" is his favorite.)

As a violist, my own longtime association with the Bach suites has given me the same reverent feeling for them. Whenever I've been asked the stock question of what

I would want with me if I were shipwrecked on a desert island, I have invariably replied that I would first like to have a book on elementary ship-building, then my viola and the Bach suites.

Yo Yo Ma makes the vital point that "if you examine a piece of music with enough depth, it will give you many clues as to how to understand and perform the work. If you just glide through, only mastering the notes, you'll get nothing."

The inspiration for the Bach Suites Project, (audio and visual), in which Yo Yo engaged, came from the writings of the multi-gifted Albert Schweitzer. "One of the things Schweitzer talked about," Yo Yo said, "is that Bach is a pictorial composer, who used specific things to tell a story."

It seems to me that there may be a close relationship between Schweitzer's thought and the one expressed by both Toscanini and Casals: "Music should have the same logic as speech."

I first met Yo Yo when he was about fourteen-years-old, one of the first young artists I brought to Seattle to perform in the "Stars of the Future" Sunday series with the Seattle Symphony. Others were pianists Cuban born Horacio Guttierez and American Murray Perahia, and violinists Miriam Fried and Korean born Kyung-Wha Chung. Each young artist was carefully chosen, either as a result of winning some competition or having been highly recommended by a respected colleague of mine. Each performed the same concerto on Sunday afternoon that the scheduled well known artist would be playing in the regular subscription series the following two nights. In Yo Yo's case, the established artist was the great Russian cellist, Gregor "Grischa" Piatigorsky.

Unknown to me, Piatigorsky slipped into the seat next to Virginia just before Yo Yo made his entrance to play the "Dvorak Concerto." Even at that early age he played remarkably well. In fact, he played so well that as soon as he had finished the concerto, Grischa bolted out of his seat and rushed backstage to berate me, "Why you bring this young China boy to play Dvorak before me? Now I am so nervous I weel not be able to play!"

Milton and Virginia Katims

But, of course, Grischa did play well both nights, although his health was beginning to fail. Yo Yo was his warm and charming self, saying he was deeply honored to have Piatigorsky attend his performance.

In a letter to Virginia and me, Yo Yo wrote: "It was after freshman week at college (Harvard) and my roommate looked at me in astonishment when I said I was going to be away for a week. It turned out to be a glorious week. We were playing as part of the 'Stars of the Future' and I had a wonderful time with Milton and with the symphony. I also met one of my heroes, Piatigorsky, who was both kind and generous to me, a much younger colleague."

A few years later Yo Yo Ma returned to Seattle to perform the "Lalo Cello Concerto" at a regular pair of concerts. He was well on his way in the cello world and I was happy to have him back. At the Monday evening concert however, something happened that caused my heart to skip more than a few beats. In one section of fast-running passages in the first movement, I suddenly became aware that Yo Yo was not playing what was in the score. He had evidently had a lapse of memory; but instead of stopping, he was improvising masterfully in the appropriate key so that only a listener following the score would have known what he was doing. After 15 or 20 seconds – it seemed a lifetime to me – Yo Yo found his way back to Lalo's notes. We both heaved sighs of relief. The rest went smoothly. Afterwards, we were able to laugh about it.

*V*irginia: I feel very much the same way about this wonderful cellist and human being, Yo Yo Ma. After a Seattle recital of his a few years later, I wrote a letter about him to the Seattle Cello Society, which publishes a newsletter four times a year: "The best phrase I can think of in describing Yo Yo Ma's playing, is 'total immersion.' During the concert I was literally transported to a higher level of consciousness, tears running down my face. I was engrossed by the whole experience. Yes, from the very first note to the last it was 'total immersion.' I have known

Yo Yo for many years. Very simply, I love him as a great artist and for his brilliant intellect and beautiful sense of fun. Put together, how could I not love him as a man?

"He recently bought a French cello bow from me, a perfect Voirin. When I went backstage to greet him that night, I was overcome with emotion. I wondered what I could say that wouldn't sound like a mere platitude. He caught sight of me and held out his arms to embrace me. His first words were, 'Virginia, I love the bow.' How typical of him to think of me and my bow at such a moment. But that's Yo Yo."

He was born in Paris in 1955 of Chinese parents and began his studies with his father at age four. Remarkably he played his first recital a year later. Yo Yo is a graduate of Harvard and in addition to concerts on every continent he plays chamber music wherever and whenever the opportunity arises. He has won innumerable prizes and records extensively for Sony Classical.

As if all that were not enough, Yo Yo takes time to teach, often at Tanglewood in the summer, and frequently gives master classes before his solo appearances everywhere in the world. Besides dabbling in jazz and bluegrass, he is also collaborating with the Mark Morris Dance Company and with Tamasaburo, the Kabuki dancer.

In reviewing his many innovative achievements, I have to conclude that Yo Yo Ma must be a complete insomniac, that he never goes to sleep at night. I'm convinced that he wanders around his house, latches on to C-Span on one of his many television sets or takes a walk outside. His fertile brain must be constantly going at top speed, bubbling over with new ideas.

Yo Yo's ceaseless creative thinking may keep him awake, but it leads to any number of fascinating innovations, as adding sight to the sound of the "Six Solo Suites of Bach" – perhaps with a with a beautiful enchanting dancer!

Milton and Virginia Katims

Virginia: As the designated cellist in the Katims family, I'm going to take over with narratives about three more cellists known everywhere in the world: Raya Garbousova, Leonard Rose, and Mstislav Rostropovitch.

Raya Garbousova

When I arrived in New York after my year of study in London, the first thing I did was to buy a newspaper to find out who was playing a recital. One ad featured a program by a Russian cellist, Raya Garbousova, in Town Hall. I had never heard of her, but I bought a ticket for her recital. The hall was full, and I heard many Russian accents in the audience. Then surprise, out from the wings walked a stunning blonde, her hair wound in a braid around her head. She was wearing a lovely, white gown with a touch of gold trim. "Well," I said to myself, "certainly she can't possibly play very well. She looks too glamorous to be a cellist, even though she is carrying the instrument. She should be a model. That's it."

She began to play – and how she played! Within a few bars, my first impression changed dramatically. I was immediately immersed in her mastery of her instrument, her fiery temperament, and her personality. I had heard many first-rate cellists here and abroad, but Raya was superior to all of them in technique and interpretation.

Raya was born in Tiflis, Russia, and began her musical studies with the piano, switching to the cello a short time later and ultimately making her debut in Tiflis. At 18 she left Russia to go to Leipzig to study with the famous teacher, Julius Klengel. He asked Raya to play many of the most difficult works in the cello literature. Afterwards, he told her he couldn't teach her anything, "You have already mastered all of the repertoire."

"If I hadn't absorbed all of the repertoire," Raya explained, "I would not have the excuse I needed to be let out of Russia."

*Leonard Rose, cellist – soloist,
chamber player and teacher*

*Two great Russian cellists Raya Garbousova
and "Slava" Rostropovich*

Milton and Virginia Katims

She left Klengel and went to Berlin to work with the celebrated cellist, Hugo Becker, but she found him too dogmatic and uninspiring and soon left him. Early on she performed with many of the world's great orchestras and also frequently played chamber music with the fabulous artists Nathan Milstein, violinist, and Vladimir Horowitz, pianist.

Raya touched many lives as a teacher. She was a faculty member at the University of Maryland's World Cello Conference. Also on the faculty was the cellist-conductor, Mstislav Rostropovich, one of her greatest admirers.

Raya appeared twice as soloist with the Seattle Symphony when Milton was its conductor. But one of the incidents concerning her that I remember best occurred much earlier in New York. We were in the apartment of violinist Bronislav Hubermann, who was visiting the city. "Come," said Bronislav, "let's play string quartets."

All agreed that would be fun. He would play first violin and Lea Luboshutz, of the Curtis Institute faculty, would play second violin. Raya was the cellist and Milton was the violist. The four sat down with the parts of the "Brahms C-Minor Quartet." They began. A few moments into the first movement, chaos reigned. They started again, but with the same result. Everybody seemed lost. After two more attempts, Hubermann said, "Enough! The only one who knows what he is doing is the viola player."

I was embarrassed for them, but they weren't, not at all. Shrugging off the failed chamber-music attempt, Raya began playing the Tchaikovsky "Rococo Variation", while Milton and I listened and marveled at her fantastic technique and passionate playing. The two violinists, their interest in playing chamber music having vanished, moved into the dining room to think of other things and to fortify themselves at the bar.

Raya died in 1997 as a result of a horrible auto accident, at age 87. Her death was a great loss to the musical world. She was a beautiful human being.

The Pleasure Was Ours

Leonard Rose

Virginia: It was almost concert time. I was backstage at the Seattle Opera House to check on Milton's full dress and make sure everything was in place – bow tie, vest, and the white handkerchief in his jacket pocket. As I entered his dressing room, I heard a lively discussion taking place.

Leonard Rose, the excellent cello soloist of the evening, had his jacket off and was pleading with Milton, "Can't I play in the second half of the concert? I haven't had time to warm up. The damned taxi had a blowout. I don't feel ready to go on in the first half of the concert."

Milton tried to placate Rose and keep the order of the program intact, as the audience expected, "Come on, Leonard, you're a wonderful cellist. You can play 'Schelomo' in your sleep. I'm going on-stage now. You can warm up a bit while we play the overture, then be ready in the wings when we finish."

In an effort to smooth things over, I gave both Milton and Leonard a big hug and gave Milton a slight push toward the stage. After the overture, Milton took a bow and came offstage. "Where's Leonard?" I looked around. No Leonard. I raced to the dressing room and found him practicing the Bloch. He had not yet donned his tails.

"Leonard, you're on!" I shouted. "Come on!"

Approaching the stage door, I saw that Leonard was carrying his cello and bow, but he had forgotten to put on his jacket! I tore back to the dressing room, retrieved it, raced back, and offered to help him on with it. Leonard, now grinning sheepishly, handed me his beautiful Italian cello to hold and slipped into his jacket. Nonchalantly, he walked on-stage to tumultuous applause, sat down, and played Schelomo like the great artist he was. He was in his glory, along with Milton, but I was ready for a tall drink. (Milton told me later that he has never been able to see the Bloch score during a performance – his eyes are too filled with tears.)

Milton and Virginia Katims

As concert incidents go, this one was relatively tame. But in Leonard's case it was an indication of the cellist's extreme nervousness just before a performance, something that happened to him every time he was about to go on. Despite his wonderful artistry, his command of the cello, and his experiences everywhere in the world, he just could never shake these bouts of nervousness. I can recall only one other artist whose pre-concert nerves were worse. That was Claudio Arrau, the Chilean pianist, whose unbelievable jitters I have already recounted.

When we were having dinner with Leonard the night before, we found him in a marvelously ebullient mood, laughing hilariously at Milton's jokes. But in the middle of dessert he stopped suddenly and said, "My God, what am I so happy about? I have to play tomorrow night!" The man was incurable.

All in all, the nervous incidents were minor phases of our association with Leonard. We spent many happy times with him, Isaac Stern, and Eugene Istomin (of the "Half-Million-Dollar-Trio" fame) in Menton, the festival site in France. One year Milton took the Northern Sinfonia of Newcastle, England, to the Menton Festival. We had our twelve-year-old daughter, Pam, with us and she promptly fell in love with Leonard, whom she had heard in concert on several occasions.

When she met him, she asked, "Why don't you ever smile on-stage?"

"Playing a concert is very serious business, Pam," he told her. "You spend many hours of your life learning to play everything as well as you can, and when you walk out on that stage, you're trying to play everything perfectly, in spite of the fact that you are often nervous. The great violinist Heifetz, once told me, 'In order to play 100% perfectly on-stage, you have to have learned whatever you've been practicing 150%, because you always lose 50% in performance.'"

Pam listened wide-eyed, but stuck to her guns, "But Leonard, you can still smile when it's over while you take a bow, at least." From that time on Rose grinned like a Cheshire cat much of the time.

The Pleasure Was Ours

During one of the eight years Milton and I lived in Houston, Leonard spent a long weekend in our guest room. He was between concerts on his Southwest tour and it gave us a chance to catch up on many events in his life and renew our long friendship. Milton and I were specially interested in hearing him practice. I wanted to pick up more bowing and fingering tips and Milton wanted to compare notes on how he and Leonard approached the "Six Bach Solo Suites." Milton's version for viola had been published by that time. The two men found that their concepts of phrasing, dynamics, and other details were remarkably similar. It confirmed the confidence of both.

When the time came for Leonard to leave to continue his tour, we bade him Godspeed with the traditional theatrical sendoff, "Break a leg." The rest of his tour was a great success. When he returned home to Hastings-on-Hudson, New York, in midwinter, he slipped on the ice one morning when he went out to get his newspaper and suffered a broken arm. We sent him a telegram: "A leg, Leonard! We said a leg!"

Leonard Rose, the extraordinary artist and fantastic teacher, who produced many of today's fine cellists as head of Juilliard's Cello Department, died an untimely death from cancer at New York Hospital. Istomin, his close friend and colleague, went to visit Leonard in his final days. The cellist, philosophical to the end despite his pain, said to Istomin, "You know, there are many forms of this rotten disease. Wouldn't you know I would get the incurable kind!"

I've been reading a wonderful book, *Widow's Journey*, by Leonard's widow, Xenia Rose. She wrote about being invited to attend a concert, her first since Leonard's death. Yo Yo Ma, a dear friend and one of Leonard's most brilliant students, was the soloist with the New York Philharmonic that evening. He had invited Xenia to be his guest.

"It was a disaster," Xenia said. "The minute I entered Avery Fisher Hall, I knew I had made a major emotional error: the audience, the orchestra players warming up, and in the center of the stage, the soloist's chair, waiting empty. I stayed rooted in my seat. Moments later Yo Yo walked from the wings, greeted by enthusiastic applause. Looking handsome and secure, he played the tormentingly familiar, brilliant Dvorak. The mantle had discernibly been passed! I was inconsolable. I felt paralyzed. Leonard's haunting cello sound had been silenced forever."

In talking about our friendship, Xenia said, "Leonard's entire career was great, amusing, and tragic. He was also a fantastic ping-pong player. He could have beaten Milton!"

Mstislav "Slava" Rostropovich

Virginia: Mstislav Rostropovitch, the fabulous Russian cellist and conductor, must be on a mission to conquer the entire musical world and his mission is succeeding admirably. His dual career has virtually seduced concertgoers wherever he has gone and that means the entire globe.

Married to the beautiful, prima donna soprano, Galina Vishnevskaya, who is also an author (Her autobiogrophy is simply entitled *Galina* and is a fascinating read) and with two accomplished daughters, Slava, is one of the most charismatic figures, captivating all who fall under his spell. Tall and rangy and the possessor of an impish sense of humor, Slava walks on-stage with his right hand held over his big heart, acknowledging the warm applause. He often blows a kiss or two to the audience. He is irresistible.

Slava soloed with Milton a couple of times, once with one of the Shostakovich concertos and once with the "Dvorak Concerto." When we learned that he was playing a recital in Vancouver, B.C., we drove up there from Seattle. At that time I was planning to sell my beautiful Cerruti cello, and I thought he might be interested in buying it, if only to add it to his storied collection. Backstage at intermission, he suggested that we bring the cello to his hotel the next morning.

The Pleasure Was Ours

At eight the next morning, Milton and I knocked on his door, knowing that he probably would have to leave early that day. When he opened the door he had his little dachshund under his arm. My first thought was that here was a musical icon in his senior years, who not only has to carry a cello around wherever he goes, but he also totes his pet dog! The telephone rang as he let us into his room.

"Veergeenia, you answer phone, please? After concert so many vimmen call me. You say you my secretary. OK?" I picked up the phone and heard a woman's voice imperiously asking for Slava. I thought it was an excellent moment for me to try my skill at acting. In a sleepy voice and feigning a Russian accent, I said, "Aaaah, uhhhh. Slava in shower."

She sucked in her voice and hung up. So did I. Seconds later it rang again and the ritual was repeated. The woman said gruffly, "In shower? Slava?" I don't know what she meant by that, but by this time both Slava and Milton were howling with laughter.

"Meelton," he said, still laughing, "Veergeenia should travel weeth me and be my secretary." I wondered if one of the two "vimmen," possibly the second, might have been Mme. Rostropovitch. After we all had a good laugh, Slava picked up my instrument and said, "We go to ballroom now and I try cello."

In the ballroom he took the cello out of the case, barely tuned it, and proceeded to rip off a couple of the Tchaikovsky "Rococo Variations." The cello sounded so marvelously that I wondered whether I really wanted to sell it. Slava stopped playing, turned to me, and said,

"Veergeenia, I like cello verry much. Tell you vat vee going to do. You weel come to Vashington to hear me conduct. After, we go to supper and drink plenty vodka. Then you sell me cello cheap – very cheap!"

I never went to Washington to close the deal.Instead, I decided to sell my instrument to the solo cellist of the Netherlands Symphony, who I was certain needed the Cerruti more than "Slava the Collector."

Milton and Virginia Katims

As an indication of Slava's human quality and humility, Milton told me that whenever he rehearsed with the cellist, the affable Russian would turn to the orchestra and say, "Please try not to make noise turning pages. But when I play cadenza, then it's OK to make much noise."

Born of a musical family in Baku, Azerbaijan in 1927, Rostropovich was homeless in Moscow until a generous Armenian woman took the family in. When the great Russian composers, Dmitri Shostakovich and Sergei Prokofieff, were being persecuted by the Stalinists in 1948, they were defended by Slava until such defenses led to the demise of his own career in Russia. The final genius of Mstislav Rostropovich is that his human qualities are exactly equal to his musical genius, probably in great part the extension of them. You don't believe it? Just ask his neighbors!

Janos Starker

Milton: If not known because of his numerous recordings and appearances on five continents, Starker is renowned because of the hundreds of his students who are concertizing, winning competitions, performing as principal cellists, playing in orchestras and ensembles, and serving as professors on four continents.

Not only cellists coach with Starker. His students include guitar, bassoon, French horn, double-bass, and saxophone players. And of course, many chamber-music groups have reaped the benefits of his coaching. This is more than ample proof of Starker's reputation as a Master Teacher. Janos has long since shown how appropriate his surname is in his chosen fields, performance and teaching; there are few, if any, who are "stronger."

Janos started the study of the cello at the age of six in Budapest, where he was born, began teaching the cello when he was eight and played in public by the time he was eleven. He was fortunate to have a mother who encouraged him from the start. At a very early age, Starker discovered the secret of great teaching – that his own understanding of music and the possibilities of his instrument grew as he helped others search for solutions, a philosophy that remains the touchstone of all great teachers.

Although Janos was successful in his native city, playing first cello in the Budapest Opera and Budapest Philharmonic, he became disillusioned with the political changes in Central Europe and moved to the United States. His reputation had preceded him, so very quickly he became principal cellist of the Dallas Symphony, then with the Metropolitan Opera and finally solo cellist, under Fritz Reiner, with the Chicago Symphony. Soon afterward, he joined the faculty of the Indiana University School of Music and re-embarked on his international solo career that has made his name a household word in music centers everywhere.

Starker has constantly been an inspiration to a number of composers who have written concertos for him. They include Jean Martinon, Antal Dorati, Miklos Rozsa, Robert Starer, and Chou Wen Ho. The latest is Hovhaness, whose concerto Janos premiered with the Seattle Symphony. As for recordings, Starker's exciting performances of many composers can be found on numerous CDs. At this writing, his fifth recording of the "Bach Six Solo Suites" is in the process of being released by BMG's RCA Red Seal label.

Always searching for ways to improve the sound he produces on his cello, Janos invented the revolutionary "Starker Bridge" for all string instruments. This device dramatically expands the quality and quantity of the tone. And, lest I forget, Janos has contributed a large number of articles on musical and humorous subjects to educational and popular periodicals. (No, I don't know what he does in his spare time.)

When Fritz Reiner asked Starker to leave the Metropolitan Opera, where he was solo cellist, and joined the Chicago Symphony, he extended the same invitation to one other musician, Alan Fuchs, a horn player.

This led to Janos telling us, "My personal contact with Alan was minimal until then – mostly poker games during intermissions or on the train while on tour. But when we arrived in Chicago, we needed each other's support and enjoyed the reminiscing of our days at the Met. Being Reiner's men was not an immediate entry into the hearts of our new colleagues. A routine of getting together in my apartment for after-concert snacks developed, as I lived close to Orchestra Hall. We were about the same age, married to musicians, and shared many similar experiences.

"After a concert one evening in the spring of 1954, I asked some of the younger orchestra members to join us for drinks. When we finished trashing the guest conductor, his program, and so forth, someone suggested that we each recall where we were and what we were doing ten years prior to our being in Chicago. Those in their mid-20s recalled their dads having been away fighting the war, rationing, watching certain movies and Rosie the Riveter.

"When my turn came, probably under the influence of whiskey, I said, 'Well, a few months short of ten years ago, while I was in a detention camp on a little island in the Danube River outside of Budapest, working in an airplane factory, 300 U.S. planes came and carpet-bombed the factory. We were in trenches. Twenty-one people near me were hit. I was one of the few to come out alive.'

"Alan Fuchs looked at me. 'What was that date?' he asked. 'Easy,' I answered. 'July 31st.' He reached into his jacket pocket, pulled out a little black book, and read, 'July 31st, 1944, bombing mission over Budapest.'

"'I was on that mission,' Alan said. I got up, shook his hand and said, 'Cheers, friend. Thanks for missing me!'"

Lynn Harrell

Milton: When I read that Lynn Harrell was also a conductor, I remembered what Maestro Toscanini said about me when he learned that I was conducting, "Why does such a wonderful violist want to conduct? Anyone can wave a stick!"

The Pleasure Was Ours

Those words were in my mind as the audience at the University of Washington's Meany Hall erupted like Mount St. Helen when Lynn came to the end of his performance of a Shostakovich "Cello Concerto," with Dmitri Sitkovetzky conducting his European Players. It was some of the most vibrantly exciting cello playing.

While he was performing my thoughts went back a number of years to a concert performance of Verdi's "Otello" I conducted with the Seattle Symphony. The role of Iago was sung that evening by a great baritone named Mack Harrell (Lynn's father). He brought to the Machiavellian role a uniquely cerebral insidiousness that only Mack Harrell could create. At the same time, Virginia, who was sitting with me in the Meany Hall audience, might have been recalling the many times she had heard concerts with Lynn's mother, Marjorie Fulton, a fine violinist. With two such parents it was inevitable that Lynn would be a consummate musician, enjoying a career as soloist, recitalist, chamber musician, conductor, and teacher.

I could list all his honors including the Piatigorsky Award, Ford Foundation Concert Artists' Award, and, jointly with Murray Perahia, the first Avery Fisher Award. I could also point to all the places in which he has played and describe him as the very warm and intelligent person he is. But nothing I write could be as moving and revealing as his own words in a letter he wrote to Virginia:

"Dear Virginia, I was eleven years old when we moved to Dallas, Texas from New York. I was lonely and bewildered, slowly turning to the cello as my soul mate, but was embarrassed to show my depth of feeling for it to my musician parents. It was my secret, until fortune brought into my life Lev Aronson.

"Lev was more than just my cello teacher. He was the teacher who opened up the windows of my soul to me, and opened mine to him and to music. I knew that he had been a superb cellist once, but that his spirit outran his fingers. I never really understood why, until the day he took me into his garage. There, in this shell of a small house in a quite characterless suburban street in Texas, he unfolded to me a world of cruelty and courage almost beyond my imagination. He showed me the woven paper clothes in which he survived Auschwitz – and told of the horrors he had witnessed in them.

"Everything with Lev was encapsulated in the one piece of music he would never work with me, Bruch's 'Kol Nidre,' the sacred prayer of the Jewish Day of Atonement. Was he protecting himself, or me, a fragile boy stranded in Texas, locked out from that experience of suffering? He would not work on the 'Kol Nidre' until many years later.

"I was 35 and playing in Chautauqua. Lev came to stay with me. And in that empty wooded place by the lake in New York State, he finally opened to me that hidden place within himself, in which 'Kol Nidre' smoldered. It was both a vision of hell and the spirit of survival. It changed me in the way my contact with Lev always did.

"Years passed. I lost him to cancer, and then I found myself in the Vatican for a special concert commemorating the Holocaust. As the violins played the opening eerie notes of 'Kol Nidre,' I looked out at the Pope and the Chief Rabbi of Rome, the first Chief Rabbi ever to enter the Vatican. My heart placed between them the vision of Lev Aronson, who had lost family, youth, and the greatest part of his musical life and buried them within his students, such as myself.

"That night I played (with a fury at what men had done to him and to each other) not only for him, but with love and gratitude for the life that he, in turn, had bequeathed to me. The breath of life was with me that night – and will be always. – Signed, Lynn Harrell."

We would give anything to have heard that performance!

The Pleasure Was Ours

Zara Nelsova

Milton: "Meine grosse held" ("My great big hero") is what a famous woman cellist called me for many years after she had appeared as my soloist in a number of concerts with the Israel Philharmonic in Israel. (No, she was not referring to my conducting.)

Israel was barely five years old in 1953 when, for the second time, I spent six weeks in that tiny country, guest-conducting its illustrious symphony orchestra. My enormously gifted soloist on that visit was Canadian-born cellist Zara Nelsova. Most of the concerts I conducted that summer were in kibbutzim in different parts of the country.

After one of our concerts in a kibbutz close to the Jordan border, Zara and I were being convoyed out of the area by armed Israeli soldiers in military jeeps. The border areas were considered dangerous, and the symphony officials felt the need to protect their soloist and guest-conductor. Zara and I sat in the back of the large four-door sedan, with ample room for Zara's cello to stand on the floor in front of the back seat. Despite my knowing full well that her cello would in no way stop a bullet aimed in my direction, I felt that crouching down behind it gave me a certain amount of psychological protection. Zara immediately began calling me her great big hero. Hence, "meine grosse held."

While the word, "hero," (or "heroic") is being bandied about, it should be applied to Zara's cello playing. Whether it was the Dvorak, the Lalo, or the Elgar concerto, or Bloch's inspired "Schelomo," her tonal tapestry was always large, always of heroic proportions. Her quality of sound was produced by a bow arm, with which she could do anything. It was matched by a left hand that moved about the fingerboard with great ease and strength. These are but the tools serving her musicality, which is most persuasive.

Although we hadn't seen Zara for many years after our music making in Israel, Virginia and I kept pace with her remarkable career. That's why we were especially delighted to have a reunion with her at the International Music Festival in Victoria, B.C., where Zara was giving a master class.

As we listened to her sage words of advice and admonition to the students who were fortunate enough to play for her in the master class, the many years fell away, revealing an even more mature artist, a virtuosa who had at her fingertips any work that the students played. We were deeply impressed with her ability to zero in on any area of the student's playing that was in need of improvement, briefly analyze it, and suggest a remedy.

Unchanged, and perhaps even more infectious than ever, was her laughter, her gentle sense of humor softening any critical comment she might make. She also adroitly avoided stepping on the toes of the student's teacher. (That's quite a trick, I can assure you. I was once observing a master class by a very famous violinist, who suddenly jumped on the student's fingering in a particular passage and shouted, "Who on earth gave you a fingering like that?" The student's teacher was sitting among the small group of auditors.)

Zara, Virginia, and I spent many wonderful hours together in Victoria, reminiscing about the many musical experiences we had had with so many artists the three of us knew. During one of our "remember when" visits, Zara came up with the following unbelievable experience, "I had just finished recording the Dvorak Concerto with a London orchestra. It had gone exceedingly well, and for once I was satisfied with the results. After listening to the final takes in the control booth, I returned to the studio to pack up my cello. The members of the orchestra, atypically disdaining their usual quick exits, had stayed to listen also.

"Suddenly, one of the cellists in the orchestra stood up and said to me, 'Miss Nelsova, playing with you has been the most fantastic experience for me. You are such a great artist. I could never ever play like you. I don't ever want to try to play this cello again. I don't ever want to see it again!'

214

"With that he smashed his cello against the studio wall. I was so shocked that I burst into tears. Then, and only then, did he confess that before the recording session he had gone to a pawn shop and picked up the cello for ten pounds. I didn't think his idea of a practical joke was funny. Not at all funny."

Eugene Ormandy, maestro of the Philadelphia Orchestra inviting Katims to guest conduct his fabulous orchestra

Chapter 15
Divas, Batons, Bows

Elizabeth Schwartzkopf, Soprano

Milton: Elizabeth Schwartzkopf was one of the most beautiful soloists ever to appear with the Seattle Symphony. Along with her physical beauty she possessed a heaven-sent voice, which she used deftly and exquisitely. Her vocal beauty was not so much natural, but more the result of a keen musical intelligence and brilliant technique. But who cared how the sounds were produced? Certainly not I! Looking at the singer's physical beauty, my thought was, "No wonder the sounds are gorgeous, look at where they've been!"

She was a veritable angel with whom to make music. The last time she sang with me (in the old Orpheum Theater, where Seattle's Westin Hotel stands today) we had programmed the "Four Last Songs" by Richard Strauss. It was a performance that made the audience forget other sopranos. I, too, was filled with wonder over her unbelievably lovely sound and marveled over how she could shape the musical phrases with unobtrusive care. Her voice had the precision of an instrument and the ethereal quality of an angel.

The summer after her appearance in Seattle, Virginia and I were in Austria for the Salzburg Festival, staying in the famous Schloss, high above the city. One day, while we were sitting on the tiny terrace next to our suite, the window in the suite directly over ours was opened by a woman who looked down and called out, "Hello Virginia! Hello Milton!"

With the sun in our eyes, we looked up at her, eyes squinting. We finally realized that it was Mme. Schwartzkopf, minus her stage makeup and with her hair up in curlers. We arranged to meet as soon as she was "decent" (her words). The pleasant time we were able to spend together, even though relatively brief, gave us a chance to be brought up to date on her amazing career. It also gave us the opportunity of bringing her up to date on the progress of Seattle's new Opera House, which would soon be ready for the World's Fair of 1962. Of course, my objective with Mme. Schwartzkopf was to persuade her to return for another appearance with the Seattle Symphony.

The old Civic Auditorium was undergoing a major facelift to turn the "Old Uglyduckling" into the handsome new Opera House when she had performed the Strauss work with us the previous year. At that time I wanted to show our lovely soloist where she would sing the next time she came to Seattle. I led her through the stage entrance onto the unfinished stage and we looked out at the vast empty space, trying to visualize what it would look like with all of the seats in place and all of the scaffolding removed.

Ever the inquisitive performer, she wanted to test the acoustics of the hall, so she sang several golden tones which wafted easily throughout the unfinished Opera House. Much to our shocked but delighted surprise, her sounds were immediately echoed by three robust tenor voices coming to us from the ceiling above the top balcony. We hadn't noticed the trio of Italian plasterers at work way up there. At least we did discover early on that the acoustics of the new hall were good in both directions!

Leontyne Price, Soprano

Virginia: On our first visit to Vienna, we eagerly looked forward to our evening at the fabled Vienna Opera House, where we were to hear Verdi's "Aida" sung by that born-for-the-role diva, Leontyne Price. The first star of the evening was Leontyne herself! The poignancy of her "Aida" was breathtaking and her voice, called by many "the most beautiful in the world," soared above the always dramatic Verdi score. It was truly spectacular. Next came the Opera House itself, resplendent in its white and gold beauty and glittering chandeliers - and the magnificent scenery, orchestra, and ballet.

As we watched and listened to this magnificent opera unfold, Milton whispered to me that he couldn't help but envision himself in the pit accompanying Leontyne. But he had to be content with wonderful memories of her appearances with him and the Seattle Symphony the previous season. How uncomplicated and easy she had been to work with. She more than confirmed what Milton and I have known for a long time - the greater the artist, the simpler it is work with them!

The next day, still mesmerized by the dazzling magic of her performance, we met Leontyne in our hotel lobby. She was beautifully gowned and coifed, a dark mink coat slung casually over her shoulders. Leontyne was every bit a glamorous diva. But she was much more. She was a warm, modest human being. When I complimented her for her masterful "Aida," she seemed vulnerable and almost shy, but receptive to everyone who spoke to her. I mentioned an interview in which she had told a reporter, "When people hear me sing and watch me as an actress, they don't realize that I am basically a very shy person."

"It's true," she said. "Sometimes people mistake my shyness for aloofness when they meet me in person. Actually, I'm a very feeling individual and find it difficult just to sit around and make small talk. I feel most at home, I suppose, right up there on the stage. That's where it's at for me!"

What was it that drove her in her career? "I'm competitive. If I can't be first, I'm unhappy. I was brought up this way. My mother always said, 'If you can't be first, remove yourself from the game.' But now I feel immensely relieved from the burden of having to prove myself. I've done it. And yet, one can never really relax or let down. Each performance, no matter where, is terribly important. A career before the public never stands still. It either moves forward or backward.

"I was born in Laurel, Mississippi. My career really began at the time of the civil-rights turmoil. I contributed a great deal of myself to that movement, although I became known as a 'token black' in the operatic world. That was then. This is now. It's nice to be accepted today simply as an artist."

She stopped for a moment, as if she were searching for just the right words, "I think success has matured me. I can handle it – and myself. I used to have to phone my mother for reassurance when my career began to take off. We were marvelously close. And now she's gone. But, thank God I have inner resources of my own."

Leontyne certainly knows who she is. So do we! One of the greatest sopranos of our time.

Roberta Peters, Soprano

*V*irginia: Milton and I have long been great admirers of Roberta Peters' singing and her highly professional stage presence. After a scene we witnessed during a performance of Rossini's "Barber of Seville" that Milton conducted with her in Seattle, we were convinced that her enormous talents as a singer were matched by her bullet-quick reaction to unexpected mishaps on stage.

One of the characters, Dr. Bartolo, was being sung by a very large, heavy man. When he sat on one of the chairs on the set, it suddenly collapsed under him. He

The beautiful soprano Elizabeth Schwartzkopf with Katims

Delightful soprano Roberta Peters admiring Katims' recently acquired Rodin "Caryatid"

Birgit Nilsson, soprano with Katims after an all Richer (Wagner-Strauss) program

*Beautiful soprano Mary Costa
being very domestic*

looked ludicrous sitting on the smashed chair on the floor and the audience couldn't help laughing at his predicament. Even after he managed, with great effort, to get to his feet, the laughter continued because of the sight of that crushed chair at center stage.

Roberta paused momentarily in her role as Rosina, concocted some believable stage business that brought her to the collapsed chair, and quickly but deftly kicked it under the desk and out of sight. That ended the audience laughter, and the performance went on to a perfect conclusion and an ovation.

Roberta made her debut at the Metropolitan Opera when she was barely out of her teens, subbing for an indisposed prima donna on six hours' notice, in the role of Zerlina in Mozart's "Don Giovanni." The rave reviews launched her career with a bang.

We met her first when she was engaged to solo with the Seattle Symphony. She sang a group of arias before and after the intermission. Roberta was both a visual and vocal sensation, appearing in two different gowns, both of them gorgeous and the height of fashion. One was a yellow taffeta and the other a startling white, studded with jewels. (I wish all sopranos would dress in a similar manner to liven up symphony concerts.)

Subsequently, Roberta returned to Seattle to wow audiences with a thrilling performance in the title role of Lucia di Lammermoor (Donizetti). What I remember most of all was her dramatic rendition of Zerbinetta's aria from "Ariadne auf Naxos" (Richard Strauss), a flawless performance of a most difficult challenge for a soprano.

It was after that spectacular evening that Roberta helped us unveil a work of art, a Rodin Caryatid, that Milton had found in Newcastle on the Tyne in the north of England. Roberta had a good laugh when I told her that when he announced that he had bought a Rodin, our daughter, Pamela, then twelve, asked, "Does it have a stick shift?"

Before the first rehearsal of her debut at the Bolshoi Theater in Moscow, Roberta's husband, Bert Fields, went to the theater to check things for his prima donna. He asked the little old man taking care of the stage door how the acoustics in the famous theater were. He replied, "If you have a voice, it has acoustics."

It is eminently fitting that Roberta Peters was awarded one of the 1998 National Medals in the Arts.

Mary Costa, Soprano

$\mathcal{V}$**irginia:** Contrary to the popular misconception of what an opera prima donna looks like, singer, Mary Costa, a beautiful blonde with a lovely voice and figure to match, was one of the most radiantly attractive singers to appear before the public. And she was one of the most feminine. In Moscow, where she sang with tremendous success, the Russians called her "The American Doll." Here at home she was dubbed "Costa the Colossal." Yet, she always retained the quiet charm and femininity of a true Southern belle.

After-performance receptions are often bright, light-hearted affairs. On one occasion we were giving a party for the cast of Seattle Opera's "La Traviata" (Verdi), which Milton conducted. Mary sang the role of Violetta. She came into the kitchen with me and was busily mixing different fruits, heating them in a pot, sprinkling in a bit of cinnamon and adding a touch of cointreau, for what was to be our dessert. At the last moment she plucked a gardenia from the corsage she was wearing, washed it and stuck it atop the fruit. While she was working, Mary hummed and grinned like a Cheshire cat. When I asked what was so amusing, she explained that she was thinking of the new bit of stage business she had tried at the end of the opera.

"Instead of dying in bed upstage, Virginia, didn't you notice how I staggered downstage so I could sing my final phrase closer to the audience before I swooned and dropped dramatically to the floor?" She started to giggle.

"I heard your Maestro in the pit whispering in a voice that must have been heard by everyone sitting on the main floor, 'My God, Mary, drop dead farther upstage. The curtain is going to decapitate you!' "I never rolled over so fast in my life!"

Birgit Nilsson, Soprano

Milton: When I invited Birgit Nilsson to appear as soloist with the Seattle Symphony, I had already decided before she arrived how best to describe the dramatic soprano's performance: She came, she sang, she conquered!

Birgit came from Sweden and not only established a quick rapport with the Scandinavians living in Seattle, but also with everyone else! Her powerful voice easily reached into every corner of the Opera House and swept all of her listeners into the palm of her hand.

Like all the great artists with whom I have made music, Birgit was immediately easy to work with. There were no prima-donna airs about her. She was basically a down-to-earth, super-friendly singer, ready to sing. A large Brunnhilde-buxom artist, she loved to drink beer, a fact we quickly learned from the social affairs we shared. We also learned very quickly that the twinkle in her eye was a very visible clue to her intriguing sense of humor.

If you need proof, Birgit herself provides it. "I was at the Met singing other roles at the time and had to learn the part of Electra (Richard Strauss). I kept going to Walter Taussig (well known coach at the Met) to learn it. How hard we worked. It is a difficult work, but it went quickly. I think I learned the whole score in about 18 hours. After singing the role in Stockholm and Vienna, I decided to write a note to Mr. Taussig's wife, Lore. I can't believe I was so daring to write such a prankish letter.

"I wrote: Dear Mrs. Taussig, I have a confession to make. I have had a child with your husband. She is very beautiful and I call her Elektra. I am absolutely sure he is

225

the father because I have not been with anyone else. I must say— I would like to have another child with your husband.' "

For her debut with the Seattle Symphony, I had assembled what could have been termed an all-Richard program - Strauss and Wagner. The final work on the program was the Prelude and Liebestod from Wagner's "Tristan and Isolde." We finished the orchestral Prelude, during which Birgit sat, no doubt absorbed in thoughts about the love-death music she was about to sing for the umpteenth time in her career. In the middle of the second or third phrase of the Liebestod, Birgit made a very minor, rhythmic mistake, easy to overlook.

I was amazed when she stopped singing and signaled me to stop the orchestra. I couldn't imagine why she would stop over such a small error.

She turned to the audience and said, "I am so excited to be in your beautiful city that I make a big mistake. You will forgive?" Forgive? Amid tumultuous applause, we began the Liebestod once more. In exactly the same spot, Birgit made the same little mistake, but this time there was no stop. We went right on.

We finished the piece and the audience rose to its feet, as one, in thunderous applause - the usually sedate Seattleites were yelling and cheering as if they were at a rock concert. I can't recall how many curtain calls we took before I suggested that, because we had prepared no encore, it might be a good idea for her to repeat the Liebestod. She agreed. This time there was no minor mistake and we finished with the audience's enthusiasm undiminished.

Among the many people who crowded backstage afterward, one dapper, white-haired gentleman rushed up to Birgit, and with youthful enthusiasm exclaimed, "Madame Nilsson, you are fabulous!. You are my favorite Wagnerian soprano. And Wagner is my favorite composer. I know every piece of music he ever wrote. What was that encore you sang?"

The Pleasure Was Ours

Marni Nixon

Milton: Some of my happiest memories are of making music with Marni Nixon. It's very difficult to place Marni into any particular niche! At any moment she could be doing concerts, tours, film-work, shows, cruises, recitals, student adjudications, master classes, or taking on the responsibilities of being President of NATS (National Association of Teachers of Singing). Marni suggests that it should be called NUTS for anyone in her right mind to take that job. Marni Nixon is first and foremost a very natural and gifted musician, no matter what she's doing. And at this time Marni has been singing in "Carouselle" at various summer festivals.

Most people do not realize that they have heard Marni sing many, many times - as many times as they have enjoyed re-runs of "My Fair Lady" with Audrey Hepburn, or "The King and I" with Deborah Kerr, or Natalie Wood in "West Side Story." Marni's singing voice is the one that has been dubbed in for each of these actresses. Marni has the amazing ability to color her voice precisely to match these actresses, so that they really sound as if they are singing.

We first met Marni Nixon when she moved to Seattle from Los Angeles after divorcing composer Ernest Gold, who is best known for writing the score to the movie "Exodus." Without pausing to take a breath, Marni immediately became an active part of the cultural scene in Seattle. She sang Arnold Schoenberg's "Pierot Lunaire" and Francis Poulenc's "La Voix Humaine" with the Little Orchestra of the SSO. For her role as the discarded mistress on the telephone in her bedroom, I suggested that she wear a suitable dress. Virginia suggested a sexy nightie. The one she wore certainly made a hit with the men in my audience. It was quite diaphanous. I said nothing, but I really had to concentrate on my score.

I decided to make use of the all important telephone as a prompting device, hooking it up to a back stage phone, manned by my associate conductor, who was armed with a score to give Marni prompting, if needed. What I did not know, and did not find out until much later, was that my bright associate had some ideas of his own. When Marni, frantically awaiting a call from her fickle lover, playing sensually with the phone cord, her long red hair spread out on the coverlet, impatiently picked up the phone after only one ring, this is what she heard, "O oh la la ma cherieee, you are so lovely, so elegante – voulez vous couchet avec moi?" All of this in a fake French accent, accompanied by very heavy breathing.

All the while Marni was singing. I'll never know how she kept from laughing or angrily letting him have it. But Marni is a real pro and she was not about to let this joker spoil her act.

It was Marni for whom I wrote the script for Richard Strauss' "Till Eulenspiegel," which she narrated so successfully on a series of Family Concerts. That was quite a switch from the Schoenberg and Poulence. Another contrasting activity was her very popular children's TV show, Boomerang, which Marni herself had created. I'm still meeting people who watched and loved that program when they were children.

Virginia introduced Marni to our good friend Fritz (Seattle's Dr. L. Frederick Fenster). It was love at 2nd or 3rd sight. Their marriage seemed quite blissful until their competing egos raised disruptive heads: Marni, rightfully aware of her uncanny ability to make people happy with her singing and acting; Fritz, with his expertise in helping people and needing all his time and tranquility to continue being one of the best gastroenterologists in the country. (Fritz was my doctor, if you need proof.) Fritz stayed on at the Virginia Mason Clinic in Seattle, and Marni fled to New York City, where she married another musician and just added more teaching to her multiple activities.

Cast of La Boheme (Seattle Opera) – Rodolfo (Luciano Saldari), Musetta (Carol Todd), Colline (Wm. Wilderman), Mimi (Beverly Sills), MK conductor

Marni Nixon in the role of the cast-off mistress in La Voix Humaine (Poulenc)

Conductor Dimitri
Mitroppoulos, reflecting the
mood of his music

"The only way to travel with a
double-bass" – Gary Karr

The Pleasure Was Ours

Batons and Bows

Milton: One evening, early in the short life of the Morini String Quartet (Erica Morini and Joseph Gingold, violins; myself as violist; and Frank Miller, cello), conductor George Szell, a close friend of Erica's, attended our rehearsal. He must have been in a nasty mood because he treated poor Erica miserably.

Nothing she did was right. She had no right to be playing chamber music. She didn't know what she was doing. She played everything too fast. He went on and on. Then he left without even saying goodnight to any of us. We were furious with him for the way he had treated Erica and for his haughty and abrupt departure. Joe Gingold, who at the time had absolutely no inkling that he would soon be Szell's concertmaster in Cleveland, summed up our feelings in the following lines:

"There was a conductor named Szell,

For whom everything was zu schnell,

He came from the Ruhr,

With his partitur,

For our part he can go to hell!"

I'm quite sure Joe did not appreciate how appropriately topical his limerick was. Many of the jokes among musicians at that time concerned a special section of hell reserved for conductors. They singled out Szell, consigned him to a tiny cell filled with the worst possible horrors in hades. His misery was only somewhat mitigated by his catching sight of Maestro Fritz Reiner in the throes of the same situation in a cell nearby. But that consolation was short-lived because Szell was almost immediately aware that Reiner held the sex goddess, Marilyn Monroe, in his arms. Szell was furious and complained bitterly to the chief devil, who silenced him with, "QUIET! Marilyn Monroes's punishment is no concern of yours!"

Milton and Virginia Katims

Dimitri Mitropoulos, Conductor, Pianist

Milton: All of the previous was a rather roundabout way of introducing the name of Dimitri Mitropoulos. He was one great conductor who definitely would not share the fate of his two eminent colleagues in the conductor's inferno. Although my musical association and friendship with Mitropolous was not a lengthy one, it was more than enough to give me a good glimpse into his monastic and ascetic lifestyle. He consistently lived the life of St. Francis, who was his model and whom he revered.

From his early youth in Greece, he was attracted by and maintained two fervent passions, music and religion. William Trotter's excellent biography of the Greek maestro is very appropriately titled *Priest of Music*. For me, the one word that best sums up this outstanding man of music is simplicity. Although he appeared to be a great showman on the podium, there was no posturing. Nothing was done for effect.

He never used a baton. His entire body was his baton. Players who looked only for the usual beat patterns would be lost. When he studied a score, he took it apart to see what made it tick. But he put it back together again so that when he conducted the music, it was from the core of the score that he conveyed his understanding and feelings to his players. There was nothing superficial about his realization of a score. I felt that his efforts to bring members of his orchestra to his concept of the music were almost telepathic. Much has been written about Mitropoulos's fabulous memory, that he never used a score at rehearsals, that he not only knew every note, but also the rehearsal numbers or letters.

I wish I could reveal his secrets. I cannot. Dimitri was kind enough to lend me his scores for study. I was aware of his markings in the scores - mnemoic aids, no doubt. I was attracted, intrigued, and ultimately baffled by them. Unlike Maestro Toscanini, Mitropoulos disclaimed a photographic memory. He said he just kept studying and living with a score with complete concentration until he was ready to conduct it, no matter how long it took. (In my own study of scores, I found that when I began to be bored, I knew that I had the score in my head.)

When Maestro Mitropoulos was appointed music director of the New York Philharmonic, Virginia and I hosted a celebration party for him in our home in Long Island, and were delighted that he came, knowing he would much rather have gone to a movie than to a party, even if it was in his honor. At the height of the festivities, we all toasted Dimitri.

His surprise response was, "Thanks very much. I'm delighted to announce that no woman helped me achieve this honor." It was the only time in our association with him that Mitropoulos made any reference to his being homosexual.

My friends in the Budapest String Quartet were among our guests at this party. Typical of musicians, they wound up in the kitchen with the conductor. And, also typically, the talk turned into a lively discussion of the orchestral repertoire. The Budapesters assailed Dimitri for invading their literature and conducting movements of Beethoven string quartets with the full string section of the orchestra. "Why do it," they complained,"when the orchestral repertoire is already so extensive?"

Mitropoulos' reply was very simple. He said he loved the string quartet music so much that, being a pianist and not a string player, this was the only way he could perform this music. I thought it was a beautiful explanation.

A few weeks later I received a phone call from Harold Gomberg, first oboe of the New York Philharmonic. Would I be interested in recording Charles Martin Loeffler's "Two Rhapsodies for Oboe, Viola, and Piano" with him and Mitropoulos, as pianist, for Columbia Records? And did I know the music? My quick, eager answer to both questions was, "Yes," but I had my fingers crossed. I rushed out to buy the music and started practicing like mad. By the time I went to our first rehearsal in Dimitri's hotel rooms, I had the work almost completely memorized.

Milton and Virginia Katims

When I walked into the conductor's modest suite at the Great Northern Hotel on West 57th St. in Manhattan, two things immediately caught my eye. One was a very large, beautiful crucifix on the wall and the other was an enormous, comfortable chair with a music stand in front of it. In the middle of the floor was a huge circular electric fan. It was July, and the hotel did not have air-conditioning.

When Harold arrived he took one look at the electric fan on the floor and immediately said he would not even take his oboe out of the case until the fan was turned off. He explained that the fan would create insurmountable air problems for him. Oboists are very sensitive people; they have to be because of the nature of their reed instrument. We had no choice but to put up with the heat and the sweat when the fan was shut off.

I was happy to be able to match Harold's beauty of sound and his intonation, and I was also impressed with Dimitri's piano playing. In the process I noticed something about his interpretive priorities that had not occurred to me before. When Harold and I began discussing the contour of phrases, a subject that is constantly in the minds of players of instruments that play a melodic or horizontal line, we talked about the tension of the music up to a certain point - then its relaxation, breathing in or out, as Harold had to do, or playing up-bow or down-bow, as I did on the viola.

What I found most interesting was that Dimitri never said a word during those discussions. I realized then that he did not have the same approach to making music. He certainly understood what we were talking about, but our concerns were not his. Perhaps he was aiming at the "larger things" in the music.

The Loeffler work we recorded for Columbia was transferred to Sony when that company took over the Columbia catalogue. More recently, it has been added to the "Debussy Sonata for Flute, Viola, and Harp" and the "Villa-Lobos String Trio" on a Pantheon Legends CD, titled "Katims and Colleagues." To the best of my knowledge, the Loeffler is the only commercial recording of Mitropoulos playing the piano in a piece of chamber music, making it quite a collector's item.

I consider Dimitri unique as a conductor, a giant who is vastly underrated and most unusual as a man - a man who thought only of others, seldom of himself. He supported dozens of musicians financially (and anonymously), many of whom later became famous, among them David Diamond and Leonard Bernstein. It was Dimitri who inspired Lenny to turn from the piano to conducting as his major pursuit.

One charming incident that is typical of Maestro Mitropoulos was told to me by Danny Kaye when he conducted the Seattle Symphony in a benefit concert. Danny had just conducted the New York Philharmonic in a benefit concert for the Musicians' Pension Fund, and Dimitri had placed a chair just offstage so that he could watch Danny conduct and listen to the orchestra. As Danny left the stage at the end of the program he noticed that Dimitri looked very unhappy. "Why so sad, Maestro?"

Shaking his head, Dimitri answered, "I'm the regular conductor of the Philharmonic, and you, who can't even read a note of music, make the orchestra sound better than I do!"

I know that my life has been made richer for having known Dimitri Mitropoulos. I remember him as the conductor, who, when told that the performance he had just completed was the greatest he had ever achieved, said, characteristically, "Such performances are gifts of God!"

Gerard Schwarz, Conductor

*V*irginia: The name of Gerard Schwarz, who took up the baton of the Seattle Symphony after Milton left for Houston, looms large in the world of music. Most people call him Jerry. He is another of those musicians who has had to prove himself as a conductor. He first made a reputation as a virtuoso trumpet player, one of the best in the nation, if not the world.

Jerry is in a class with other great instrumentalists who put aside their instruments in favor of a baton. In addition to Milton, the class includes cellist "Slava" Rostropovich, pianist Christoph Eschenbach, violinist-composer Lorin Maazel, and many, many more – all of whom would have drawn Maestro Toscanini's comment that "anyone can wave a stick."

Jerry's conducting career has blossomed on both sides of the continent (New York and Seattle) and has extended to Japan, where he is principal guest conductor of the Tokyo Philharmonic. He serves as conductor of the New York Chamber Orchestra and is music director of the Mostly Mozart series at Lincoln Center. With the Seattle Symphony, he has made a large number of recordings for DELOS. He has also extended his career into opera, conducting a varied repertoire for Seattle Opera with members of the Seattle Symphony in the pit.

Jerry reminisces, "I'll never forget my opening concert with the New York Philharmonic, my first concert in New York as solo trumpet. One of the compositions on the program was Richard Strauss' "Also Sprach Zarathustra." There are two very difficult trumpet solos in the work, both forte and in a high register. I was very nervous about the two spots. Messing them up would have been a disaster.

"I arrived very early, and was handed a note from the press director, Joanna Fiedler, (daughter of famed Arthur). The note read: 'Dear Jerry, Before the concert, please call the following number. It's very important!' Being quite young and naive, I immediately thought it might be the *New York Times* wanting my reactions and impressions of my first concert in the big city.

"At 7:15 I went to the pay phone outside the brass room, put in my dime (in those days it was only ten cents for a local call), and dialed the number on the note. I quickly discovered that I had reached Dial-a-Prayer! I also realized that my good friend, John Cerminaro, the solo French hornist, and Joanna had played a practical joke on me. But, maybe, it may not have been a joke after all. Perhaps the prayer did help. The concert went swimmingly."

What do cellists talk about (Leonard Rose and Virginia)?

The Katims being serenaded at first Symphoneve by an elite group of SSO strings

The Katims with pianist Leon Fleisher about to play a Candlelight concert.

I'm convinced the prayer worked - and that the humor of the practical joke also helped relax a very nervous, young trumpeter so he could "do his thing" well.

Gary Karr, Bassist

Milton: Several decades ago, when I was an undergraduate at Columbia University, I was the music reviewer for a college magazine. One of the concerts I covered was the Carnegie Hall performance of Serge Koussevitzky, a virtuoso on the double bass.

Up to that time I had known him only as a conductor, but I soon discovered he was an exceptional instrumentalist, as well. What a rich, vibrant sound he coaxed from his bass, an Amati made in 1611. Many years later I would again hear beautiful sounds from that same instrument, this time under the superb hands of Gary Karr at the first Victoria International Music Festival, in which I participated.

How that marvelous, old instrument came into his hands is a story best told by Gary himself. "In 1962, I played my debut recital at Town Hall in New York City to a packed house of friends, colleagues, and curiosity seekers. Among them was Olga Koussevitzky, the widow of the famed Boston Symphony conductor (and double-bass virtuoso), although I didn't know about her presence until later. When I received a phone call the next day from a woman with a strong Russian accent, my immediate reaction was that someone was playing a practical joke on me.

"'This is Olga Koussevitzky calling,' she said in a whisper I could barely hear. "'Oh, yeah,' I said, 'Sure, baby, I'll bet.'

"I don't think she heard me, because she then invited me to her apartment for something important. Curious to find out who was playing the joke on me, I went to the apartment indicated and quickly found from the name on the door that it was indeed Madame Koussevitzky who lived there and who had invited me. The reason, she said, was to show me her late husband's Amati double bass, which was now more than three centuries old and better than ever.

"She then said something I shall never forget, because it gave my life new meaning and focus. 'After hearing you play, I am convinced that you are the one to carry on the legacy of Serge Koussevitzky. To do this I should like to present you with this bass.' Winning the lottery could never have equaled the surge of excitement I felt at that moment."

One of the major reasons I had looked forward to traveling to Victoria, British Columbia, to take part in its festival was to meet Gary. For years I had heard about him and knew many of his recordings. I didn't believe it possible for anyone to accomplish what he did on that large brute of an instrument. But seeing and hearing were believing. He moved around that large fingerboard with the ease of a Jascha Heifetz on the fingerboard of his violin, producing a cello-like sound.

Before meeting Gary I had pictured him as very tall and heavy-set. Imagine my surprise at finding my eyes at the same level as his - and I consider myself to be on the short side. He is also slight of build. But even more important, from the moment we met, he made me feel that we had been friends for years. With a sharply honed sense of humor, he has a clever quip on the tip of his tongue almost every moment. In performance, some people might consider him to be a ham, but I always enjoyed his clowning because he never sacrificed his superb level of performance. Small wonder that *TIME* magazine hailed him as "the world's leading solo bassist."

Gary did for the double bass what Casals and Feuermann did for the cello, and what Segovia did for the classic guitar. In the years since his debut in New York's Town Hall, Gary has made believers of those who didn't realize what feats of virtuosity could be achieved on that huge instrument.

In one particular area, as much as I admire Gary Karr, I have never envied him. That is his need to lug that goliath of an instrument when he goes out on the road. It requires not only a great deal of muscular output, but also demands the purchase of two seats whenever he flies. But Gary faces his professional life with enviable equanimity and good humor.

Here's how he describes it: "About the only compensation for 35 years of tortuous travel with an unwieldy double-bass is the reward, after forking out the fare for two large first-class seats, of being served two meals – one for me and one for Mr. B. Fiddle, which is the name on the other ticket. On one trip, having looked forward with great expectations to the sumptuous airline feast, I was greatly disappointed when an obstinate and humorless flight attendant refused Mr. B. Fiddle his share of the vittles.

"From that day forward, I always ordered a special meal for my strung-up companion. One day, as I was wheeling my double bass through the massive corridors of Chicago's O'Hare Airport, I was surprised to hear the following announcement: 'Will Mr. B. Fiddle please report to the ticket counter at Gate 52?'

"A few minutes later, I stood facing the ticket agent at Gate 52. He looked first at me, then at my buddy, Mr. B. Fiddle. He then astonished me by asking very seriously, 'Which of you is Mr. B. Fiddle?' When I nodded toward my wooden friend, he said, 'I regret to inform you that we have run out of kosher meals!'"

An unlikely quartet – Igor Stravinsky with Danny Kaye, Katims and Lou Guzzo in new Opera House

Chapter 16
Musica da Camera

Milton: As a violist I found the opportunities for solo recitals and concertos with orchestra quite limited because of the lack of repertoire. Playing chamber music became the major part of my professional life as a violist.

Almost from the beginning of my life in music chamber, it has been an integral part, starting when I was in my early teens. My violin playing must have been fairly acceptable when one evening I substituted for the second violinist in a doctor's string quartet when he was called away in an emergency. (Those were the days when doctors made house calls) The chamber music bug bit me that evening; I have been a devotee ever since.

As an undergraduate at Columbia University, I founded the Chamber Music Society. The first thing we did was to form the Columbia College String Quartet. Naturally I played first violin in the quartet. I have fading memories of this youthful foursome, the most vivid being the New Year's Eve when we decided to celebrate by reading through 77 Haydn string quartets. It took us the whole night and half the next day to complete. Intoxicating as it was, we felt that it was a most enlightened (and sober) way to welcome the New Year.

Some years later, as a violist, I well recall playing string quartets with Mischa Elman, specifically the first movement of the Brahms "A-Minor." At the opening of the movement, the viola accompanies the first violin. Then their roles are reversed, with the first violin taking over the accompanying figure. Elman didn't see the role reversal that way. When I began playing the major melody, I was shushed, in no uncertain terms. Even if he had been correct, with his big luscious tone, I couldn't begin to compete with him. Mischa was fond of telling us that he didn't know a particular quartet at all, then proceeded to play it without looking at the music!

Another rather well known violinist with whom I found myself playing quartets quite unexpectedly one evening was Henryk Szeryng. This happened in Chicago. Henryk was supposed to be appearing as soloist at Ravinia. I was scheduled to conduct at Grant Park. Torrential rains cancelled both concerts. Luckily, I just happened to have my viola with me, and later that evening when Henryk and I met, along with other musicians, we all gathered at a mutual friend's apartment. We spent the entire evening playing string quartets.

One of my most memorable evenings of ad-hoc chamber music was playing viola quintets with a most notable cast – Itzhak Perlman and Pinchus "Pinkie" Zukerman (violins), Walter Trampler (2nd viola), and Danny Saidenberg (cello). As if playing with such illustrious colleagues were not enough, the walls of the Saidenberg Park Avenue apartment were covered with Picassos and Braques. (Eleanor Saidenberg was the American representative of both artists) It took much of my concentration to keep my eyes on the music.

During our New York years (and in Seattle), with my having married a fine 'cellist, all we had to do was invite a couple of violinists over for dinner and we could spend the rest of the evening playing string quartets. Later, when I became conductor of the Seattle Symphony, one of the ways we helped raise funds for the orchestra was to invite the current symphony soloist to join Virginia and me in an informal chamber music evening (Candlelight Musicale) for the benefit of the orchestra. These were all ad hoc affairs. But in New York the two important groups that were to mean the most to me were the Budapest String Quartet, with which I was frequently identified as the "fifth member," and the New York Piano Quartet, of which I was a charter member.

My close association with the Budapest String Quartet began when I was engaged by Ira Hirschman (director) to play a Mozart violin-viola duo with violinist Roman Totenberg at a New Friends of Music concert in New York's Town Hall. The world-famous Budapest was performing at the same concert. Ira asked if I would join them for a Mozart viola quintet. The work was the "C-Major Quintet, K.515." I remember how warm and cordial the four men were – violinist Joseph Roisman, violist Boris Kroyt, and the Schneider brothers, 'cellist Mischa and violinist Alexander "Sasha."

We sat down and, almost without a stop, read through the quintet. I felt as if I had been playing with them for years. The ensemble, intonation, the manner of bowing, and concept of phrasing meshed beautifully as the wondrous music unfolded. They seemed to be delighted – and, of course, I was supremely so. Little did I realize that this meeting was to be the first in a 15-year association of concerts and recordings (Columbia, now SONY) in New York, the Library of Congress in Washington, and elsewhere around the country.

Among the many unforgettable experiences I had with the Budapest was a date in Indianapolis, where we were to play three viola quintets. When I arrived I was told that Boris (their violist) was ill, and that his doctor would not permit him to leave his bed to rehearse. However, that presented no problem because we had played (and recorded) the programmed works so often that no rehearsal was necessary. Boris would surely recover for the concert by evening. I practiced for a couple of hours, had lunch, and went to a movie.

Milton and Virginia Katims

When I returned to the hotel late that afternoon, I found that Boris was still confined to bed and would have to stay there – doctor's orders. The concert was about to be canceled when one of the members of the Indianapolis Chamber Society spoke up." You have one healthy violist. Instead of the viola quintets, why not play a program of string quartets?" There was no time to rehearse, the three healthy members of the quartet looked at me and I at them. We said, almost in unison, "Why not?"

We picked out a program of Mozart, Beethoven, and Brahms and talked through the music – where they made repeats and other details I needed to know. The concert must have gone well because afterwards Roisman said to me, "After we started, I completely forgot that you were not our regular violist." I don't think I have ever received a greater compliment. The next day one of the newspapers carried the headline: "Budapest String Quartet carries a spare."

When our recording of Mozart's great' G-Minor Quintet" was released, *The New York Times* published a review, accompanied by a photo of me alone. That night I had a dream. Mischa came to me and said solemnly, "All you play is.....," he sang the very short solo the second violist plays in the slow movement, "and you get your picture in the paper!"

What made the Budapest String Quartet great? Each artist in that foursome contributed his own unique musical gifts and personality that added up to an artistic whole of chamber-music perfection. The first violinist, Joseph Roisman, was a very reserved – a very private man. In all the years I played with the quartet, I never really had any social contact with him away from the rehearsals and concerts. He was an elegant violinist, with a beautiful tone and a technique that allowed him to play everything with apparent ease. Joe guided the ensemble with a sure hand. It was a joy to play with him, because there was never any mistaking his musical intentions. (Incidentally, he was the fastest page-turner I've ever seen).

Sasha Schneider was a perfect foil for Joe. He was a great second violinist playing the most challenging part in a string quartet. The second violinist, with the excep-

Violist Katims (2nd from right) recording Mozart with the Budapest String Quartet
(Joseph Roisman, Edgar Ortenberg, Mischa Schneider, and Boris Kroyt)

New York Piano Quartet –
Alexander "Sasha"
Schneider (violin),
Frank Miller (cello),
Milton (viola),
Miecio Horsowoski (piano)

tion of occasional solo passages, has to adjust his playing to match the tone and musical ideas of the first violinist, who is the prima donna of the group. In addition to that, the second-violin part is almost always in a lower, less-grateful register.

Sasha had a very outgoing, volatile personality. He added zest and much life to the performances. When I played quintets with the Budapest, I was continually catching Sasha's eye winking at me across the tops of our music stands, like a Till Eulenspiegel of the chamber-music world. His joy in bringing music to life – and life to music – was most contagious. (Whenever I phoned Sasha, I invariably was greeted with, "The world's greatest second violinist!")

Boris Kroyt was an excellent violist who provided the ideal, vital bridge between the violins and cello. He had a warm viola sound and technical prowess that had carried over from his days as a fine violinist. Boris had a great sense of humor. He would double me up when retelling (mangling!) some of the stories I had told him. His twisting the jokes around would make them even more hilarious. He was also a fanatic collector of gadgets – a loyal member of the Gadget of the Month Club. Among other things, on the dashboard of his car he had an altimeter. He and his wife Sonia were wonderful caring friends.

Without a doubt, Mischa Schneider was the most complete quartet cellist with whom I have played. He gave the Budapest its solid foundation as the cellist must. He drew a warm and marvelously sensitive sound from his instrument, and those are exactly the same adjectives I would use to describe his personality. Virginia and I treasured his close friendship.

Mischa was the scribe of the quartet. He took care of correspondence and kept track of their performances of every quartet played by marking the date on his cello part. There were so many dates marked (particularly Beethoven) that it was almost impossible to see the notes. Another chore that Mischa undertook was to keep a scrap-book of their reviews, but he taped in only the negative critiques. He always thought that they might possibly learn from them. That scrap-book was mighty thin!

The Pleasure Was Ours

The Budapesters never permitted differences of opinion about phrasing, dynamics, or whatever, to take any time away from rehearsals. Musical disagreements were almost immediately resolved by taking a vote. To avoid the possibility of a tie vote, they took turns giving each man two votes. (I wonder if there isn't the germ of an idea there for a democracy to adopt?) Of course, the quartet's two-vote strategy wasn't necessary when I played a quintet with them. From the very beginning of my being "the "fifth member" of the Budapest, the foursome gave me a vote.

I will not soon forget the time Joseph found himself very much on the minority side of a vote. Actually, it was four to one. Acknowledging the result of the vote we resumed rehearsing, but just before giving us the signal to start Roisman said very quietly, "Doesn't Mozart get a vote?"

During the years I played with the Budapest, I was also doing more and more conducting at NBC and in various cities around the country and abroad. In fact, I was doing so much that Mischa's wife, June, was inspired to create a tile for me. It depicts a viola being stabbed out of shape by three batons. I still have it.

In my entire career as a conductor, I have never exploited the fact that I once conducted the Budapest String Quartet. One day I received a phone call from Mischa, asking if I were available on a certain date to conduct a recording session of the quartet.

"Are you kidding?" I asked.

"No. I'm very serious. Let me explain."

In great detail Mischa told me that they had recorded Darius Milhaud's "14th and 15th Quartets," which he had composed to be played separately or together as an octet! The engineers at Columbia Records could not fit them together. So, with each player wearing earphones, they listened to their recording of the 14th while attempting to play the 15th. The result was chaos.

That's when I was called to the rescue to help them synchronize the two works so they would mesh perfectly. With no baton in hand and wearing earphones, I listened to their recording of the 14th and conducted while they played the 15th. It worked! Columbia Records didn't even send me a copy of the recording! (Which, incidentally, is ML-4332.) And I never received even the Musician's Union minimum fee for the session!

My association with the New York Piano Quartet started sometime later. A very pleasantly voiced gentleman phoned me one day, "This is John Hammond calling." Although we had never met, I was aware that he was the head honcho of Mercury Records. He had an idea which was to realize his dream of forming the ideal foursome to record the three Brahms piano quartets. My colleagues to be were pianist Mieczyslaw "Miecio" Horszowski, violinist Sasha Schneider, and cellist Frank Miller. Fortunately, I already knew them and had had marvelous associations with all three artists.

I had first met Horszowski at Maestro Toscanini's home in Riverdale. The two were longtime friends. And, of course, I had known Sasha well through my collaboration with the Budapest String Quartet, and I had had a long personal and professional association with Frank Miller.

I'm quite sure that John Hammond was aware of these close associations when he had his idea of bringing us together. Four more diverse musical personalities would be difficult to find. However, each of us admired and respected the musicianship and instrumental capabilities of the others. It goes without saying that we immediately warmed to the idea of making music as a foursome. We couldn't wait to get started.

"Mieco" (Mee-atcho), a nickname I was happy to learn I could use instead of Mieczyslaw, was the senior member of the quartet. Having started his career as a young prodigy, he had been before the admiring public for many decades and enjoyed an enviable reputation as a recitalist and chamber musician. He was truly a poet at the piano. Mieco produced a beautiful sound and was always sensitive to the need to balance the sound of his nine-foot Steinway grand with our much smaller instruments. Although he was small in physical stature, he was a giant in the musical world.

The Pleasure Was Ours

Mieco was surprisingly shy and offered his opinion only when it truly mattered. He was always careful to avoid any confrontation. I found out later that he had once been a most avid mountain climber. As a testament to his physical fitness, he played his final New York recital at the age of 99!!

Although outwardly Frank Miller was a benign giant of a man, I sensed that he was seething within. He had no patience with stupidity and trivia. At times he expressed an interest in sports, particularly baseball, but his attention was centered on music alone. He would not read or even touch a newspaper because he refused to dirty his hands with the newsprint. In his hands, 'the cello looked like a viola, in much the same way as a cello appeared in the grasp of equally big Gregor Piatigorsky.

Frank produced a beautifully vibrant sound with immaculate intonation, plus a technical facility to match. His solid musicianship may have been on the conservative side, but the sheer perfection of his playing brought every note, every phrase to life. I have always felt that Frank was not fully appreciated, and that, if he had ventured into the world of the soloist and recitalist, he would have had great success. We had proof of that time after time when he played solos with the Toscanini NBC Symphony.

Sasha was the diametrical opposite of Mieco and Frank in temperament and in his approach to making music. For the sake of giving life and emotion to the music, Sasha didn't hesitate to sacrifice the quality of his sound. He would often taunt me during a rehearsal for my viola tone, employing the German word for sweetness – "süsskeit" – like an arrow to my heart. Of course, he always said it with a smile, which blunted the arrow somewhat.

One might assume that when a second violinist in the Budapest String Quartet moved over to become the sole violinist in the New York Piano Quartet, there would be some sort of metamorphosis. But no! Having observed both Sashas first hand over several years, I can attest that no metamorphosis ever occurred. He was always his inimitable self, always sure of and ready to defend his often rebellious but exciting musical ideas, whether playing second or the only violin. Whether one agreed with him didn't matter, other musicians always knew exactly where they stood with him.

Sasha brought to his music the very same attitude he had toward life. It was to be lived to the fullest – a very Bohemian life. His array of friends was fascinating, and most of them were non-musicians. Among them were actresses Uta Hagen and Geraldine Page (his second wife), actors Paul Robeson and Jose Ferrer, photographers Margaret Bourke-White (with whom he had a torrid affair), and his friendships with Djon Mili and the celebrated New Yorker cartoonist, Saul Steinberg.

Mention of Sasha's Bohemian lifestyle reminds me of the time during our rehearsals of the Schubert Trout Quintet with Phil Sklar, first bassist in the NBC Symphony. Discussing his Bohemian life-style, Phil asked me if Sasha were happy. I told him I had no idea, that he should ask Sasha himself. The next time we were relaxing after a rehearsal at Sasha's apartment on Beekman Place, Phil asked the question. He received no reply. Four days later I had a phone call from an exasperated Sasha. He complained, "That son-of-a-beetch, Sklar! He asked me if I'm happy. I haven't slept for three nights, asking myself if I'm happy – if I'm not happy!"

As one might guess, rehearsals of the New York Piano Quartet were never boring. There were many disagreements at rehearsals, and some of them developed into shouting arguments. Unfortunately, we did not employ the democratic voting system the Budapest String Quartet depended upon to resolve arguments quickly and without bloodshed. Most of the time the differences of opinion were between Sasha and Frank, with me in the middle.

And Mieco? He usually left the room during the very vitriolic brouhahas. But I remember one occasion at a rehearsal in Buffalo, when the confrontation slipped beyond the verbal and the antagonists literally came to blows, with me in the middle once again. This time, Mieco did not leave the room; he ducked under the piano, earthquake-style!

In spite of the disagreements, the four of us did like and admire each other and we did get along 99 percent of the time. Unlike the Budapest, we traveled together when we went on tour. Once, on the way to Louisville, Kentucky for a concert, the conversation turned to the subject of the "movable do," as in do-re-mi. Frank couldn't resist saying to Sasha, "We haven't even reached the Kentucky border, and you're already speaking with a Southern accent." (Translation: "movable do" = "movable door")

On this occasion we were playing the "Copland Piano Quartet" in the very old musty concert hall at the University of Louisville. While negotiating the fast sixteenth note passages in the middle movement, with my peripheral vision I noticed a very large black spot on the floor between Frank and myself. I thought I saw the spot move, but I didn't dare take my eyes off the music for fear of losing my place, until I had a whole bar of rests at the same time Frank also had rests.

At the very moment I swung my head around to take a better look at the large spot, Frank's left foot swiftly emerged from behind his cello and, with deadly accuracy, squashed a hapless cockroach with a terrific bang. Without missing a beat, we went on playing as if nothing had happened. We thought better of asking Aaron Copland to write the impromptu percussion note into the score as a tribute to Frank's prowess. But it did add a definite fillip to the concert.

I've always been grateful to Johnny Hammond for creating his and our dream piano quartet. It was as exciting as it was musically rewarding to be a part of that gifted foursome. Once in a while I indulge in nostalgia and listen to the recordings we made – not only for the pleasure the music gives me, but to help me relive many of those memorable moments.

The authors cutting up in San Marcos Square (Venice)

Chapter 17
More Musical Gems

Milton: One of the prized, autographed photos in my album of artists with whom I have had the joy of making music is clarinetist Benny Goodman, the "King of Swing." Nadia Reisenberg, the wonderful Russian pianist and pedagogue, who was not only a good friend, but also a colleague on the Juilliard faculty, invited me to join her in an evening of chamber music. I always enjoyed playing with her. She and I had just finished a series of weekly broadcasts of viola-piano sonatas on WOR (Mutual Broadcasting System). I didn't realize I was about to meet an American legend.

The whole world already knew and enjoyed Benny Goodman as the greatest jazz clarinetist of all time. I envied his virtuosity and improvisatory brilliance in the jazz idiom in which he was Prometheus unbound, able to take off unrestrained by a printed page. Although I had not heard him play the classics, I was told by the members of the Budapest String Quartet that he was just as good with Mozart as he was with Gershwin.

Milton and Virginia Katims

Playing chamber music with Benny and Nadia that evening introduced me to the side of his musicianship to which I could relate – being a square, bound by the notes on the page. He was more than welcome to my world of "squares," into which he slipped with ease, playing with a gracious sound and a keen sense of phrasing. We matched tone and intonation without any difficulty. Having Nadia at the piano had much to do with our being in sync.

That evening I was also introduced to Mozart's Kegelstatt Trio, for our three instruments. It was so named because Mozart is supposed to have written it in a bowling (kegel) alley (statt). I'm not sure about the authenticity of that tale, but it does make a neat story. Like most of the great artists I've met, Benny made me feel that we had been friends for years. We were on a first-name basis before we played a note.

Friends had told me that when he was courting his wife Alice, he was so shy and inhibited that he finally had to propose to her with his clarinet. But that night at Nadia's, I found it hard to believe the stories about his shyness and inhibitions. He was articulate and talkative. I also enjoyed his positive approach to music. We had so many friends in common in our world of music that we thoroughly enjoyed each other's company. It was the beginning of a cherished friendship that endured until he died.

Although Virginia and I were not in the habit of night clubbing, we did go to the ballroom of the New Yorker Hotel a few weeks later to hear the Benny Goodman Band. Benny was in fabulous form. As a lark we sent him a note telling him how very much we were enjoying his playing and asking whether he could include some Mozart when he returned to the stage. Much to our surprise and delight, in the next set he interpolated phrases from the Mozart clarinet quintet and improvisations on themes drawn from the Kegelstatt Trio. His inventiveness was astounding. Virginia and I were probably the only ones in that big room who recognized the Mozartian origin of his inimitable improvisations. But that was the beauty of it. He had brought two distinct worlds of music together.

The Pleasure Was Ours

Benny Goodman's name was at the top of the list of soloists I wanted to bring to the orchestra when I became conductor of the Seattle Symphony. My first efforts were foiled by Benny's busy schedule. But I persisted. In time I found a date he could accept. News of his coming was welcomed warmly by Seattleites, just as I expected. The sold out house that greeted Benny was a mixture of the old guard (matrons and patrons) and the younger devotees of the "King of Swing." The evening provided something from both sides of the musical coin, although I'm sure young and old alike were thrilled by everything they heard.

In the first half of the program, Benny played the "Concertino" by Weber, and to close the concert he performed Aaron Copland's "Clarinet Concerto." Fortunately we were prepared for the tumultuous ovation at the end of the printed program. After we took a half dozen bows, the stage crew moved our Steinway grand out in front of the orchestra. Beverly Hamway, the orchestra's expert pianist, took her place at the keyboard, and Randy Baunton, our percussionist, brought his set of drums forward. Mori Simon, bassist, moved to a spot next to the piano. Benny went on-stage for the planned encore, gave the three a toe-tapping downbeat, and they were off!

I've never heard anything like the happy thunder that audience let loose for the 15 to 20 minutes Benny and his ad hoc jazz group stomped at the Seattle Symphony! The Seattle Opera House is still reverberating from that spectacular evening in which the classics and jazz were wed in Seattle.

Virginia: I really love good jazz, with its combination of sophisticated arrangements and brilliant improvisations. What great musicians we had: Benny on clarinet, Harry James on trumpet, Lionel Hampton on the xylophone and vibes, and Gene Krupa on drums. Each was a virtuoso. I also recall some of the singers I'd heard and admired so much: Rosemary Clooney, Martha Tilton, Frank Sinatra, and more, each of them with a fine voice and a distinctive style. Many of my musician friends and I openly admired, in particular, Sinatra's instinctive sense of phrasing. Beverly Hamway, the symphony pianist, always alerted me whenever Frankie was within reach – whether in person, on the tube, or on the radio.

How different those jazz musicians were from the cacophonous rock bands that have assaulted our ears with the aid of electronic amplification at full throttle. My ears ache at the thought. I find it to be barely organized chaos, not beguiling at all and not honestly sexy, like mellifluous, ingenious jazz. I find no romance at all in rock. Yet, this is what our younger generations have been growing up with, an insistent bombardment of noise that poses as music. And the audiences? Jumping up and down, throwing themselves at the players and at each other. It is so restless, never a lovely tune to relax with.

Give me some wonderful jazz any time with its gifted performers, to say nothing of the peace and fulfillment of listening to a wonderful piece of classical music, performed at a high level, a level which allows the listener to sit back relaxed, letting the music flow into body and mind and dispelling some of the day's stress. (I had an unhappy chuckle one day when I came across a yellowed newspaper clipping of an interview my maestro had given many years ago. The journalist asked Milton what he thought of "rock'n roll." The astute prophet to whom I'm married replied, "It's a passing fad – it won't last!"

Musical Cruise – S.S.Mermoz

Milton: My single experience performing on a music cruise as conductor and violist was aboard the S.S. Mermoz. Each evening the director usually asked me if I were familiar with a particular score. The next morning I would rehearse it with the Polish Chamber Orchestra and perform it that evening. On board was an enviable array of international talent that included French trumpeter Maurice Andre, Irish flutist James Galway, Hungarian pianist Tomas Vasary, and Russian violinist Victoria Mullova.

The King of Swing –
clarinetist Benny Goodman
after soloing with Katims and SSO

A light moment during the
music cruise on the SSMermoz
– James Galway, flute with
violist-conductor Katims

SSO premiere of Lees' "Vision of Poets"
Virginia, Noma Copley, Lee Lees with the composer

Sitarist Ravi Shankar with Symfunics in Katims' home

The Pleasure Was Ours

Maurice was a familiar sight on the upper deck where, still in his bathrobe with his slippered feet resting on the railing, he would warm up his trumpet in the sea breezes. He told me that although the acoustics of his studio were a bit less than perfect, he enjoyed its spaciousness.

We almost never saw Jimmy Galway without his flute in one hand and a drink in the other. He certainly looked more like a leprechaun than any of the pictures I've ever seen of those Irish elves. I don't know if he imbibed much of the liquid in the glass he carried, but whenever he performed, he produced the most fantastic silvery sound I have ever heard. As a violist, I'm the first to confess that I've borrowed a good deal of the repertoire from other instruments. But Jimmy has me beat by a mile in that department. Among his "thefts" there is even an arrangement for flute of my beloved Schubert "Arpeggione Sonata," a delightful surprise.

The day came when I was able to surprise him. After a performance Jimmy played in Seattle, we gave a party for him. Upon his arrival at our condo, he rang the doorbell and reacted with delighted surprise. I had programmed our doorbell to play the opening phrase from Debussy's "Afternoon of a Faun." It's just solo flute!

Ravi Shankar, Sitarist

Virginia: The lights in our living room were turned low and I had burned some incense for atmosphere as the front door opened and Ravi Shankar entered. He wore a flowing, white robe and sandals and carried his beautiful sitar inlaid with silver and mother-of-pearl. About 80 young people were waiting to meet and hear the extraordinary Indian musician. They were members of my "Symfunics," a group of young professional single men and women who gathered before concerts to hear about upcoming Seattle Symphony programs. Most were seated on the floor, some on pillows, and others had assumed the lotus position. They were sipping wine, nibbling crackers and cheese, or smoking.

Milton and Virginia Katims

I introduced Shankar. He bowed to the applause, and then arranged himself on a cushion that had been placed in the middle of an area rug of vivid orange and hot-pink hues.

"Please," he said softly but firmly, "I would like no one to sip wine, eat, or smoke while I play." Immediately two girls dashed to the kitchen to get trays to collect all the glasses. "Now," Ravi intoned, "I will begin."

He played a raga, which he explained was a piece of music written to "color the mind." It took about 45 minutes to perform and all of us were completely entranced. When he had finished, a young man asked, "Do you improvise that entire piece of music or is it written down – something you have memorized?"

"Both," Ravi answered. "One improvises in between the melodic ideas. You know, there are ragas for the morning for adoration. There are ragas for the evening for merriment. And there are ragas for midnight for calm and mystery." The young people asked him about gurus and about the drug culture. Their questions no doubt prompted by the fact that Ravi had appeared with rock groups.

"The guru fad in the United States has become too commercialized," he replied. "Very often, young people in America become interested in things superficially, like gurus. Indian spiritual development must be worked for, long and hard. I spent many years with my guru. They were years of discipline, devotion, and isolation. That's the only way.

"As for drugs, I am strictly against them. Drugs don't go with Indian music, nor do they go with Bach and Beethoven. Music which is pure requires a pure mind. If you are on drugs and you are listening to me, we aren't honestly communicating."

It was a fascinating evening, and I hoped that Ravi's message got through to all those young people, and that they passed along his wisdom to those who were not in our home that night.

Ravi was born in the holiest of Indian cities, Benares. He is one of the few artists in the world who has played at Woodstock, the Monterey Jazz Festival, Lincoln Center, and in London's prestigious Festival Hall.

The Pleasure Was Ours

Milton: Conducting the Ravi Shankar "Concerto for Sitar" was a unique experience, visually and aurally. My Indian soloist preceeded me on to the stage, dressed not in white tie and tails, but in a handsome Indian costume. He carried his sitar (it is simply a Hindu guitar) carefully in front of him and headed for the riser placed downstage next to my podium. The riser, usually used by cello soloists had only a prayer rug with a cushion on it. Shankar stepped out of his slippers and sat cross-legged, with almost bare feet on the cushion. I say almost because on the big toe of his right foot was the largest diamond ring I have ever seen. It sparkled brightly under the stage lights.

When I first looked at the score of Shankar's concerto, I was intrigued by the marriage of our Western orchestra (albeit somewhat reduced) and the fascinating rhythmic patterns of his native music. I wondered whether I would have any difficulty accompanying him precisely. But I soon found that my concerns were groundless. As Ravi played he moved, his bejeweled foot rhythmically back and forth like a veritable metronome. All I had to do was to keep my eye on it!

In all my years in music, both as a violist and particularly as a conductor, I have always been aware of my responsibility toward the American composer, to program his/her compositions. That responsibility has necessitated a continuing balancing act, figuratively walking a tightrope between performing new music and holding on to my audience, as well as expanding it.

If I've heard the old saw once, I've heard it 1,000 times, "I don't know much about music, but I know what I like." My response has always been, "No, you like what you know!"

The recognition factor is vitally important in the enjoyment of new music and, for that matter, any work of art. In guiding the taste of any audience, the conductor and/or the composer should not be so far out in front that he is out of sight. Composers should leave their research and experimentation in the laboratory, the studio, unless they are just writing for themselves or for other composers. I feel strongly that new music should retain some thread, some connection with the past so the listener will recognize some facet of the music, some connection between the past and the present. The progress of art should be evolutionary, not revolutionary. It should be evolutionary in the way Beethoven and, much later, Debussy were in turning the direction of musical composition.

Benjamin Lees, Composer

Milton: I first met the American composer Benjamin Lees when members of the Budapest String Quartet introduced us. From the beginning I recognized that he had a strong individual voice with something to say. I also realized that he was influenced by the music of Bartok and Prokofieff. Not bad influences!

This is how Ben himself remembered our first meeting: "I recall vividly this incident the time I first met Milton. The Budapest String Quartet had just played my 'String Quartet No. 1' in New York. Mischa and Sasha Schneider told me that Milton was looking for a short new work for his forthcoming NBC Symphony broadcast and suggested I telephone him. I followed their instructions. Milton asked that we meet at the New York Public Library and that I bring along a score.

"The only piece I had was 'Profile for Orchestra,' which is about five and one half minutes long. We met. I found Milton warm and friendly, and gave him the score. He called 24 hours later and announced, 'You're on.' I could hardly believe it. Here I was, fresh from California and just out of the student stage, about to have my composition played by the greatest orchestra in America and on a coast-to-coast broadcast! I was ecstatic, but also a nervous wreck.

"On the appointed day of the rehearsal I was in the famous Studio 8H at NBC. Milton came over and I called his attention to a place in the score where the trumpets have a rapid passage, somewhat tricky. I cautioned him to be careful of that place. He smiled at me, as one would at a pathetic moron, and said, 'Look, don't worry. This is the NBC Symphony.'

"I felt as if I had committed a real faux pas and decided to shut up and enjoy the rehearsal. Everything went smoothly, or, I should say, brilliantly. Milton looked in my direction and mouthed, 'See!'

"Came the evening of the performance. The invited audience filled the studio to capacity. Milton leaped onto the podium, gave the downbeat, and the orchestra launched easily and confidently into my 'Profile for Orchestra.' I waited, breathlessly, for the approaching passage in which the trumpets, fairly exposed, began their precarious climb. The passage arrived and suddenly the trumpets cracked! I couldn't believe it. The vaunted NBC Symphony! Well, Milton confessed later that he couldn't believe it either.

"This experience taught me a valuable lesson. A composer should never take any orchestra for granted and should always be prepared for the unexpected. In any event, this was the first of many happy collaborations with Milton Katims over the years. He was one of the few brave conductors who always championed the American composer."

There was another valuable lesson Ben should have absorbed from that experience: Always check the feasibility of any difficult passage with a good player of that instrument. My reaction to the "cracking" incident was that if my fine NBC Symphony trumpeters had difficulty with that passage, just imagine what troubles lesser players would have. I don't remember whether quickly changing meters were part of the problem, but I do remember having many discussions with Ben about his fondness for writing that way, constantly changing the meter. My suggestion to him was that a judicious use of accents in a steady meter might also adequately express his musical ideas.

When I conducted the Japan Philharmonic in Tokyo, I discovered that, unlike Americans, the Japanese musicians had absolutely no difficulty with rapidly changing meters, perhaps because of the character and style of their own music and their training in solfege, not a regular staple in American music studies.

I failed to influence Ben on the meter issue, but I still admired his talent for bringing fresh ideas to his music. I programmed more of his music. Two of those new works stand out in my memory: "The Trumpet of the Swan" and "Vision of Poets." The latter was commissioned and premiered by the Seattle Symphony.

If Ben had not chosen composition as his life's work, he could have been a tremendous success in public relations. I have never met anyone who was as persevering in promoting his music as Ben. But he has every reason to believe in his own creations. Ben was not only influenced by Bartok and Prokofieff, but also by another American composer with whom he studied, George Antheil, who was called "the bad boy of music" because of his far-out thinking. Antheil was a close friend of Noma Copley, who became a patroness of Ben's.

When Noma married Bill Copley, a wealthy painter, they decided to establish a foundation for musicians and painters, combining both of their interests. Bill was an avid collector of surrealist art. (Virginia and I had the opportunity to see Bill's fantastic collection when we visited the Copleys in their domain in Longpont, not far from Paris.)

Ben was the first recipient of a grant from the Copley Foundation, and he certainly made the most of it.

Concert Managers

Milton: An important component of the music business is the concert manager and his role in that rarefied world. In this age of CDs, computers, the Internet, TV and radio, the concert manager is playing a gradually diminishing role in structuring and influencing the careers of performing artists. For example, the primary force in furthering my own conducting career was the series of more than fifty coast-to-coast broadcasts as guest-conductor of Toscanini's NBC Symphony. It was that series, not the activity of a shrewd concert manager, that led directly to my being invited to appear with a number of symphony orchestras in the U.S. and abroad. Those appearances with the NBC Symphony played a most important role in my move from New York to the podium of the Seattle Symphony.

I have had two primary managers, C.A.M.I. (Columbia Artists Management, Inc.), with Arthur Judson and Ronald Wilford, and Sol Hurok, Inc., with Walter Prude and Max Gershunoff. But the majority of my engagements have been the result of recommendations of colleagues or of having been in the right place at the right time. I believe concert managers are at their best when they are working for artists who need little or no sales pitch. All that's really needed is a congenial, efficient secretary and/or a good working computer.

Toscanini had already quite regularly invited me to guest-conduct his NBC Symphony when Virginia and I decided it might be advisable for me to have a manager if I wanted my career to develop. At the time, Virginia was a touring cellist for Community Concerts under the C.A.M.I. management. It was quite natural for us to think of Arthur Judson, the agency's founder, as the man to manage my career. He was also known as the czar of the world of conductors.

I made an appointment to meet with Judson in his spacious office on West 57th Street, across the street from Carnegie Hall. He made quite an impression on me. Judson was white-haired, quite tall, and heavily built – an imposing figure. I'm sure I was influenced by the fact that he was the most powerful mogul in the world of music and had the reputation of being able to make or break an artist. He was the perfect image of the successful CEO of a very large industry. I remember being intrigued by the Dickensonian standup desk in his office.

There were no wasted words. The reason he had agreed to see me was that he had evidently tuned in some of my NBC Symphony broadcasts. He quickly let me know what he thought of that "achievement": "Anybody can stand on the podium of that great orchestra and look pretty good. The real test would be to conduct a second or third-rate orchestra, make it sound pretty good, and build it into a first-rate ensemble."

Although I had my own ideas on that subject, I was soon given the opportunity of putting that thought to the test. When Maestro Toscanini retired and the NBC Symphony was disbanded, I decided it was time to leave the big city and accept the invitation of one of the orchestras I had guest-conducted. That's how I chose Seattle and it chose me, without the help of management.

One evening, violinist Alexander "Sasha" Schneider introduced me to a visitor from Seattle, Dr. J. Hans Lehmann. The good doctor was on the search committee of the Seattle Symphony, which was in need of a conductor. The previous music director, Manuel Rosenthal, had arrived from France with a mistress. Evidently, his wife back in Paris had blown the whistle on him. On a subsequent trip through immigration, he was denied entry on the grounds of "moral turpitude," and had to return to France. The Seattle Symphony had been queried about the Rosenthal case, but gave the French conductor no brief.

Previously the Seattle podium had been graced by Sir Thomas Beecham, who was sitting out the war in Seattle. With a typical Beechamism, Sir Thomas hurled a poison barb at Seattle when he asked the Symphony Board for better support, saying, "Do you wish to be considered an aesthetic dustbin?" That remark may have been a blessing in disguise, because it received wide coverage and shocked Seattle's cultural community into taking action to see to it that the "esthetic dustbin" label would not become a reality.

I had guest-conducted a few concerts in Seattle and the orchestra members and I liked each other. Encouraged and smitten by the beauty of the Puget Sound city, I accepted the orchestra's offer to become its music director and moved my family from New York to Seattle.

Only twice during the time I was under Judson's management did he show what appeared to be an active interest in my career. After I had been in Seattle but a few months, I began receiving offers from various orchestras. Judson flew out to Seattle to meet with the symphony board. He was greeted with pleas such as, "Please don't take Maestro Katims away from us." Obviously the members of the board had heard that the powerful impresario could move conductors around like pawns on a chessboard. Little did they realize that possibly one of the strongest motivation for these maneuvers was to generate the commissions received by the Judson office.

Symphony officials in Rochester, New York had made overtures to me to take over their orchestra. I had guest-conducted several times in that city and Judson showed up one night unexpectedly, introduced himself to the symphony board, and attended the party after the concert. Board members there assured Judson that they would do everything in their power to make me an offer I couldn't resist.

I might have seriously considered the Rochester proposal if the board had been able to meet one important condition: Their total support of a solid plan to gradually convert the orchestra into a completely professional one. Half the musicians were professionals and the other half were Eastman School students, who were constantly graduating and moving on. I would be facing the problems of a college football coach. However, the board members were unable or unwilling to undertake that financial responsibility. Judson tried hard to persuade me to accept the position. The most potent argument he offered was that Rochester was close to New York. I remained unconvinced. Besides, my heart was already in Seattle, and I felt indebted to the wonderful orchestra people I had met there.

A few years later, Judson decided to retire. He was succeeded by Ronald Wilford, who took over Columbia's large stable of conductors. If there had been little activity on my behalf at the agency up to that point, there was even less afterward. Wilford and I didn't get along. He evidently didn't think too highly of me, and I didn't trust him. In his defense, I must say that he does give tender loving care to several conductors, particularly those with major orchestras in the large cities.

Milton and Virginia Katims

Roberta Peters and Isaac Stern suggested that I visit their manager, the renowned Sol Hurok, with the thought of switching to his management. He was most certainly the other powerhouse in the world of music. Physically, he couldn't have been a greater contrast to Judson. Sol was short and chunky, but most impressive. I made an appointment to see him and, after a few moments of small talk, took the bull by the horns and plunged right in, "What do you think of the idea of my leaving Columbia Artists to come under your management?"

Without hesitation he replied, with a smile, "Well, it all depends on whether you prefer being with a supermarket or with a 'Mom-and-Pop' outfit." Of course, I opted for the latter and Hurok welcomed me into his prestigious family of artists. He assigned Walter Prude, husband of the noted choreographer Agnes de Mille, to look after me. Walter was easy-going and very personable, but unfortunately I never found him very effective as a manager. He was much better on the tennis court and I did enjoy playing with him.

My guest-conducting assignments in the U.S. and abroad continued for the most part to be the result of efforts outside the Hurok office. However, being under the Hurok banner with so many illustrious artists had a tremendous value that is difficult to measure. What I hadn't expected was the amazing speed with which the comparatively small "Mom-and-Pop" operation also grew into a sizable supermarket.

There's not much more to the story. After Sol Hurok died and his company was dissolved, all the vice presidents traveled their own separate ways. I went with Max Gershounov. He failed to change my mind about managers.

Chapter 18
On and Off the Record

Milton: Whenever my beautiful granddaughter, Michelle, talks too fast for me to understand even one word, I tell her that she's speaking at 78-rpm while I'm listening at 33! The first time I said that to her I had to explain the reference. She had never heard of 78s and was barely conversant with LPs at 33.

With the exception of one brief foray into recording in the late 1930s, when I played the Handel-Halvorsen "Passacaglia for Violin and Viola" with Eddy Brown (Royal 1840), my affair with that temperamental, but fascinating lady really began in the early 1940s. I had quite forgotten that single disc of long ago, so I was amazed to discover that it had reappeared on CD in "The Recorded Viola, Volume 3" (Pearl). Details of how and where in New York, Eddy and I made that record are lost in the mists of time.

What I remember most of all about 78-rpm discs was the challenge of having literally to play in short spurts, of having to divide the music into segments of either 4:20 or 4:40 minutes, depending upon whether Columbia or RCA Victor was producing the record. However, the time limitations of 78s presented no problem when I conducted albums with the beautiful soprano Gladys Swarthout, and the glamorous mezzo Rise Stevens, as virtually all the songs fit quite snugly into the time slot.

It's with much affection that I remember the Victrola with the record changer that my parents bought when I was quite young. I was fascinated by it, but how frustrated I was when the music came to the end of a side. I had to wait until the next disc dropped on to the turntable before the performance could continue. I recall, too, the unfortunate surface noises of those old 78s, and how easily they could be scratched or broken. I was happy to leave all that behind and welcomed the progress that was being made in the art of recording.

In the early 1930s, in the interim between successfully making the transition from violinist to violist and becoming solo violist and assistant conductor on the staff of WOR (a New York radio station) with Alfred Wallenstein, I was active as a freelance musician in New York City. Leon Barzin, my viola and conducting mentor, had been so right in advising me to become a violist. When I was a violinist, no contractor ever called me for a commercial recording date. But as a violist, after initially being introduced to one or two contractors, I found myself admitted to membership in a tightly controlled group of recording musicians in New York.

The contractors were the men to know. Each sponsoring company (Camel, Palmolive, Lucky Strike, City's Service, Firestone) had its own contractor to hire the players for its radio program or recording session. I soon found that a good deal of back-scratching went on. Contractors hired each other to play their dates and scheduled the sessions so that they did not coincide.

On one of my very first dates I was given an excellent piece of advice by my much more seasoned desk-mate. He noticed that I was quite nervous (my shaking knees were in danger of intruding on the percussion section) and, to calm me down, he said, "There is only one thing to remember, when in doubt, leave out!" Early on I was given a rather expensive lesson in this freelance world. I was engaged to play on the Palmolive program, conducted by Nathaniel "Nat" Shilkret, whose brother sold life insurance. I was soon made to understand that if I wished to continue playing on that program, I had better buy an annuity from brother Shilkret.

Playing the Camel program (this all took place long before we became aware of the dangers of smoking) was fun because of the talented and delightful Xavier Cugat, who conducted. Another maestro with whom I enjoyed playing was Andre Kostelanetz. Perhaps I feel so well disposed towards Andre because he subsequently invited me to guest conduct a number of his Promenade Concerts with the New York Philharmonic. Although he never joined the ranks of the leading conductors, he was much more than a good business conductor. He was quite knowledgeable, made most intelligent arrangements and conducted very efficiently. (Besides that, he was married to lovely soprano Lilly Pons.)

New York City and Los Angeles (Hollywood) were the two main centers of commercial recording in the 1930s. When I visited the violist Louis Kievman in L.A. at that time, I was amazed at how pale-faced he was, despite living in that sunny climet. I soon found out why. He had to stay close to his phone in order not to miss a call from a contractor. I'm sure that with today's answering machines and cellular phones my colleagues on the West coast now have nice tans.

It was usually quite easy to recognize when a commercial recording session was about to take place. Players were not in their seats until moments before they were to begin, just long enough to tune their instruments. Unlike the usual bedlam, the chaotic sounds of players 'woodshedding' prior to a symphony rehearsal, the commercial recording players would not dream of having any of their peers think that they needed such preliminary practice. In any case, they were very good sight readers. (My friend Don Gillis, composer and NBC Symphony producer, was fond of saying that some musicians were better readers at second sight.) This led certain conductors to begin recording right from the start of a session, and fine tune as they made subsequent takes. Rarely was there any real effort to go beyond having proper balance, playing with good sound, intonation, rhythm and ensemble. There was no time (or effort) to reach for musical heights, sublime or otherwise. I recall one 'conductor' whose mantra was: "Boys, watch your 'rits' and 'ralls'!"

When Sasha Schneider was concertmaster of Hamburg Opera, he noticed that his colleagues in the cello section usually dashed back to their seats after an intermission with just enough time to tune their instruments. Sasha decided to play a practical joke on them. At the start of the intermission he remained in the pit. He rewound the pegs of the first four cellists so that they were backward. Then he tuned each cello within a hair of being perfectly in tune. He sat back and watched as the four cellists started to tune their instruments frantically, as the conductor returned and began the next act.

You can't imagine the sounds that emerged from that unfortunate foursome! Sasha said it was worth the month's pay he was fined by the musician's union just to watch those agonized moments endured by his colleagues.

In 1943 I joined the NBC Symphony under Toscanini as first-desk viola and subsequently became assistant conductor. I recall many a time when Maestro would storm off the podium in a rage, but on one occasion there was ample justification for his stalking off in a fury. It was when he finally became aware that individual members of the orchestra were surreptitiously being beckoned by the personnel manager, H. Leopold Spitalny, to sneak out because they were scheduled for a recording session in another studio. Because of his complete concentration on the music he was conducting (and his extreme nearsightedness), Maestro had not initially noticed what was going on.

Leopold Stokowski, the enormously gifted, flamboyant conductorof the Philadelphia Orchestra for many years, was completely frustrated by the limitations of recording on 78s. He hated having to cut up the music into short segments. and when he insisted on playing much longer sections of the score, his engineer set up a series of recording tables so that when the music reached the end of one side, he faded the sound while simultaneously fading in the same music on the next side. Stokowski was able to think in longer lines and the listener had the impression of greater continuity, albeit there were unintended diminuendos and crescendos that were not in the score. Unfortunately, this procedure was employed only on a limited number of releases.

"Stokie" (a nickname we all used) insisted on having the control panel placed immediately in front of him so that he could adjust the knobs to control the balance of the various choirs and solo instruments, especially when a multiple-mike setup was employed. He had earphones on in order to monitor the results. All of this was within a glassed-in cubicle, where we could easily watch him conduct.

What Stokie did not know – and no one was about to tell him – was that the panel of knobs he had in front of him was a fake! The recording director controlled the real panel. Nevertheless, there can be no doubt that Maestro Stokowski has left us a legacy of superior recordings that captured the unique flowing sound he drew from his musicians. (I'll have quite a few more words about "Stokie" in a later chapter)

Balance has always been one of the most important aspects of a recording. Whether it is a symphony orchestra, a chorus, a chamber-music group, or just two players, balancing the sound so that each musical line emerges at its proper aural level is so vital. I have always believed that a successful recording should sound as if the listener were sitting in the ideal seat in an acoustically perfect performance hall. I did not agree with Columbia Records when it came up with "Stereo 360 Sound," because I did not want to be sitting in the middle of the orchestra when listening to a record.

Toscanini actually did not like to make records. He showed no apparent interest in the problems involved and rarely, if ever, went into the control room to check the results of a take. But he was aware of the difference in the quality of sound of his recordings and those of other conductors.

Milton and Virginia Katims

When Maestro was visited by composer-conductor Morton Gould, he complimented Morton on the sound of his recordings. He also told Gould that he would like to record in the same hall, but Morton diplomatically dodged the issue. He had no wish to go into an explanation that he and his orchestra were recording for a different label. (Gould was with Columbia, now SONY, and Maestro was with RCA, now BMG.) Of all the chamber-music recordings in which I have played, the "Debussy Sonata No. 2 for Flute, Viola, and Harp" was the most challenging to balance. (John Wummer, flutist, and Laura Newall, harpist) It was difficult because of the complete diversity of the three instruments.

To a lesser extent, other trios in which I have played also presented some challenges. They would include the Beethoven "Serenade for Flute, Violin, and Viola," with Wummer (flutist) and Alexander Schneider (violinist), and Charles Martin Loeffler's "Two Rhapsodies for Oboe, Viola, and Piano," with Harold Gomberg (oboeist) and Dimitri Mitropoulos (pianist).

When LPs at 33 rpm and recording on tape made their appearance early in the 1950s, they brought with them many obvious advantages over the earlier 78s. Finally, we were able to breathe more freely in the recording studio. And speaking of breathing, I remember one experience I had while playing viola in a commercial recording session. At one point the producer, speaking to us from the control booth, asked,"Who's making all that noise breathing out there?"

I had to confess that, with my deviated septum, I was the culprit. From then on I had to breathe through my mouth for the remainder of that session. With my viola right under my chin, that proved to be somewhat tricky.

Recording on tape solved many problems. It freed us from the confines of 4:20 or 4:40 minutes on one side of a record. We could play whole movements and succeed to a greater extent in duplicating the feeling of a performance in the concert hall. An entire quartet or symphony could be put on one record. But the greatest improvement we now had was the safety net of editing and splicing of the tape, which brought us much closer to putting our best on a recording.

I was amazed at what an expert editor could do with his scissors. There are many tales on this subject. One of them was when Toscanini was unhappy with one high trumpet note on one of his recordings. The director had Harry Glantz, first trumpet of the NBC Symphony, re-record that one high note. With relative ease, the editor replaced the unwanted note with the perfectly played note.

During one period we performed in Carnegie Hall on Saturday nights. The performance was taped and broadcast Monday night. On one of those broadcasts, which I conducted, Alex Williams, first clarinetist of the orchestra, performed the Debussy "Rhapsody for Clarinet." Toward the very beginning of the work, Alex squeaked very badly on a high note. The following Monday night he sat before his radio with great apprehension, dreading the moment of that awful squeak. But when the high note arrived, there was no squeak!

In his mail the next morning, Williams found a letter from Don Gillis, the production director of the program. Enclosed with the letter was a piece of tape about seven or eight inches long. The note read: "Dear Alex, here is your squeak."

Of course, there were other important strides made with the advent of LPs. The quality of sound was improved, the dynamic range was expanded, and surface noises were reduced. The listening experience for music lovers was renewed, and when CDs arrived some years later, ever newer territories of listening experience were opened up.

Toward the end of my tenure as artistic director of the University of Houston's School of Music, I had an opportunity to record the "Six Solo Suites" of J.S. Bach in my transcription for viola. George Mendelssohn of Vox and Pantheon Records had shown interest in my undertaking. I had discovered a young professor in the School of Communications, who had had experience in producing recordings. He also had access to stereo recording equipment and the use of the university's organ hall for an entire weekend. (International Music had published my edition of the "Suites for Viola" a few years earlier.)

I had been giving master classes devoted to the Bach suites so I was well aware of the enormous musical and technical challenges these wonderful suites presented. I was somewhat familiar with the acoustics of the organ hall. They were "church-like" alive!

The word "acoustics" triggers different memories. Among them is our attending a performance of a play at Epidaurus in Greece, which left us absolutely amazed at the very clear and audible sounds of the actors' voices on that outdoor stage. I was almost convinced that some sort of amplification was being used. The amphitheater had been built long before the word "acoustic" was in use. In an article about Lincoln Center in *The Sunday New York Times*, Bernard Holland wrote that "acoustics was a crap-shoot." He was absolutely right.

I have found that if an acoustician is really honest (and I have known some), he will admit that he can do only so much to assure good acoustics. He can design the shape and size of the hall and he can choose the appropriate materials to be used. Beyond that, it's sheer luck if the resulting acoustical target is what he was aiming at. (Most recently the new Benaroya Hall in Seattle reflects the great strides that have been made in the art of acoustics. The sound in the hall is so alive that the solo cellist of the Seattle Symphony, Ray Davis, remarked, "When I play in Benaroya Hall, I feel naked!")

When Herculean efforts were made to correct the sound in Lincoln Center's Philharmonic Hall (now Fisher Hall), Maestro Stokowski was called in as consultant. Stokie walked to the center of the hall and clapped his hands twice. Then, as he turned on his heel to walk out, he said, "Too late!"

One unforgettable brush I had with acoustics was in Sherwood Hall in La Jolla, California, where I conducted a series of concerts with a chamber orchestra for the Musical Arts Society of La Jolla in the 1960s. I was constantly frustrated with the very dry, non-existent reverberation time in the hall. In desperation I phoned acoustician Paul Veneklasen in Los Angeles. I had introduced Paul to Benny Priteca and Jim Chiarelli, architects of the Seattle Opera House. I explained my problem to Paul and asked him to come down to La Jolla to take a listen to the hall.

Paul was, as always, very sympathetic and drove down. Unlike Stokowski's hand-clapping test in Philharmonic Hall, Veneklasen brought several testing devices with him and spent a good deal of time in the hall. When he finally finished, he turned to me and said, "Milton, there is only one solution to the acoustical problems here. Tear down the hall!"

Unlike many of the halls in which I had played or conducted, the organ hall at the University of Houston was alive – in fact, too alive. I chose a spot next to the railing in front of the seats in the hall so that I could hang some heavy blankets there. I also brought in a thick piece of carpet to stand on to cut down the reverberation time. Then I varied my distance from the mike, depending on the style and demands of each movement of the Bach suites. At times I turned the back of my viola to the mike to eliminate unwanted rosin sounds on the strings, to say nothing of my unwelcome loud breathing. It worked! The result was "Pantheon-CA-PEN 2063" – three cassettes, since transferred to two CDs for Pantheon Legends.

My experience "conducting" the Budapest String Quartet recording sessions was to be very helpful years later when I decided to have the Seattle Symphony record both orchestral parts in a work called "Venice" (An Audiograph for Double Orchestra and Brass Choirs), which I commissioned Morton Gould to compose for the orchestra. My idea had been to invite the orchestra of any city in which we were performing to join us in the closing work of the program.

We played the world premiere of "Venice" in Spokane, with its symphony when Don Thulean was the conductor. Don rehearsed the second orchestra part with his group while I prepared the Seattle Symphony to take care of the first part. It was designed as an all-Washington State affair. When the Seattle Symphony and I arrived

279

in Spokane for the final rehearsal, I found that each of the Spokane musicians was wearing an Avis (car rental) button with the legend, "We Try Harder."

The next performance of the Gould work, before we recorded it for RCA (LSC 3079), was with the Seattle Youth Symphony. Both performances went well and were enthusiastically received. When RCA decided to have us record "Venice," I recalled my experience with the Budapest String Quartet and the Milhaud Octet and decided to have the Seattle Symphony play both parts. At the first session we recorded one part. Then, the next day, again using earphones to listen to the previously recorded part of the score, I conducted the part to be superimposed. Although my task was somewhat simplified because I had the entire score before me, my greatest challenge was to recall, as precisely as possible, the rubato with which I had conducted the previous day. I had to devise a counting system to help me over that hurdle.

When I recall the halls, studios, or rooms in which I have performed and/or recorded, only a few stand out in my memory. They stand out because they were so superior acoustically that they made me sound good and I enjoyed making music in them. Whether I was playing my viola or conducting the NBC Symphony, Carnegie Hall had all of the necessary ingredients to make it my favorite. When I was playing the viola, the sound under my ear was what I wanted to hear. When I was conducting, there was no problem in projecting my ears from the podium to any seat within the hall to assess the sound and balance. Perhaps my feelings about Carnegie Hall are somewhat biased by the fact that it was the site of my very first important conducting experience, my graduation debut with the National Orchestral Association in 1935.

Next on my list of favorite recording sites was Liederkranz Hall. Situated at the top of a building adjacent to the New York Public Music Library on East 58th Street in Manhattan, it was a rather large, irregularly shaped room made almost totally of old, seasoned wood. When I recorded there I felt as if I were playing within the very large body of a gigantic, old, Italian string instrument. It was perfect. But – and this is a vital "but" – Columbia recording engineers decided to "improve" the hall. They put up panels and baffles and a control booth. They succeeded in ruining not only the natural ambiance of the hall, but also the joy of playing in it. The engineers obviously hadn't heard the phrase: "If it ain't broke, don't fix it."

The third and final of my favorite recording sites, nestled in the foothills of the Pyrenees in the south of France, not far from Prades, is St. Michel de Cuxa. It's an old church in which I spent many joyful hours playing and recording Schubert and Brahms chamber music with Pablo Casals, Myra Hess, Isaac Stern, Joseph Szigeti, Sasha Schneider, and Paul Tortelier, all part of a Casals Festival.

Although I marvel at the wonders of today's ability to recreate a performance faithfully on a recording, I still believe it is no substitute for a living performance. I keep remembering what a musician friend of mine said many years ago: "Compared to a live performance, a recording is like kissing your best girl over the telephone!!!"

The one and only Jack Benny reacting to the gift of an appropriately topped totem pole on the occasion of Katims'
"tinth" anniversary with the SSO

Chapter 19
Innocents Abroad, Part One

Virginia: One of the great joys of being a musician has been the opportunity to visit other countries. Milton was invited to hold two weeks of viola master classes at the Conservatory of Music in Shanghai when China was opened up to Americans.

We landed there at midnight. A tall young man stepped forward to greet us. "Mr. Katims, welcome to Shanghai. I am Pao Jung, your interpreter. Did you have a nice flight?"

As Milton nodded and smiled, a petite woman accompanying Pao interjected, "I am Professor Shen, and we have 20 viola students who will play for you at the Shanghai Conservatory."

Her English was not quite as fluent as Pao's. She quickly explained some of the details concerning Milton's chores with the viola master classes, his schedule of conducting the orchestra, and his coaching chamber-music sessions. The conservatory had embarked on an ambitious series of programs to bring the world's leading instrumentalists, vocalists, and conductors to Shanghai for programs and master classes. Included among those who had preceded Milton were violinist Isaac Stern (the film, "From Mao to Mozart," was one of the results of his visit), pianist Vladimir Ashkenazy, soprano Roberta Peters, and pianist Rudolf Firkusny.

With Pao's expert help we breezed through immigration and customs and were driven to the guest house on the grounds of the conservatory. It was the end of March and the weather was raw. Most of the buildings had no heat, including the one in which we were to stay. Our room was plain and basic; the beds had cozy comforters and thick cotton sheets that bore a cheerful floral print. Two trays of toast (the Chinese dub it "burnt bread"), green tea, butter, and jam were laid out on a table for us, but we were bone weary and not very hungry, so we quickly piled into bed.

The plaintive sounds of a Chinese flute being played beneath our window awakened us at 7 a.m. What else could we expect at a conservatory? (Certainly not a musical rooster!) I ran water into the bathtub. It was hot, but it poured out in a dark brown color. Oh well. When in Rome! I tossed two capsules of aromatic pine into the water, producing a fascinating tint no artist's palette could ever hope to capture.

Refreshed, brown bath and all, we adjourned to the dining room of the guesthouse for breakfast. Pao soon appeared and walked with us to the conservatory building. En route we passed a few lines of laundry fluttering in the early morning breeze in front of small cubicles, not quite motel size, where families of students and teachers were living. Wildflowers were starting to burst into bloom along the way near a row of lovely trees.

On one side of the campus was a large grassy soccer field, and ahead of us were many types of exercise equipment on which music students and teachers were working-out with great concentration. Over on the other side of the grounds were shops, in which violins, violas, cellos, harps, pianos, and even strings were being made. Imagine having such gifted artisans working immediately adjacent to the Juilliard or Curtis Schools of Music?

The Pleasure Was Ours

We were deeply impressed with all the activity, and the instruments on which we were to hear the students play would amaze us even more.

As we entered a large music room of the conservatory, we found Milton's first two viola students warming up. The room was so chilly that I wondered if their fingers would be flexible enough to handle the technical demands of the music they had chosen to perform. In the room there were many other string players to take notes as Pao translated for Milton. Professor Shen introduced us to the two violists who were to play and said firmly, "We do not want praise. We want criticism."

The first player was a petite, doll-faced girl with gleaming black hair and bangs cut straight across her forehead, accenting huge, almond-shaped brown eyes. She adjusted her music stand, tuned her viola, glanced quickly at her piano accompanist, and announced, "Bartok Concerto." Without further words she launched into the challenging work. Beautiful! Milton and I applauded, astounded by her playing. Then she moved toward Milton gracefully and said, "May I find a time to speak with you some of a time, alone?"

Milton said, "Of course," and I resolved to be on hand when she did. The next violist was a tall, good-looking fellow with a disarming smile. He ambled over toward the piano accompanist and announced, "Walton Concerto." He too, was absolutely first-rate.

"My God!" Milton murmured to me. "I have to go back to our room and practice!"

The viola repertoire is relatively limited in comparison with the literature of the violin, cello, and piano. But the two concertos by Hungarian Bela Bartok and Englishman William Walton are among the most important and are very demanding.

Day after day, gifted players appeared and performed. It was not only their marvelous technique and quick understanding of phrasing and bowing suggestions that were amazing. We marveled at their incredible grasp of our Western music. I wondered if we Americans could ever begin to understand their Eastern musical language and feel it the same way.

Milton and Virginia Katims

I was asked to listen to some elementary cello students. Eight youngsters awaited me, along with their accompanist, in a large room of the guesthouse. All stood respectfully as I entered. The youngest, five, played first. The teacher helped her tune her half-size cello. Then the child gave the pianist a very professional looking signal and they started. Swaying back and forth with the music, her pigtail keeping time with the rhythm, she attacked every note with aplomb, strong intonation, and a facile bow. Wonderful! Next came a six year-old, then others of similarly young ages, until all had played. They were remarkably mature for their ages, extremely serious about their chosen instrument, and were uniformly well taught.

"Please criticize them," their teacher implored.

I offered suggestions, then added, "Some of you will play in good orchestras. And some will be fine chamber-music players."

Before their teacher could respond, the five-year-old spoke up, "No, no. Me play solo!"

Alas, I thought, sooner or later they will learn that there's never enough room at the top. But they will discover that in time, even in a nation of more than a billion!

When I think about Shanghai, I recall walking down a busy street one day, followed by a group of young boys. Had I heard one word of English, I would have turned around and told them I was an American who was accustomed to strolling around in a foreign country without a crowd. But I didn't. Their constant and excited babbling finally annoyed me. I crossed the street, hoping they would go on their way and leave me to do my browsing alone. They followed me as I crossed. I looked around hoping that a smile would dissuade them. One of them quickly approached and asked, pointing to my hair, "Clairol?" It dawned on me that we had been searching in the wrong places for a universal language, not realizing we had one all the time: Advertising!

Composer Sang Tong and pianist Li Mingqiang were among the highly respected directors of the school. Professor Li was an accomplished recording artist with a solid reputation among musicians. One night we were invited to dine with two Seattle friends aboard a cruise ship that was docked for two days in Shanghai. We had no idea how complicated it would be to accept their invitation to join them for dinner. It provided us with our first strong realization that we were in a Communist country. Professor Li had to apply for special visas for us to go aboard. He informed us, "You must take your passports and these very special visas to the ship and hope that the authorities will let you pass."

We set out with the car and driver that was always at our disposal. It was a very dark night and we seemed to ride for hours toward the river. Finally, the driver found the right pier and took us within sight of the ship. We approached several uniformed Chinese standing watch, and produced our "very special" visas and our passports, only to have the officials shake their heads briskly, which had to mean, "No!" We pleaded, flashing our most beguiling smiles, but to no avail.

Desperate, I went through the motions of playing the cello and Milton followed suit, pretending to play the viola. My mother had told me many times that music would open every door, but this was ridiculous. We gave the impression that we were playing together and performing the same piece of music – and feeling terribly silly! But it worked! It was not so ridiculous after all.

The officials must have had some notice that musicians were to arrive to board the ship because one of them grinned and, bobbing his head up and down, said, "Ah, you musicians. You teach Shanghai Conservatory, yes? Enter, please." We boarded the ship and had a lovely time with our friends and we had no trouble getting back to the conservatory guesthouse later that night.

Ensconced in a tree near the guesthouse was a loudspeaker, which burst forth with music at noon and again at dusk. The fare included American ballads, Russian love songs, Mexican cha-chas, and, sometimes, Pavarotti belting out an aria. Between selections, we heard a female voice speaking.

"Is that propaganda?" I asked.

"No," said our translator, Pao. "She tells us how bad it was during the Cultural Revolution."

I accepted his explanation, reminding myself that politics can get dicey. Besides, we liked Pao and needed him and his translating ability. However, I found myself looking forward to hearing the music that echoed through the square twice a day. I tried to imagine a loudspeaker in Seattle's Pioneer Square, playing a Brahms symphony, perhaps followed by the voice of our always optimistic, charismatic leader at the time, President Reagan.

I spent one afternoon in a Shanghai museum, eager to see what kind of Chinese art might appeal to me. I rode on the back of Pao's bicycle, up and down crowded thoroughfares and alleys until we came to an impressive building, to get there. I was surprised to see that the entire exhibit was devoted to Chinese scrolls, an art form of which I had never been particularly fond. But these were gorgeous. Each scroll was a riot of all the colors of the rainbow, of mountains, waterfalls, exotic birds, and beautiful landscapes – all the scenes the Chinese admire.

"This is an exhibition by China's most famous painter, Ying Ye Ping," Pao told me proudly.

"I love so many of these," I told him. "How would I go about buying one?"

"Here comes the artist now," Pao said, pointing to a distinguished-looking elderly gentleman entering the main doorway. He was followed by a group of young art students who were hanging on his every word as they followed him through the gallery.

"May I buy this scroll?" I asked him, pointing to one on the wall.

With Pao translating for me, he answered, "Yes, but it is expensive. So much money, 70 percent has to go to the government, you know."

Indeed, the price was far beyond what I had hoped for and certainly more than I was prepared to pay. I had an inspiration.

"Ask him if he would care to attend my husband's concert tomorrow night."

Pao understood. The two conversed. After a minute or so, Pao assured me the artist would be delighted to attend the concert.

The following evening Milton played a viola recital and also conducted the conservatory orchestra in the "Schubert 5th Symphony." The 300 students of the conservatory were there, as well as a large number of local residents. I remember how noisy that audience and others before it were, many with children and some with babes in arms.

Milton was backstage, trying to warm his hands by caressing a hot water bottle supplied by the thoughtful Professor Shen. The audience applauded a couple of seconds and stopped as Milton walked on-stage. They seemed unaware of what was expected in a concert hall. The applause at the end of a composition and at the end of the concert was just as minimal.

How unlike our own public or the European audiences, with their cheerfully enthusiastically shouted, "Bravo!" and prolonged applause – or, on some occasions, boos and catcalls. But, and this is important, how intensely the Chinese listened to the music once it began! Those who sat in seats at the far end of rows leaned far out to observe and make certain they wouldn't miss anything. Some of them leaned so far out, I was afraid they would fall into the aisles.

When the concert ended, students and members of the audience poured backstage. Among them was the artist I had met the day before, who was accompanied by his handsome son, a professor at the local university. The painter grasped Milton's hands, his eyes brimming with tears, telling him how much the music had touched him. Then he turned to me and, as his son translated, said, "I wish to present you with the scroll you loved. My son will be happy to send it to you."

At a reception hosted by the students and faculty after the concert, we experienced the generous giving of gifts, a longtime Oriental custom. We were overwhelmed with the variety and creativity of the carefully selected offerings. Five of the students helped us carry the treasures back to our room. The next day we bought an additional suitcase to hold all the gifts. One gift Milton had no difficulty carrying was a decorative pin which indicated that he was a full professor of the conservatory.

Milton and I fervently hope the Chinese people will remain our friends, people to people and country to country. We can learn so much from each other. As I painfully tried to copy the Chinese characters that stand for "U.S.A." on each postcard I sent home, I was happy to learn that those characters translate into "Beautiful Country." We return the compliment with all our heart.

Milton: Our Chinese adventure began in my final year as artistic director of the University of Houston's School of Music, when I received a group of distinguished visitors under the guidance of Shen Zhen, the Chinese consul in Houston. It included Dr. Wang Zicheng, China's minister counselor for cultural affairs, and the wife of a high government official. After showing them around our Fine Arts Building, I expressed interest in visiting China one day and meeting its musicians. A few months later, I received an invitation from composer Sang Tong to come to Shanghai to offer viola master classes and to conduct at the Conservatory of Music.

But what repertoire to cover? I had no idea of the capability of the young Chinese violists, nor what music they would be playing for me. I had just edited the three Bach gamba sonatas and re-edited the Bach solo cello suites, so they were fresh in my mind and fingers. I dusted off works I hadn't taught for some time, from Boccherini and Handel to Bartok and Hindemith.

I have only a few additional comments about the performances of the first two viola students I heard. One was tall, soft-spoken Liu Yun Tie, who spoke just a little English, but needed no words to interpret the first movement of the "Walton Concerto" beautifully. The other, Chen Ziang, was so attractive that I could hear some of my American colleagues saying, "She doesn't have to know how to play —

and how!" She tackled the Bartok Concerto with all the confidence and sweep of an experienced professional.

I congratulated Professor Shen and told her that any viola teacher would be proud to claim them. Not all the violists I heard were of such a high caliber. Professor Shen had shrewdly started the master classes with her prize pupils. The others, however, had much to offer, as day after day we explored the viola music of Bach, Handel, Brahms, Schumann, Bartok, and Bloch. One young man essayed the Bloch Suite, but I felt that the Hebraic style of music had completely eluded him. The music was quite foreign to him, although he handled the viola well enough. I tried to help him but I'm not sure I succeeded in inculcating an empathetic feeling in him for Bloch. (A transfusion of Jewish blood might have helped.)

I was delighted to learn that a number of the violists were using my editions and transcriptions. The fact that there were a number of photocopies among them did not disturb me. Some of my recordings were also to be found in the music library.

I had brought with me a video cassette of "Mozart in Seattle," the TV special I had made with violinist Henryk Szeryng, but I didn't know whether the conservatory had the necessary equipment to show it. Not only did it have the equipment, it had a fully equipped and staffed recording studio, where concerts by visitors, faculty, and students were recorded. The conservatory's recording engineers made a good copy of "Mozart in Seattle" and asked permission to make it available to their national TV network. Without waiting to contact Henryk, I gladly gave them my OK. Later, when I told Szeryng about the incident, he was very pleased.

In the master classes the students welcomed my remarks and stories about my experiences with Toscanini, Casals, and others. They were hungry for information about the West, particularly of its artists. When we turned on TV in our room, we found a surprising number of serious educational programs teaching English and math at all levels.

291

Milton and Virginia Katims

In the evenings we would walk over to the concert hall where visiting artists or faculty members were playing concerts. It was always easy to anticipate the size of the audience by the number of bicycles parked outside. If no concert were scheduled, we would stay in our room and sample the TV fare during prime time. In addition to viewing ping-pong and volleyball matches and the highly regarded Chinese Opera, with its extraordinarily athletic performers, we were treated to concert performances by singers and instrumentalists.

One evening we tuned in to hear a young violinist play the Saint-Saens' "Havanaise," a work that is a challenge for any violinist. She performed with a virtuosity that belied her young age. The next day at the conservatory orchestra rehearsal, I raved about the young lady to Pao. He didn't say a word, but gestured and took me over to the third stand of the first violin section. There she sat, warming up. I told her how much we had admired her performance. I was amazed that she was sitting at the third stand in the section.

I wondered how all of these remarkable young talents had started on the path to such excellence. It surely was not in their homes, although discipline was certainly a strong part of their upbringing. Even if there had not been the devastating, so-called Cultural Revolution (which should actually have been called the Anti-Cultural Revolution), I don't believe their parents could have provided a home environment conducive to such understanding and dedication to Western music.

I was told that during the trying seven-year period of the revolution, the conservatory was closed and that not a single note of music was permitted to be heard. The faculty and directors were "re-educated" by peasants and soldiers. Most musicians and intellectuals were sent to work on farms or in factories. China would well have lost two or three generations of cultural endeavor if it had continued much longer.

One answer to my question about how the young talents got their inspiration may lie in the fascinating Children's Palace, which we visited the day before leaving

Shanghai. This impressive building, once the home of Sun Yat Sen's widow, houses a very special school for gifted children. In that spacious facility, both Chinese and Western music, dance, and the visual arts are taught. We were escorted through the building by a 14-year-old boy who spoke English quite well. He took us from room to room to witness the training given the alert young people.

We visited a piano class, a string orchestra, an orchestra of ethnic instruments, an orchestra of accordions, a chorus, a wind ensemble, and a ballet class. We were impressed with the students' skills, but even more by their obvious joy in what they were doing. I was quite sure that the best of the young musicians were sent on to the conservatory to continue their training. Of course, I was just as sure that the Children's Palace was being used as a propaganda vehicle.

At the beginning of our second week at the conservatory, I began afternoon rehearsals with the orchestra of the middle school, the equivalent to our high schools. Just before leaving Shanghai, I planned the final concert to be given, with the first half devoted to my playing works by Bach, Beethoven (the "Eye Glass Duo for Viola and Cello," with the gifted young cellist, Vivian Gu, now a member of the Seattle Symphony), and a Brahms sonata.

The second half was devoted to the orchestra's performance of Schubert's "Fifth Symphony." From the very beginning of the rehearsals, the young players responded very well to all of my requests and suggestions, which were translated for them by their regular conductor, Professor Wang. Early on, the string players seemed to be better than the wind players in performance and understanding; but, by the time we reached the day of the concert, they were all with me and came through beautifully.

One added word: The name of the artist who made us a gift of his beautiful scroll is Ying Ye Ping, one of China's most celebrated painters. That inspirational reminder of our all-too-brief visit to Shanghai now hangs on the wall of our living room. What a beautiful way to remember our warm Chinese friends.

With Spanish cellist Pablo Casals in Puerto Rico in 1958

Chapter 20
Innocents Abroad, Part Two

Virginia: In August 1971, we took advantage of being between concerts to visit Morocco, a country we had never visited. We flew from Paris to Rabat, the capitol, an all white city glistening in the hot summer sun, but still blessed by a hint of a breeze wafting in from the nearby Atlantic.

With no concert dates to keep, we were free to do whatever we wished and take our time doing it. Escorted by a new friend we had made while breakfasting in our hotel's coffee shop, our first outing was to visit the main palace in the city. But alas, Milton was not permitted to pass through the ancient gate because he was wearing shorts. So I breezed through without him and proceeded to walk through two impressive edifices aiming our new movie camera at sights along the way.

As I was strolling through a spacious garden on my way back to the main gate I noticed a man in a red fez and the traditional long djbella coming toward me. He had his hands in a prayerful position before his face. As he drew near he said, "You give me money lady? I take nice picture." Nearsighted as I am, I didn't realize who it was until he spoke. It was Milton. A sheik in borrowed clothing! So, with him in tow I went back to tour the palace all over again.

The following day, in a rented car, we drove inland through oppressive heat to Fez. As soon as we were settled in our hotel, we picked a guide who had been recommended to us. Surprise! His name was Abdullah. He looked rather distinguished, so we put ourselves in his hands, while mumbling a silent, hopeful prayer. The Medina (Old City of Fez) is such a maze of narrow alleys that we began to appreciate Abdullah. We wound down the hill into the souk, where all of the tiny shops competed for our attention. A not so small seed of suspicion was planted in my head as I noticed that every stall owner greeted Abdullah with excessive enthusiasm. (Hmmm – how much of a commission was he collecting?) Milton bought an attractive Moroccan shirt and I bought a caftan, the traditional dress for women. Abdullah kept up a running commentary about his ancestry.

Finally, hot and exhausted, he led us into a beautiful mosaic-walled courtyard. "A former palace," said Abdullah. The walls were hung with many stunning carpets. Four hassocks were brought forth by two small boys and we were introduced to our "host," a good looking man, his head swathed in a turban and dressed in a white djbella. We assumed he was a friend of Abdullah. The boys also brought glasses of hot, very sweet-minted tea. As we sipped the tea, Milton asked our "host" questions about this apparently historic spot. Seated in the lovely courtyard, we conversed in French, my high-school French rising brilliantly (I thought) to the occasion. (Milton was quite silent, his French was not to be believed.)

At 9 o'clock or so, we rose to thank our host for his hospitality, but he firmly but gently pushed us back down in our seats. "Just a minute," he said in surprisingly good English, "Boys, throw down the rugs."

It suddenly started raining carpets from the balcony and, within seconds, our "host" unrolled ten or 12 of the carpets before our startled eyes.

"You are rich American, yes? You buy two or three, yes?"

The Pleasure Was Ours

Disillusioned, feeling like simpletons, we managed a hasty retreat back up the hill to our hotel with Abdullah following us, either in embarrassment or disgust. We weren't sure which.

Next, it was on to Marrakech, another of Morocco's famous cities. It was an unbelievably torrid drive in mid-summer. A wise traveler should visit Morocco between October and May, but we had to travel as our concert schedule permitted. We didn't have the luxury of choice.

Suddenly we found ourselves in a swirl of a dirt cyclone that went on for about five miles of driving. Intelligent Moroccan drivers were parked alongside the road, waiting for the winds to subside, but Milton careened on. A few more miles ahead, we did a double take when we saw a Moroccan man walking along the road completely nude, except for a brilliantly jeweled fez atop his head.

Marrakech is a city of dreams, poverty, wealthy expatriates, beautiful gardens, palaces, and, of course, tourist attractions. You name it, and Marrakech has it. To the eye, it is really a pink city in a pink environment. All the buildings are a pale strawberry shade, and the surrounding hills are of pink rock. When we checked into the famous Mamounia Hotel, we found that their air-conditioning had broken down. August in Morocco without air-conditioning? We made some flimsy excuse for canceling our reservation and checked into the Holiday Inn. Americans!!

We went sightseeing the next day, and in the evening visited the wildly improbable Place Dmemma el Fna. This square is either the delight or nightmare of tourists, hundreds of whom are attracted by day and by night to watch the "happenings." The visitor sees men playing wooden flutes, as cobras rise from their urns or baskets to sway with the music; bearded fellows, with scorpions that run up and down their faces and often into their mouths; storytellers; acrobats; and "dentists," with samples of false teeth spread out on rugs in front of them (they were extracting teeth on the spot and immediately fitting new sets for size!).

Milton and Virginia Katims

We left Marrakech with some regrets and drove on to Casablanca ("Humphrey, Baby, where are you?) and along the cool coast to Tangiers, where we were to board the ferry for Algeciras, Spain. Before boarding we spent a couple of hours bargaining with shopkeepers. In one small shop Milton found a soft leather jacket that he liked very much. He was doing very well in his bargaining with the shop owner, forcing the price down to where he would buy it. I almost felt sorry for the sweating owner. He turned to me at one point in exasperation and said, "I think all Americans have much money. Not your husband? What does he do for a living?"

"He's a musician – plays the drums!" Just then a couple from Tacoma entered the small shop with exclamations of, "Maestro, imagine meeting you here." The price of the jacket zoomed right back up!

In another shop I bought one more caftan for $10. As I was trying it on the shop-keeper said to Milton, "You have beautiful blonde wife. Is she for sale? I like to buy her. How much you want?" He was serious.

Milton, the jokester, paused for a moment in his imitation of Jack Benny, and then said, "How much you give?" Even though I knew he was joking, I wanted to kick him in the shins for the all-too-interested gleam in his eye.

"Forty camels," the shopkeeper answered eagerly.

With camels going for a cool $500 apiece, I thought that wasn't a bad price for a 49-year-old American cello player. Do I have to note that no sale was recorded? Milton, still playing Jack Benny later said, "What was I going to do with 40 camels in Seattle?"

On to Spain.

Virginia: Near midnight, I was sitting in a box in Madrid's incomparable concert hall, El Teatro Real, listening to the Orquestra Nacional, with Milton conducting and appearing as viola soloist with violinist Jaime Laredo in the Mozart "Sinfonie Concertante."

En route to
Caracas (Venezuela)
to guest-conduct
1975

Virginia at "Great Surries" with hosts,
Fleur Cowles and husband Tom
Meyer (a lumber baron)

Milton and Virginia Katims

Did I dream that tremendous ovation and six curtain calls? No! By the time I made my way back to the conductor's room and found a line of young people waiting for autographs, I noted the time was close to 1 a.m. Evening concert time in Spain is 10 p.m., and most concerts are S.R.O. This particular series had a long list of subscribers.

A supper party was held in the elegant townhouse of Princess Baviera y Borbon, who is an aunt of Spain's Queen Sophia, after Milton's second Madrid concert. We had first met the Princess at the Menton Music Festival in France.

Milton's debut concert at his first Menton Festival was a night to remember. The square in front of the beautiful Church of St. Michelle high on a hilltop was packed with people, as were all the steps leading to and from the area. Princess Grace of Monaco arrived shortly before starting time, and the audience rose to greet her with applause. A vase of orange roses indicated where she would sit, and her simple orange chiffon print matched the bouquet. We all thought it a fine tribute to Milton and his American soloists that she choose to attend this concert. (Among the other notables that evening was Marc Chagall, the renowned artist and good friend of Isaac.)

Afterwards, the princess came back-stage to greet Milton and the celebrated soloists – violinist Isaac Stern, cellist Leonard Rose, pianist Eugene Istomin and French flutist Jean Pierre Rampal. Princess Grace was not only a vision of beauty, but extremely gracious, as well. Her radiance was infectious. How proud we were of our American beauty. (What a tragedy to lose her a few years later in that terrible auto accident!)

Earlier, we had been luncheon guests of Princess Baviera at her Madrid home, and on that occasion we were served cocktails on the patio. The "bartender" was a tall, dark, handsome young man, Prince Juan Carlos, now the King of Spain. I was impressed with the sparkling gold dinner service and the two liveried, white-gloved waiters who attended to every wish of the 14 guests. During the party the Princess cuddled in her lap a tiny dachshund that lay happily supine, covered with a cloth of

French lace. As to the future king – we were pleased when the good-natured, compassionate monarch received the World Statesman Award from the Appeal of Conscience Foundation for his wonderful policy of pursuing peace and tolerance among Christian, Jewish, and Islamic leaders.

Between concerts we spent some glorious frolic time at a condominium in Marbella on the sparkling Costa del Sol. The keys to the condo had been given us by its owner, Lorin Glickman, one of our musician friends (bassoonist) in the New York Philharmonic. Milton now had plenty of time to study a new score by composer William Bolcom, which was to receive its world premiere with the Seattle Symphony.

Having the Hilton Hotel right next door was most convenient. The manager sent a large pitcher of the potent punch, sangria, to our table at our first lunch on the hotel patio. As we tried sipping it with our paella, we glanced around at the various nationalities on the terrace. "The only Americans I can see," I said to Milton, "are at the table next to us." Just then they rose to leave. As they passed us, Milton stopped them and said, "How would a couple of fellow Americans like to help us finish this murderous punch? We can't begin to handle it."

The man answered with a strong German accent, " Sorry! We are not your countrymen. I am Klaus Menzel from Switzerland, but this will not keep us from helping you finish your wine." He turned out to be a concert manager from Zurich, and we had so much in common that we quickly became friends.

We were invited one evening to dinner at the Marbella Club. I wore a vividly printed shift, slit up the side to "there," and different orange pants. I thought I was terribly daring. But I found I was the most conservatively dressed female there. Milton wore a flowered Hawaiian shirt and was right on target. A stunning senorita tucked a flower behind Milton's ear when we arrived. The most exotically and creatively gowned woman at that dinner was a gorgeous young blonde with hair falling to her hips. She wore a tiny bra and a flowered skirt that hung from those hips.

Below her bra was a painting of a sunrise, and in the scooped out back, a sunset! (Oh, yes, and in the navel, a jewel.)

The next day I went shopping. I had forgotten to take along a black slip for a dress I had brought. The only one I could find that fit me had a price tag of $70! When I told the shopkeeper the price was ridiculous, she responded, "But, Senora, it is a special slip. No electric currents!" Static electricity!

Ah! And those handsome Spanish men. They smelled good, too. Whenever I ran into elegantly dressed Spaniards in the hotel elevator, I had to restrain myself from asking what cologne they were wearing. I recalled the experience Milton had had when he first went to Spain to conduct. At a party after one of his concerts a handsome young Spaniard bridled when Milton overtly admired his beautiful wife. In response to Milton's asking if he weren't flattered by having his good taste confirmed, he said, "It's okay as long as your eyes are not in your fingertips!"

On our last day in Madrid, we decided to try a small offbeat cafe frequented only by the natives. Our problems began when we realized that no one spoke English and Milton's high school Spanish was sadly inadequate, even when supplemented with gestures and sign language. When Milton blindly picked an item from the menu, the waiter motioned us to wait while he brought us a cold chafing dish to inspect. It was filled with a few dozen raw, red cockscombs. We both gulped and everyone in the cafe started to laugh. We quickly, hysterically joined them. We swallowed our pride and a nice Spanish omelet.

Fleur Cowles, Painter

Virginia: The last time we saw Fleur, Milton and I were house guests of Fleur Cowles and her husband Tom Meyer, at their country home, Great Surries, in Sussex, England. Fleur was the creator and editor of the short-lived magazine, *Flair*, and was the former wife of Gardner Cowles, publisher of *Look* magazine. My friends in Seattle will remember her especially because of her visit there, when her imaginative canvasses of flowers and animals were the features of Symphoneve, the annual benefit ball staged just before the opening of the Seattle Symphony season.

We left London for the one hour ride to Sussex where Tom Meyer met us at the station. As we approached Great Surries, a fine mist was falling, lending the soft ambiance of a Corot landscape to the lush, green countryside. Fleur was waiting, dressed in a brilliantly flowered pantsuit. She took us in hand immediately, guiding us into the huge and stunning main area called the Pool House. It was once a barn, built 400 years ago, and has the distinction of being one of England's historic monuments, as is the Meyers' London home, Albany, in the heart of Piccadilly. As historic preservationists know, any structure designated as an historic site in most nations may be altered inside, but the exterior must be left intact. Vogue magazine is one of the periodicals to pay tribute to the fantastic Great Surries with pictures and story.

The Pool House stands beside a magnificent swimming pool that is tiled in varying shades of aquamarine. At each end are banks of white Iceberg Roses. One wing of the building has a huge sauna and several dressing rooms, all equipped with beautiful choices of robes, shower caps, colognes, and sofas for relaxing. The other wing has a master bedroom for the Meyers' own use; it boasts one of the most artistic bath-and-dressing room combinations I've ever seen. The huge tub of deep jade is surrounded by copper planters, all with exotic flowers and foliage. Fleur had painted the dressing-room walls with multi-colored flowers and trailing vines of ivy and wisteria. I could have spent the entire weekend soaking blissfully right there.

Fleur took us to the main house, which was across the driveway from the Pool House. There we were assigned the entire third floor, which was to be our home for the weekend. The suite consisted of two bedrooms, a bathroom, and a charming sitting room done in Chintzes. The predominating color scheme was scarlet. Only an artist like Fleur could have created a dream house like that one. We felt like royalty.

Milton and Virginia Katims

We were surprised to discover that the Great Surries staff had already unpacked all of our luggage and neatly placed our things in drawers and on hangers. Milton and I looked sheepishly at each other and wished we had packed more carefully that morning. What must the maids have thought when they saw our thrown-together assortment of clothing?

It was soon time to change and return to the Pool House to meet the other guests. The Meyers, whose Wednesday-night salons in London are renowned, had brought together a fascinating group of people. I know it's somewhat risky to indulge in the pastime of name-dropping, but I just can't help myself when I come upon personalities like those with whom we mingled at Great Surries.

We first met Sir Leon and Lady Bagrit. He was a pioneer in the international development of the computer, but we quickly found we had a strong common interest in music. He was a fine amateur violinist and had created the Friends of Covent Garden, a major support group for the arts at the famous London theater. Next came businessman Norbert Baillen, whose wife, a psychiatrist, had just published her book, *The Life of Coco Chanel*. I haven't read it yet, but a book about that famous designer by a psychiatrist should be a fascinating read.

Last, but most certainly not least, were the famous Duke and Duchess of Bedford, whose home, Woburn Abbey, about 40 miles from London, was open to the public at that time and had become one of the most popular tourist attractions in England. We were enchanted with both of them. They were quick-witted and unaffected. We found the Duke to be truly "mod." The next morning he showed up for breakfast in a long, Chinese peasant type outfit. In the evening he wore a marvelous Indian print, which I was sure had come from Asia — but he insisted he had "simply plucked it off the rack at Liberty's" (a London department store famous for its Liberty Prints).

Woburn Abbey has been in the Duke's family more than 300 years. Twenty-two of its principal rooms, as well as an antique market and game park, are open to the public. It is so large that it takes a staff of 400 to run. The main dining room is a veritable museum, whose walls are graced by the paintings of Van Dyck, Rembrandt, and many other European giants of art. Three restaurants are open to the public. For a mere $200 a person, visitors can have a room overnight, and tea and dinner with the Duke and Duchess in the fantastic dining room. No more than 20 guests can be accommodated there at a time.

At lunch the next day, while all the guests were being introduced, our host Tom whipped up a formidable mint aperitif that had dynamite in it. Perhaps that was the main reason the conversation sparkled from then on. In the midst of the merrymaking, the butler appeared with a wicker wash-basket full to the brim with freshly picked garden peas. We were all invited to sit on the floor and shell the darned things. The pea-shelling chore was conquered in a jiffy thanks to our glasses being refilled as soon as they were emptied. The fruits and vegetables we were soon served were from the Abbey "farm."

We had the afternoon to ourselves to sight-see or nap. After dinner that first evening, someone suggested we play Scrabble, and with a broad smile on his face, Tom Meyer asked, "In which language?" This thoroughly cowed Milton, who had leaped to his feet, convinced he would "take all," which he often does at home.

I sat in a corner chatting with Fleur, while she painted away, holding her canvas on her lap and pausing from time to time to hold it away a bit to observe her handiwork. She mixed her own paints from a combination of oils and plastics. With great pleasure, she informed me she was preparing for exhibitions of her work in Sao Paulo, Brazil, and Dallas, Texas.

It was with great regret that we left Great Surries for Heathrow Airport and the continuation of our European trip. That night at the airport, we slept in one of those airtight, noiseless, little hotel "cells." What a comedown, contrasted with the luxury of our previous nights with an entire mansion floor all to ourselves! C'est la vie.

Virginia and Milton off to Paris for some guest-conducting

Chapter 21
Innocents Abroad, Part Three

Virginia: Under a cluster of crystal chandeliers, she stood dressed in a long gown of the palest pink chiffon, embroidered here and there with silver sequins. Although she wore no jeweled tiara in her shining black hair, she wore a fantastic diamond ring on her a finger of her left hand and a sparkling diamond bracelet on her wrist.

It was the mid-'70s, and I had to go all the way to Venezuela to meet the Empress Farah of Iran and her husband, the Shah. There were 2,000 others there, as well. Milton was in Caracas, the attractive city of many hills, dramatic vistas and unbelievable traffic jams, to guest conduct the Orquesta Sinfonica Venezuela. One of our invitations was to the gala reception honoring the Shah and the Empress. Milton begged off, claiming he had scores to study, so I went alone.

The party began at 10:30 p.m. and the receiving line was so long that by the time I made my curtsy it was 1 a.m. I'm sure the long wait to meet the Iranian royal couple would have seemed much longer if it hadn't been for the free-flowing champagne and gourmet delicacies provided to us in the line.

Milton and Virginia Katims

A diplomat's wife said to me rather haughtily, "I don't intend to curtsey. I'd feel decadent." (Venezolanos are fiercely independent.) Finally reaching the honored guests, I sank to the floor – prima donna style – and I thought quite elegantly, too, until I heard the sickening sound of a split extending the length of the slit already in my fitted skirt.

"Empress Farah," I said boldly, to cover my confusion, if not my thigh. "My husband and I loved seeing your beautiful concert hall when we were in Teheran last January." She gave me a radiant smile. I bowed to the Shah, murmuring in a quite un-American fashion, "Your Highness."

Was I dreaming or did he give me a tiny wink as I blushed?

"Certainly not," Milton said later. "Shahs don't wink, they think. They think oil, especially when they are visiting Venezuela."

It costs a fortune for a wife to follow a popular conductor around the world, but I couldn't resist that visit to South America. On the flight from Los Angeles to Miami, on our way to Caracas, Milton had been studying the score of the Beethoven "Eroica" when he sensed someone looking over his shoulder. As Milton turned to look up at the interested spectator, who looked rather familiar, the stranger said, "Ah, the great 'Eroica.'"

It was Ray Bolger, the Strawman of "Wizard of Oz" fame. He was now a bit portly and craggy-faced, but he had a keen interest in and obvious knowledge of music. He was no longer making films, but was appearing in TV commercials for companies like Sony. Bolger, an engaging personality, made our cross-country flight most enjoyable.

What memories I have of that South American trip: the marvelous playing of the Caracas orchestra, whose roster included so many first rate musicians; the large number of young people at the concerts, thanks to the very reasonably priced tickets and the uninhibited way in which they behaved, shouting their bravoes; the volatile behavior of the Caracas University male students, who, when the Ballet

Africain appeared at the campus theater with the ballerinas who were bare from the waist up, rushed headlong toward the stage, causing the dancers to flee in panic and the curtain to be lowered quickly; the weight I put on drinking those super-delicious batidos (milkshakes made with mangoes, guavas, and papayas); our last night in that exotic tropical city, when I was dozing off to the combined sounds of crickets and the radio next to my bed that finally lulled me to sleep. And what did I dream of? The Shah of Iran's intense brown eyes? Milton's great performance of the "Eroica?" No. My dream was that I was back in my beloved Seattle in time to see the rhododendrons bursting into bloom in our garden.

Leon Barzin, Conductor, Violist

Virginia: Twilight was descending on the beautiful City of Lights as our plane touched down at Orly Airport. Ah, Paris! Is there a woman in the world whose heart does not beat a bit faster at the mere mention of that city? Milton was not conducting on this trip; we were on vacation, but music follows us everywhere.

At the hotel we found a note from Leon Barzin, former conductor of the National Orchestral Association in New York and, before that, solo violist of the New York Philharmonic. Leon was Milton's first mentor and a longtime friend. In his note Leon invited us to spend the weekend at their out-of-Paris retreat and included precise (we thought) information on which train to take from the Gare St. Lazare. He had included his phone number so we called him immediately for more instructions. Milton and I threw a few things into our backpacks and walked to the train station, where we proceeded to board – the wrong train! Two stations later, a sympathetic conductor practically took us by our hands like two lost children and walked us to a train taking us back to Paris. There he literally placed us in front of another track, saying, "Don't move from this spot until the right train arrives. Remember, you're going to Vaux, not Baux."

Milton and Virginia Katims

It was then that we realized we had misunderstood Leon's pronunciation of the little town on the Seine. After a 45-minute ride, we arrived at Vaux-sur-Seine where we were met and hugged warmly by Leon and his lovely wife Eleanor, who had been waiting patiently. They laughed heartily when they heard why we were late.

"Wait until you see our place," said Leon. "When you do, you will understand why I dislike going into Paris these days. Paris has been ruined. Too many autos and three-deep parking everywhere make it a hassle no matter where you live."

We entered a chauffeur driven car and within minutes arrived at a chateau-like estate. Huge grilled iron gates swung open to reveal a very large circular court. "What do you call this place," I asked Eleanor, "a chateau, a domaine, or maybe a castle?"

"No, no, Virginia. This is known as a Pavillon. It's a place to which royalty used to come to hunt."

Charles X, I learned, had used this Pavillon as his personal hunting lodge when he was king. As it happened, I slept in Charlie's bed that weekend and found myself wondering — why, I don't know — if he had snored. Nevertheless, the royal bed, draped in lush velvet, was very cozy. Charles must have slept well.

The beautifully sculptured doors of the Pavillon opened into a large rotunda with a high vaulted ceiling. Eleanor, a discriminating collector, showed us through at least a half-dozen suites, each decorated in a different style and each with its own sumptuous bath. King Charles must have had many hunting buddies and a huge staff to serve them. My favorite place to spend daytime hours was the Versailles Room, which had a golden harp standing in one corner and a massive fireplace that always had a roaring fire come twilight.

The grounds of the Pavillon seemed endless and included huge vegetable gardens and orchards, which supplied much of the food for the Barzin table. A well-manicured lawn, about the size of a football field, reached from the rear of the Pavillon to the bank of the Seine.

Awestruck, I asked Leon, "How many rooms are in this place?"

His answer, "I don't really know. We've never counted them, but I do know that there are all sorts of secret passageways, libraries filled with precious first editions, and even a concert hall. Come, I'll show where our concerts take place." We crossed a small, immaculately kept garden and entered an adjacent building.

"This was originally the king's private chapel," Leon explained. "I turned it into a concert hall that seats almost 100 people." The large rectangular room was resplendent in gold leaf and a rich red-velvet drape graced the stage. We had a chance to see the concert hall filled, because the very next day Leon presented a violinist and harpsichordist from Paris to perform for many of the villagers and their children.

"Most children today listen only to rock music," Leon said with disgust. "I present four of these musicales each season. At least the young people have this much of an introduction to classical music." Leon was indeed the Prince Esterhazy of Vaux-sur-Seine.

We had one more day to enjoy Paris. I was looking forward to seeing the latest collection at one of the big fashion houses, so we stopped first at Givenchy' on Avenue Montaigne. An attractive Cambodian hostess greeted us as we entered. She glowed with pleasure when I told her that my husband was a chef d'orchestre, "I adore symphonic music." Then, to our delight, she said, "Come, I will take you to Monsieur Givenchy."

Sure enough, there on the second floor was the handsome, world-renowned couturier adjusting a white organdy hat with rippling brim almost half a foot wide on the head of a ravishing Chinese model. (I imagined what would happen to such an enormous chapeau in the Seattle rain.)

"Monsieur Givenchy," said the hostess, "this lady is the wife of a symphony conductor from Seattle in the U.S.A."

When I started to say, "You won't remember me," he interrupted. "But of course I remember. You and I were in the *Life* tableaux together."

Milton and Virginia Katims

Hubert de Givenchy had traveled to Seattle at the invitation of one of Seattle's department stores to show his collection at one of our Symphoneve benefit parties. Both of us had appeared in full-page photos in *Life* magazine. "Madame," he added. "can you come back to see me at 2:30 thees afternoon? At thees moment, as you can see, I am so veree beezy. We are having our spring showing next week."

I quickly agreed to return later while thinking, "Good Gawd, spring collection? I haven't even thought about my clothes for this winter yet."

As we left the golden-caged elevator on the first floor, our hostess spied a lissome blonde looking over gowns in the boutique. "Oh," said the hostess happily. "Here is another symphony conductor's wife."

She approached Madame von Karajan and introduced us. "Pardon, may I present Maestro and Madame Katims?" Her husband, Herbert von Karajan, one of the world's best-known conductors, had recently died.

She nodded with the briefest of smiles and said hurriedly, "I must see Givenchy immediately. I am going to Japan to do some public relations for my husband's recordings, and I must have something to wear for morning, afternoon, and evening." And she dashed off. (Not a thing to wear??)

We slipped into Nina Ricci's for a short while and then it was time to return to Givenchy. He was waiting for us in a small office, his white starched coat pressed immaculately. As we chatted, at least 50 of his employees with questions darted in and out. After reminding him once more of his visit to Seattle, I asked brashly, "What are you showing for spring? What about skirt lengths?"

"Short," was his quick response. "Short. Short. Short."

"What about me? What about women of my age?"

"You have good legs, Madame. Why not show them? Why make a beeg secret?" He paused a moment, looking over my body. "Well, maybe a leetle longair, just below the knee for you, n'est-ce pas?" I wanted to kick him in the shins.

Instead, I asked, "How about the shoulders? Will we still look like football players?"

"Yes, broad shouldairs. They make your waist look very leetle, yes? We show lots of white for spring. Linens, beautiful prints, some sheer wools from Milano. And lots of fantasy."

I changed the subject. "What do you remember about Seattle?"

"Ah, what a beautiful city. I love the hills, the watair, and all of the lovely sailboats."

"Would you come back?"

"Eef you ask me, of course. You just have to geeve me the invitation, yes?"

Givenchy is immensely popular. He travels a great deal, lending his charismatic charm to various affairs, particularly for charitable purposes.

"I weel be in New York early in Novembair. There weel be beeg party at the Museum of Modern Art to honor my friend, Gary Coopair. You know his daughter, Maria?"

I nodded quickly. Maria is married to Byron Janis, the wonderful pianist.

"She is a good friend of mine, too," Givenchy continued, "and we weel be part of the tribute to the great actair, Gary. I was hees beeg fan."

As I left, I made a mental note to myself: Call your friend Maria, and wangle an invite to that one.

Milton and I also had an opportunity to visit once more with a couple of long time friends, Noma and Bill Copley (benefactors of young composers and artists), at their small domaine in Longpont, about 15 miles outside Paris. They had one of the finest collections of surrealistic art in the world, and their lovely garden was dotted with sculptures by Jean Arp and Max Ernst.

Each night their beautiful dining table was decorated in honor of the guest of the evening – statues of musicians for our first night, and on other nights there were African sculptures, Mexican or Iberian pieces, and so forth, depending upon the interests of the sculptor or artist who was being honored. Huge paintings by Dali, Tangey, and Magritte decorated the walls of the dining room. The piece-de-resistance in the stunning, white living room was a gigantic painting by Man Ray of a pair of red lips. It covered almost one entire wall.

Finally, I must pass along a tip to hostesses that I learned from Noma: Keep a guest log in which menus, wines, table decorations, and flowers are recorded so that no guest experiences the same menu or decor twice.

The most fascinating dish of this night was trout served in white wine, garnished with almonds and shallots and decorated with sprigs of green leaves from the garden, followed by a luscious dessert of small French melons, each served with its cut-off top pinned back on with a yellow rose. We removed the top to find tiny cointreau-soaked strawberries poured over vanilla ice cream. Ummm!

Some other memories from that amazing French trip include scenes of collectors scrambling madly for African sculpture, beauty operators teasing hair like mad and leaving clients looking as if melted butter should be poured over their heads (the "artichoke"), three wonderful days spent in the breathtakingly beautiful Roussillon home of our long time friend, Sasha Schneider, and the small restaurant nearby at which Picasso and Casals often signed the guest book. Vive la France!

On one late-summer trip in the early '70s, we headed for the British Isles to combine pleasure and business, although I confess I've never been able to differentiate one from the other while seeing the world. Our first stop was London, a city we love so much. We arrived just in time for the only London showing of Arthur Rubinstein's film, "Love of Life." The pianist had alerted us to the event and we were able to combine the London visit with plans to attend the Glyndebourne and Edinburgh Festivals.

At the Rubinstein film showing, we chuckled, wept, empathized with Arthur's words of wisdom, and lost ourselves in the beauty of his playing. It was a rewarding evening. One of the pleasures of attending concerts in the British capital was arriving early at the hall (many young people go directly from their jobs) and having a choice of a snack bar, cafeteria, or dining room. It was all so natural and easy and it made concert-going a much greater delight.

The highlight of our concert-going in England on that trip was a performance of Richard Strauss' "Ariadne auf Naxos" at the Glyndebourne Festival. Glyndebourne, a most charming little town in Sussex, had become famous for its brilliant opera productions in July and August. It was all a kind of "happening." Ticket holders left London's Victoria Station in mid-afternoon in formal dress — long gowns for the ladies and tuxedos for the men. It felt weird trotting through the huge railway station at two in the afternoon looking like characters in search of a play.

Most of those bound for Glyndebourne, which is about an hour's ride from London, carried picnic baskets complete with two or three bottles of wine which they began breaking out the minute the train started. When they arrived at the festival site, via busses that met the train, many of the formally dressed opera-goers were already in a mellow, very receptive mood.

The performances began at 6 p.m. and allowed for a supper break after the first act. Those with baskets strolled out into the beautiful gardens, spread tablecloths, and picnicked. Some of them took along butlers to take care of this arduous chore. Others dined inside at attractively decorated tables in the dining room, for which reservations were required.

The only American singer in the cast, Helen Vanni, who sang the role of Ariadne, did herself and her country proud. She had a rich, opulent voice with beautiful intonation and excellent technique. When we went backstage to congratulate her, Helen told us the production was one of the highlights of her singing career. "Where else," she asked, "can a singer have the opportunity to sing 16 performances in a six-week period?"

In Edinburgh, we checked into our hotel, quickly donned our wrinkled formal wear and set out to find Usher Hall for the first night's concert of the Edinburgh International Music Festival, Scotland's cultural jewel. As we exited the hotel, we saw Yehudi Menuhin, who was to be the soloist, and his wife Diana, waiting for their car. Milton went quickly toward the violinist, his head down, and bent over as if to pick up Yehudi's fiddle case, saying, "Carry your violin for you, Sir?"

Absent-mindedly, Yehudi answered, "No, thank you. I like to handle it myself." Then as his eyes met Milton's, he exclaimed, "Good Lord, Milton. What are you doing here?"

The four of us went to Usher Hall, lobby and stage of which were banked with exotic flowers. We watched the chic audience and the musicians of the Scottish National Orchestra take their places. The Edinburgh Festival Chorus was seated behind the orchestra in a section that was usually used to accommodate overflow audiences. Directly behind the chorus was a giant pipe organ.

Sir Alexander Gibson conducted. Yehudi brought an incandescence and purity of tone to the musical riches of Elgar's "Violin Concerto." On the second night, the London Philharmonic performed with its conductor, Bernhard Haitink, with piano soloist Andre Watts. Hearing Watts was a first for me, and his playing of the "Tchaikovsky Concerto" was a glowing experience.

Later, back at our hotel for tea with Andre, we heard a man across the room singing the Tchaikovsky melodies to his companion with great ardor. Intrigued, we went over to him and learned he was Sir Neville Cardus, former music critic of the Manchester Guardian. He told us of the time that he, as a cub reporter, and the noted English critic, Ernest Newman, were reviewing the same concert. As they left the hall, Sir Neville had tears streaming down his face.

Newman remarked, "Don't you know it's a heinous crime for someone in your position to love music that much?"

Sir Neville answered, "But I've always felt that I had to have a love affair with great music if I am to involve and imbue my readers with that same emotion."

I agreed heartily with him and wondered how an esteemed critic like Newman could know the quality of a performance if he really had no great love for music.

The Pleasure Was Ours

The soloist at the next night's concert was the Spanish songbird, Victoria de los Angeles, who always established an instant charismatic relationship with her audience, and she certainly did that evening. When Milton and I visited her the next day, I asked her what the greatest moment of her career had been, she replied without hesitation, "Having a child. I waited 15 years for that supreme experience of my life. Other emotions can change, but those of motherhood never can."

The next concert was a high spot for us. Pierre Boulez, then music director of the New York Philharmonic, put the National Youth Orchestra of Great Britain through its paces in a program that began with Bartok's challenging "Music for Strings, Percussion, and Celeste." With Boulez's mastery of the score, the huge, youthful orchestra was able to fully realize the character of the work. The orchestra then accompanied Yehudi's introspective reading of Alban Berg's somewhat astringent "Violin Concerto," followed by a surprisingly mature performance of Webern's "Six Pieces, Opus 6," and finally sailed into Debussy's "La Mer."

My eyes filled with tears over the wonderful musicianship and concentrated efforts of the young players. It was also thrilling to come out of the hall and watch a sea of young admirers waiting to get the autographs of their talented peers. Later on, Boulez told us that only 20 percent of the youngsters go on to become professional musicians, that the others had their eyes on careers as scientists, doctors, engineers, and other pursuits.

That same evening we attended the Military Tattoo high on the hill above the city, where Balmoral Castle sits. It was a rousing spectacle, with Scots cheering wildly as their regiments and clans performed. It was raining hard, but no one seemed to care or even to notice.

It was on to Kings' Theater the next night to hear the Scottish Opera Company perform Wagner's "Die Walkure," which was distinguished by a near ideal Brunnhilde sung by soprano Helga Dernesch. Thanks to the dry wit of Scots and Brits, every experience in their land produces moments of humor. After the final curtain of the Wagner opera, I overheard a woman comment, "I don't know. It's a long pull. Wagner only puts in a couple of tunes every now and then."

I immediately thought of what Mark Twain wrote in his autobiography: "I've been told that Wagner's music is better than it sounds."

Chapter 22
Some Final Travel Words

*V*irginia: It was the middle of winter when we arrived in Finland, and it was time to crawl into bed when we checked into Helsinki's ultramodern Hotel Vaakuna. It was Milton's 15th trip abroad to conduct, this time to direct the first-rate Helsinki Symphony. Like most Americans, we admire the staunch Finns and associate them naturally with snow, saunas, and Sibelius. One of the many visual tributes to their favorite composer is a provocative sculpture of him by a gifted woman artist. It stands impressively on a rock in one of Helsinki's lovely parks.It is one of many of the composer, Sibelius, for whom the Finns have an almost religious regard. The dark, brooding quality of Sibelius' music reflects the nation's character, its people, and the rugged, challenging environment.

Rehearsals were held in the House of Culture, which had been built by the Communist Party, but the concert itself took place in the stunningly contemporary Finlandia House, built by the government. One realized with some concern that the country was still divided politically, but certainly not fragmented.

Milton and Virginia Katims

The men and ten women musicians of the orchestra were eager, friendly, and quick to respond, although few were fluent in English. But music is international and, with the help of a fine violinist as translator, all went smoothly. I realized, happily, that a guest-conductor in Helsinki was welcomed as eagerly as a new bride.

Helsinki turned out to be a rather expensive city, so I appreciated the fact that our hotel opened directly into a large department store where I could conveniently buy fruit, yogurt, cheese, and other foods to eat in our room rather than dine regularly in restaurants.

Inflation was far worse in Finland and other European nations than it was in the U.S. Yet, we were told that the Swedes traveled to Helsinki on weekends for produce and meat, because their own inflation had ballooned even higher.

During rehearsal breaks, I enjoyed conversing with a fine cellist in the orchestra who had been a pupil of Slava Rostropovitch, who was scheduled to play a recital in Seattle a few months later. Between rehearsals, Milton and I took sauna baths at mind-blowing temperatures, grateful that there was no snow for us to dash into. We'd heard about the foreigners who indulged in that routine and suffered heart attacks.

After the concert, which was very well received, Kai Massalo, director of Finnish Radio, and his wife whisked us off to a rooftop restaurant where we were joined by a fun-loving young lady, Seija Haavisto, who not only kept us in stitches with her witty comments, but then served as our Helsinki guide. As we enjoyed the view of the twinkling lights of the city and gorged ourselves on blini (pancakes with a touch of caviar and chopped raw onions), topped off with frozen strawberries, our host Kai spoke of his love for the "Rachmaninoff Second Symphony," which Milton had just conducted. (It was the first performance of it by the orchestra.) His eyes were full of tears as he spoke.

The next morning we bid "hyvasti" to Helsinki and jetted off to Persia, that fabled land now known as Iran. Our Seattle-built Boeing 727 glided gently on to the runway of the Tehran airport, lubricated not by grease and oil, but by snow. We had to travel from snowless Finland to usually sunny Iran to encounter snow!

What were we doing in the sometimes unfriendly Iran? Milton was a member of the State Department music-advisory panel and had been asked to go on a discovery mission to find out what Iran was doing for the arts. Ambassador Zahedi of Iran had arranged for us to meet with the minister of arts and culture. This was when the Shah still ruled.

The Tehran airport was bulging with people jetting in from all parts of the world. I'd never seen anything like it. The crowds were moving with an almost hysterical rush. The scene was virtually the same in the lobby of our hotel. And the city itself was a swirling vortex of visitors, traffic jams, and daredevil taxi drivers – a condition that would not have surprised us in Rome, Paris, Vienna, New York or London. But Tehran?

We spent an interesting few hours with the minister, finding out that Iranian money was indeed flowing into the arts. The scorecard of recent additions included three handsome new buildings for the arts, a newly established 100-member symphony orchestra, an opera company, and a beautiful new concert hall with a special box for their majesties.

At the residence of the minister, we dined on Iranian caviar, hot crunchy Iranian bread, and spiced lamb. This was done while sitting, Persian style, on velvet pillows oriented to take advantage of the view of the gorgeous scenery outside.

The next day we were taken to see the crown jewels, housed in a basement bank vault. I don't have adequate words to describe the unbelievable splendor and beauty of that priceless collection of gems, with diamonds and rubies from the encrusted Peacock Throne. The jewels were so piercingly bright that I was literally blinded by them so much so that I ended up with the second migraine of my life.

We flew to Shiraz, a city of roses, for a brief look at its spectacular floral displays and visited Persepolis nearby to see the ruins of the great ceremonial palaces still bearing witness to the splendor of the Persian empire under Darius. Unfortunately, the unrelenting snows forced us to cancel our trip to Isfahan, the jewel of Iran, with its blue domes and minarets. It was doubly disappointing because we were afraid, given the volatile conditions in the Middle East, that we might never have the opportunity to feast our eyes on the treasures of Isfahan.

Our final stop before returning to Seattle was Beirut, that continually strife-torn Lebanese city once known as the Paris of the Middle East, with its beautiful harbor reminiscent of the French Riviera. The 18-hour return flight from Beirut to Seattle provided a bonus on the Rome–New York leg, when William Harness, a Seattle tenor, strode aboard our 747. Bill, fresh from operatic triumphs in many European cities, had an early date to solo with the Seattle Symphony in Verdi's dramatic "Requiem." We had enjoyed our latest travels a great deal, but now we were looking forward to getting back to our home in the glorious Emerald City.

BERGEN, NORWAY

It wasn't long before Milton and I were headed back to Scandinavia, this time to Norway, where Milton had a date to guest-conduct the Harmonien Symphony Orchestra in Bergen. I wondered whether women's liberation had arrived in Norway, a nation I had always thought was so progressive and modern. Looking out of the plane window I could see the myriad of snow-covered islands dotting our approach to the Norwegian coast. Moments later, we glided gently onto the icy Bergen runway. We were met by a sweet-faced, attractive blonde, who said shyly, "I am Laila Kismul, the symphony manager."

Almost as if she had been reading my mind, she told us she belonged to a group that was working hard for equal opportunity for women in Norway! I had to bite my lips to suppress a laugh. But her marvelously feminine and efficient approach to her duties as manager, coupled with the complete and selfless dedication she demon-

Mutual admiration in Houston, Texas – Virginia with Henry Kissinger

Gov. Dan Evans appointing Maestro Katims Cultural Ambassador of the state of Washington

strated to the Harmonien Symphony Orchestra and its conductor, showed us quickly that she exemplified the professional woman at her best. I wanted to say "Bravo!" to her – or, rather, the feminine form of the exclamation, "Brava!"

Bergen is a fairy-tale town surrounded by mountains and embracing inlets carved out by the sea. Both a funicular and a tramway scale two of its highest hills, transporting tourists and townspeople who live up above the city, as well as skiers who take off in all directions once they reach the summit. The views at the top of the world are magnificent. Our hotel was immaculate,

We had a typical Norwegian meal of herring with assorted sauces, a dash of aquavit, and a bowl of tart, but delicious, cloudberries. I looked around and discovered I was the only woman in the dining room! Most assuredly, I thought, Bergen and Norway were as rumor had it, a man's world.

The next morning I awoke, green to the gills with eight-hour flu, and I promptly gave it to Milton, who turned even greener. We must have been made of stern stuff, thank goodness, because we were both back to good health in time for the beginning of orchestra rehearsals a day later. It was love at first sight between Milton and the musicians, and there was a strong feeling of mutual trust. That is frequently the case when one guest-conducts. Perhaps it's because both the conductor and the musicians know the association is temporary. Milton insists the it was more like a brief courtship, in which both sides are open to each other's virtues and unaware of any faults.

Milton chuckles now about the one incident that threatened to interrupt the courtship, but at the same time confirmed my belief in the women's liberation in Norway. One thing that most irritates a conductor is to see a player with legs crossed. During the second meeting with the orchestra, Milton noticed a player with crossed legs. He stopped conducting and, without looking at the errant player, he said very quietly, "You know, for me, making music is very much like making love, and I have never figured out how to make love with my legs crossed!"

The Pleasure Was Ours

Those erring legs were uncrossed immediately. After the rehearsal Milton apologized to the young women in the Harmonien for his remarks. One of the young women quickly said, "There is no need to apologize, you're in Norway!"

In our first free time after a rehearsal, the chairman of the orchestra took us to visit the home of Edvard Grieg, the composer who is to Norway what Sibelius is to Finland. From the tidy, simple, and well preserved home, we clambered down a steep cliff in deep snow to the small remote cottage that stands beside a lake and in which Grieg composed in utter seclusion.

Without boots and panting heavily, we struggled back up the hill, our eyes riveted on the cozy taxi awaiting us. Whew! That hill seemed three times longer and more precipitous climbing up than it was when we slid down its slope. Our guide-driver then took us to the opposite side of the mountain and through the woods until we came upon Grieg's tomb, carved into the rocks overlooking the other side of the lake. With great feeling, the guide said reverently, "See what a beautiful view he has. When the Moscow Symphony was in Bergen last year, all the musicians hiked down here and wept with emotion. Russians cry a lot. They are very emotional." Our own eyes were not exactly dry.

We were escorted the next day to the half-completed Grieg Hall, a dramatically original architectural project that had been started way back in 1967, but now sat forlornly unfinished because of the usual arts bugaboo, lack of funds. When finished, Grieg Hall would house all of Bergen's artistic productions.

Then they were using a movie house and the concert had to begin promptly at seven in order to be finished in time for the start of the movie at nine. I noticed that the feature was "The Arizona Kid," but happily, the marquee had given top billing to the orchestra and Milton.

Precisely at seven, Milton gave the orchestra a downbeat to begin the performance of Brahms noble "Third Symphony," one of the most beautiful works in the symphonic repertoire, and the concert was off to an auspicious start before a capacity audience, all of whom were informally garbed, by the way. Norwegians treasure casualness. The Harmonien played a subscription concert every week, in addition to fulfilling other musical assignments, all for a population in a city of only 100,000.

Before the final work, a symphony by American composer Peter Mennin, my impetuous husband turned to the audience, raised his hand for silence, and said with a tear in his voice, "Please, beg, borrow, steal, and write your politicians or phone King Olav, but find the money needed to finish your beautiful Grieg Hall and give your fine orchestra the home it deserves."

The audience applauded with gusto, and Milton breathed a sigh of relief, because he wasn't sure how the words of a brash American conductor would be taken. At concert's end, they showed him once more how much they were in his corner with a vigorous, rhythmic hand clapping that was deafening and so characteristic of many enthusiastic European audiences.

After the third or fourth bow, the orchestra's chairman, who was also the percussion player, came from the wings with a large bouquet of flowers for Milton and gave him a warm bear hug. At that moment, Milton could have run for mayor of Bergen – and won!

Later, at a supper party with the players, an invitation was issued to Milton to bring the Seattle Symphony to play at a forthcoming Bergen Festival. Thus, our love affair with Bergen ended, one might say, on a delightful note. The next morning we departed for home. Before boarding the plane, I picked up a Bergen newspaper and found the name Katims in a lead story. I turned to a Norwegian gentleman sitting next to me and asked him if he would translate for me.

He studied the article for a few minutes, then said very seriously, "It says Bergen will always have happy memories from the happy music concert of last night." That's all I needed to know.

The Pleasure Was Ours

KENNEDY CENTER

Some of our most memorable moments were in a special visit to our own capital. The occasion was the 1971 opening of beautiful Kennedy Center, whose architectural brilliance finally gave Washington, D.C., the magnificent national cultural home it long needed.

When we learned the center's opening date, I phoned John Ehrlichman, (whom we had known well in Seattle) at the White House and was lucky enough to get through to him. These were the brighter, early days in his life as an aide to President Nixon, before all the political problems began. We had always known John to be an exceptional lawyer and a warm, caring friend, who had a profound interest in music and all the arts. After I told him that Milton and I wanted very much to attend the Kennedy Center opening, he said, "Of course. Come right ahead. And call me when you check into your hotel. I'd like to show you my office in the White House. Also, I want you to be my guests at the opening ceremonies of Kennedy Center and the dinner afterwards. First there will be a cocktail party in Georgetown, and I'd like to take you both there."

When we arrived at our Washington hotel, appropriately named The Intrigue, we phoned John, as he had directed, and he alerted White House security to expect us. He was happy as a youngster with his official status and his new responsibilities. "This is going to be the greatest administration this country has ever known," he assured us.

We believed him, too, especially if all other appointees in the Nixon administration were as bright and full of integrity as John was. He showed us through the White House. As we walked down a corridor, we saw Secretary of State Henry Kissinger coming toward us. Without waiting to be introduced I said to him, "Dr. Kissinger, I'm happy to meet you I'm a great admirer of yours."

With a smile, he said, "You have very good taste."

Those were the good, upbeat, beginning days of the Nixon administration. It was 5 p.m., and we had to get back to the hotel because John would be picking us up at six for the cocktail party. Milton and I scrambled to get ready. While he was in the shower I opened my suitcase, found my silver slippers, and looked for my formal. In desperation I dumped all the contents of the bag onto the bed. My Gawd! Where was my formal? I began to panic, my heart pounding. I picked up my purple nightie, hoping the gown might have been entangled within it. I couldn't go to the Kennedy Center opening, as well as a chi-chi party in Georgetown without an evening gown!

Could I borrow something from the hotel? No, this place wasn't elegant enough to supply guests with anything more than a toothbrush or a pair of shoelaces. Milton came out of the shower and I told him the horrible news. He spied my nightie. "What's that purple thing? Wear that!"

I looked at it, looked away, and then turned back to it. Did I dare? Well, I thought, I've always loved purple. Could I carry it off? At that late hour I didn't have a choice. I donned the floor-length nightie, which was lined with chiffon, and slipped into the matching coat, which buttoned to the floor. Then I put on my silver slippers, some gobby earrings and we dashed for the hotel entrance, where John was awaiting us with a private limo. It was all so frantic I didn't have time to worry about what might happen. The limo headed for Georgetown.

We approached a large, elegant home and John rang the doorbell. A short, stocky man opened the door. I assumed he was the butler, until John said, "Stanley, these are the Katims. Milton is the Seattle Symphony conductor and Virginia, his wife, is a fine cellist. This is Stanley Marcus."

My God! I should have known. I did know! He was the Marcus of Neiman-Marcus, and I blushed beet red as he ignored the introductions and looked me up and down. Oh, please I thought, this is it! I also thought I heard him gasp slightly as he said, "Well, I don't believe I've ever seen an outfit quite like yours." Then, as if trying to make amends for his negative tone, he added, "We'll have to try something like that at the store."

I shook his hand weakly and said, almost inaudibly, "Uh, purple is my favorite color," then hurried in to meet our hostess. I saw so many beautiful gowns at the party and again at the Kennedy Center ceremonies and the dinner, but no one was dressed in a nightie!

We made a tour of the concert hall and the Eisenhower Theater, each with fantastic sparkling chandeliers. At the dinner I was fortunate enough to sit between Dr. Kissinger and Martha Mitchell, both of them extremely witty and warm, and obviously not knowing or caring about the difference between a Parisian evening gown and a purple nightie. Martha was especially charming and made me feel very much at home.

And best of all, after two or three glasses of wine, I felt like the most elegantly gowned woman there.

Virginia on the deck of Seattle home, overlooking Lake Washington

Chapter 23
The Seattle Years

Milton: Two of the questions heard most often in the lobby after my concerts with the Seattle Symphony were: "What will he think of next?" and "How is he going to top this?" The questions were not surprising since I was following a belief that I had long held: that the most vital responsibility of a music director is creative programming.

A conductor's greatest challenge is to offer a delicate balance between the known and the unknown, the comfortable and what makes an audience stretch and grow — a balance between conservative programming and what some would term avant garde. One might also say that it is important for everyone who loves music to be exposed constantly to a good mixture of the past, the present, and the future, because they are all vital parts of the whole and important to a well rounded enjoyment of music.

Although I had assisted Toscanini and was principal guest-conductor in the last seven of my eleven years with the NBC Symphony, I realized that the programming challenges would be totally different in my new role as conductor and music director of the Seattle Symphony. In radio broadcasts, I didn't have to be concerned with box office. But if I were to be successful in building an audience, something Seattle had been struggling with for a number of years, I had to keep an eye on ticket sales.

The orchestra was in need of continuity in musical direction and inspiration after the strain of guest conductors. In addition, I realized that the symphony concerts faced heavy competition – ski slopes, hiking trails, sailing, boat launches, and gorgeous water and park sites in "God's country." To get live bodies into the concert hall was no small challenge. Concert goers would have to be attracted not only by exciting quality performances, but also by unusual programming.

In Seattle, as in most other cities, a conductor has to face the challenge posed by the inevitable resistance to new music. One man, who loathed contemporary music, pleaded with me to either open programs with the new work so he could arrive late, or close with it so that he could leave early.

I constantly clung to the conversation between two octogenarians after they heard their third performance of Stravinsky's "Le Sacre du Printemps." One remarked to the other, "Millie, do you remember when this music sounded modern to us?" I wondered about the irate lady who wrote to me saying that Gyorgy Ligeti's "Atmospheres" had been badly misnamed, that it should have been called "Air Pollution." Had she ever changed her mind?

Still I remained dedicated to the composers of our time, especially to American composers. In many circles these efforts were considered successful and worthy of recognition. Our programs included enough new music to bring me the Alice M. Ditson Award and an ASCAP Award.

I was music director of the Seattle Symphony for 22 years. After ten years of concentrating on the old and comfortable symphonic literature, the time was ripe to add more creative ideas to stimulate loyal subscribers and to attract a more diversified audience by adding other dimensions to the symphonic experience, such as painting, dance, narration, and mini- and semi-staging.

Years before the advent of multimedia events, I began to add these other art forms to our programs. In one of our very first forays into multimedia, we presented a program of music inspired by paintings: "Reger Böcklin Suite," "Hindemith Mathis der Maler," and the "Moussorgsky-Ravel Pictures at an Exhibition." I provided brief commentary before we performed the music while we projected slides of the paintings on a screen above the orchestra. In a subsequent program we played Gunther Schuller's "Seven Studies on Themes" by Paul Klee. But that time we offered the music and painting simultaneously, believing they would complement each other.

There was one visual event that stirred quite a bit of conversation and controversy and brought a large number of Northwest painters into the Opera House. Virginia and I had long enjoyed the friendship of many of the area artists. We were always intrigued by their habit of filling their studios with the sound of music while they painted. I wondered if a couple of them could be persuaded to "go public" and put paint and brush to canvas in the Opera House while we played a symphony. Two artists, Bert Garner and William Mair, were fascinated by the idea of painting on the two side stages while we played the Bruckner Seventh Symphony, which was long enough (almost an hour) to give them enough time to fulfill their artistic ideas.

On the first of three successive nights, the artist "soloists" appeared on stage not in white tie and tails, but in paint-smeared slacks, each with his "instruments" – paint, brushes, palette, and a 6-by-10-foot canvas. I had programmed the "Bruckner Seventh" for the second half of the concert. During the preceding summer I had sent each painter a recording of the Bruckner so that they would be familiar with the music. Not that I expected to see a visual concept of the music, but to get it into their hearts and minds might prove inspiring.

Milton and Virginia Katims

During the intermission the artists set up their easels on the two small side stages, one painter on the left and the other on the right. Unfortunately – or perhaps fortunately – I could not see them, even peripherally from the podium during the performance. I was told later that the experience was quite similar to watching a tennis match, with the audience turning their heads from side to side to see what each painter was doing. All seemed to go quite smoothly until about the middle of the final movement. I became aware of furtive whispering in the audience, whispering that became more and more agitated, then became mixed with barely stifled laughter. I couldn't figure out what was happening. The music certainly wasn't the cause. When we finished the symphony I rushed backstage for an explanation. I soon got one.

Bert Garner had decided to give his painting a dimension in time to mirror the temporal dimension of music. Having familiarized himself with the recording of the Bruckner over several weeks and handling his brush like a baton, he timed his strokes on the canvas to the rhythms of the music and covered the entire canvas with juxtaposed, vivid blue vignettes on the white canvas. Then he returned to the first vignette and, still painting in time to the music, he filled in all the white spaces with blue paint, then covered the last white space precisely with the final chord of the symphony. Thus, there was no longer a painting. The canvas was totally blue. This wasn't exactly what I had anticipated, but the idea was creative and stimulating.

Realizing that Bert intended to repeat his performance the next evening, this time with a bright orange over the blue, I decided to explain his creative idea to the audience (as well as to the critics) to avoid the confusion of the previous evening and to make everyone aware of his very innovative aesthetic intent. For those in the audience who were unhappy with the visual distractions of the painters, I suggested they remember that God had provided them with eyelids, not ear lids. "Just close your eyes," I suggested.

*Katims with Vera Zorina, after
her brilliant performance of
Jeanne d'Arc by Honneger*

*Dedication at a Katims lying-in of
Bruckner 7th Opera House Painting
by William Mar*

Milton and Virginia Katims

Two other pieces that brought an unusual visual dimension to programs were Varese's "Deserts" and Scriabin's "Poeme d'Extase" – not on the same evenings, of course. I was fascinated by the raw power of the Varese work, but concerned about its acceptance by the Seattle audience. I knew the music was supposed to conjure up mental images of all kinds of deserts – sand, snow, water, deserted streets, and the desert of some minds. But I wondered if it would be enough merely to project appropriate slides on a screen during the performance.

My solution was to engage the Regina Circus, a group of three young light-painters (photographers) to create on-the-spot visual images on a screen hung above the orchestra. I gave them a variety of desert slides to intersperse and combine subliminally with their light show. It came off beautifully. The audience was intrigued with the mixture of sight and sound. It was gratifying to note that the program attracted so many young people not usually seen at symphony concerts. That gave us the opportunity to introduce them to Beethoven and Ravel, the other composers on the program.

As for the Scriabin, commissioning an original movie to accompany the score seemed like a good idea at the time. But, although it aroused quite a bit of interest and conversation, the project didn't fulfill my expectations. I had hoped that the passionate music filling the pages of the score would inspire the young moviemaker to create some romantic imagery and even some eroticism. It did not!

At one performance Virginia read Shakespeare's lines for Mendelssohn's "Midsummer Night's Dream," with the soloists and women's chorus performing their parts, followed more traditional paths in symphonic fare. It was quite successful. For Family Concert performances of Strauss's "Till Eulenspiegel," I felt that our audience would enjoy the score much more if they knew exactly what the music was describing as the tale unfolded. I wrote a script for soprano Marni Nixon to read at the appropriate moments. It worked like a charm.

The Pleasure Was Ours

We had the same result with Charles Griffes' "The White Peacock," with the original William Sharp poem that had inspired the music. In another vein we programmed Allan Rawsthorne's score to T. S. Eliot's "Old Possum's Book of Practical Cats," with Virginia narrating. The Family Concert audiences loved it. (I never realized how many people were owned by cats!!)

Because the world of ballet has provided much music which is performed at symphony concerts, I could see no reason, other than the requirements of space, that dancers as soloists should not occasionally be added to the symphonic experience. Our first steps in this area came with Tamara Toumonova and Wladimir Oukhtomski dancing to Debussy's "Jeux" and Tchaikovsky's "Romeo and Juliet." The combination went so well that a couple of seasons later Melissa Hayden and Andre Prokowski were invited to appear as soloists in music by both Delibes and Sousa-Hershey Kay. Later, Hayden and Conrad Ludlow danced to parts of Mendelssohn's Italian Symphony and Tchaikovsky.

Our most unusual and exciting dance-symphonic experience was American composer William Schuman's "Judith." I had conducted this powerful score with the Detroit Symphony (without dancers) after seeing Martha Graham (to whom it is dedicated) dance "Judith" in New York at the Julliard. ((I always get a chuckle when I recall Schuman's characterization of ballet audiences. He said that they had so little discernment that if you put a half dozen hand-clappers in the pit, they wouldn't know the difference.)

By the time we were ready to program "Judith" in Seattle, Martha was no longer performing. On her recommendation I engaged Yuriko, a dancer who had worked with her. I met with Schuman in New York to plan the presentation. We decided to have Yuriko make her entrance on a shoulder-high ramp behind the orchestra. At an appropriate spot in the score she made her way around the orchestra to the downstage area to conclude her dance in front. A spotlight revealed a small tent down-stage left – the tent in which Judith, at the end of her macabre dance, beheads the tyrant Holofernes.

Milton and Virginia Katims

In planning such concert diversions, we made selections not only for their musical values, but also because they lent themselves to mini- or partial staging. Among the former were two monodramas of operatic genre: Poulenc's setting of Jean Cocteau's play, "La Voix Humaine," and Schoenberg's "Erwartung." For the Poulenc, Marni Nixon, wearing a beguiling, diaphanous gown, sang the solo role of the castoff mistress in a small bedroom that had been built in front of the orchestra. The room was furnished, as one would expect, with a chaise lounge and the all-important telephone. In case any prompting might be needed, the phone was actually connected with another one backstage, where my assistant conductor was on the alert, score in hand. All went well.

The set for "Erwartung" was less literal. Schoenberg himself had made some paintings for the monodrama. I borrowed the paintings from Mrs. Schoenberg, so that the stage manager could create the needed decor for the 10-by-16-foot stage on wheels. With the imaginative use of netting and styrofoam suitably painted, desk lights for the orchestra and myself, and a small bench with dramatic lighting aimed only at the soloist, Helga Pilareczyk, we were all set. Helga told me later that it was the most successful way to present "Erwartung" – preferable even to a fully staged performance. Here, her physical movements were confined to a very workable area.

However, the entire audience wasn't exactly in perfect harmony. As the performance ended, a man sitting directly behind Virginia hissed into her ear, "Tell your maestro that if he ever again subjects me to anything like this, I'll never come to another concert."

The rest of the audience made it clear he was in a distinct minority. I refused to be deterred from the course I had set, programming between the extremes of the very conservative and the very far-out.

It was clear to me that semi-staged works required more imagination on the part of the audience, because they had to furnish their own ideal images of the action and the scenery.

The Pleasure Was Ours

The most elaborate semi-staging was planned for Honegger's "Joan of Arc at the Stake." The entire cast of actors, soloists, chorus, and orchestra was surrounded by a light-blue cyclorama, on which very large gold fleurs-de-lis had been sewn. To the immediate left of the podium, an appropriately robed Vera Zorina played the title role, standing on a platform symbolizing the stake. Frere Dominic, in the robe of his order, sat at her feet. To the right of the podium was a table at which the other members of the speaking cast sat. In their usual places behind the orchestra stood the soloists (Joan's heavenly voices) and the chorus.

Appropriately colored lighting was used for each scene – sky blue for the Voices of Heaven, purple for the King and Royalty, yellow for the Court and the Beasts, and flaming red for the final scene, Joan of Arc in the flames. The enthusiastic response of the audience reflected its appreciation of all the labor and imagination that had gone into the production. In retrospect, perhaps a descriptive tape pointing out the action of each tableaux should have been played beforehand. However, we counted on the sophistication of our audience.

When our manager, Lanham Deal, learned that I had programmed Rimsky-Korsakoff's "Scheherazade," he suggested, "Let me try something different, something visual for this old war horse. I would like to have an attractive young lady impersonate Scheherezade and re-create a scene from the 'Arabian Nights' in the lobby of the Opera House."

I agreed, but I was surprised, nonetheless, when I entered the lobby the night of the concert. There, atop a platform of Oriental rugs, sat the very attractive daughter of the manager, gowned in crimson and gold. She looked very much like the Scheherazade of our fantasies. As can be imagined, this was the subject of considerable conversation, pro and con. One newspaper critic wrote a scathing review of the tableau.

Over the years we did build an audience, and we were sold out much of the time. Whether that was due to, or in spite of, some of our daring forays into creative adventures I don't know. Still, in spite of my belief in the value of offbeat, imaginative programming, I also continue to be a firm believer in the challenge of building interesting, "conventional" programs that are emotionally fulfilling for the audience, the members of the orchestra, and certainly for the conductor.

Virginia: The concerts took on a much different appearance from where I sat as the conductor's wife from what Milton saw and heard as the conductor. For example, on symphony nights the dinner hour was quite placid and humdrum for him, but for me it was always an anxious adventure.

"Why, oh why," I'd ask myself, "does he always insist on having steak covered with a generous blob of yogurt, plus the inevitable radishes, before a concert?" Then the doorbell would ring. At last the tailor would arrive with Milton's dress suit that I thought would never again look spanking fresh and clean after the gallons of perspiration it had absorbed just the week before. But the tailor would do it — the man was a genius. Milton lost two to three pounds at each concert! Who would believe it?

At last we'd start out for the Opera House. The conductor always liked to go early, because, as he always made sure to tell me, "We should avoid getting snarled up in that Mercer Street mess." (The Opera House is on Mercer Street, the Seattle Center's main thoroughfare.) Backstage, the pre-concert dynamic was definitely "tempestuoso." Milton would head for his dressing room; I'd straighten his white tie and brush a stray blonde hair from his shoulder (mine?). He couldn't sit because he didn't want to crush his tails. So, he'd pace, and pace, and pace.

Ruth McCreery would enter. She didn't look like an orchestra manager, but she was one, an imaginative one. She moved quickly, wearing a satin theater coat. She'd confer with Milton on lighting, length of intermission, and the number of extra musicians for future programs. She co-ordinated box office and audience arrival activities with back stage — curtain time, etc., etc.

The Pleasure Was Ours

Concertmaster Henry Siegl would arrive, checking some last-minute changes in his part and other details. They'd be all the afterthoughts that the conductor had added between the final morning rehearsal and the evening performance. You'd think it would upset the musicians; it didn't. They absorbed the turmoil because they were used to it and they were pros.

Phil Boltin, the librarian, would appear to ask, "Mr. Katims, which publisher should I contact for the music for the next concerts?" They'd settle the publisher details and some others for the next three programs. Then the assistant manager would appear, "Maestro, if you're ready, the lights are down."

I'd give my husband a quick kiss and, with a thumbs up and a smile, toss, "Hals und Bein Bruch," at him. Those words are traditional on concert stages all over the world. What do they mean? Something like the similar good-luck wish in the theater, but with a slight difference. They mean "Break a neck and leg!" I'd dash up to Box B, making it with just a moment to spare before Milton walked on stage. I'd wonder if he'd miss the podium on this night? "Nope, maybe next time." His trademark entrance always consisted of a sort of short leap, never using the first step, from the floor to the podium. I've never seen him miss it. (His tennis playing kept him agile and conditioned him for that jump, almost as if he were jumping over the net.)

I'd look around the audience at this point: Say, where was Annette? She's not in her usual seat in the tenth row. Darn it! She missed the overture and she would have adored this one, too. Verdi's "La Forza del Destino." She'll arrive just in time for the Bartok. Hope it won't jolt her husband too much. At least he can't sleep through the "Concerto for Orchestra."

It's difficult to build a program that satisfies everyone. Difficult? It's impossible. You can't build one that will excite the audience (usually Tchaikovsky does that), titillate the critics (good reviews help sell tickets), and interest the musicians enough so that they sit on the edge of their chairs while playing.

After the concert there was a feeling of "sentimento" backstage. Musicians and conductor alike would be keyed up. I wonder why more people don't go backstage in Seattle? Are they shy? Don't they know that the guest artist and conductor feel they have not communicated, nor aroused, nor moved anyone if no one goes back to grasp their hands afterwards?

Milton: Whenever she headed for the Seattle-Tacoma International Airport, Ruth McCreery, our orchestra manager, inevitably was asked where she was going. Her reply always was, "I'm going to New York to buy a new hat."

I didn't find out until I had been in Seattle for a number of months that I was once the "new hat." Conductors have been called many things, but never a "new hat." (Perhaps old hat?) Our first exploratory meetings in New York were rather formal. I had never dealt with a woman manager before (she was the only woman at the major orchestra managers annual meetings, and her presence probably softened the language during heated discussions). She was probably wondering what kind of a temperamental baton-wielder she was going to have on her hands.

As happens in most first meetings, the manager and I verbally sparred a bit while we took each other's measure. My conclusions were very positive and led to 15 years of provocative and productive working together with her to build the Seattle Symphony. La Belle McCreery was an artist in almost everything she touched. Her thought processes never slowed down. Creative ideas were constantly bubbling up and flowing over. During all the years we worked together we supported each other in whatever ideas either one of us suggested, no matter how hare-brained!

Ruth was always a source of great strength in her support of my programming philosophy. (How I missed her in an unfortunate experience I had recently guest-conducting an orchestra I will not identify. When I expressed my wish to precede the opening work on the program with an unseen voice reciting the poetic words that had inspired the music and would set the mood for the music, I was not permitted to do so. I was told to adhere to the usual concert format and not to stray from the beaten path.)

As part of the Rockefeller Foundation's Festival of American Music, Ruth arranged for the orchestra to take up residence and perform on the campuses of universities in Montana, Idaho, Oregon, and Washington. The three- or four-day visit was climaxed with a formal concert by the full orchestra. Leading up to it were open rehearsals, readings of compositions by faculty composers, master classes of all the orchestral instruments, and seminars in composition, chaired by the director of the music department.

On our visit to the University of Montana we had the luxury of having two American composers to participate in the seminar. They were Morton Gould and Alan Hovhaness. In response to a question from a composition student seeking clues to the inspiration needed for composing, Gould showed him the music notebook he always carried (a la Beethoven), in which he jotted down thematic ideas as they occurred to him. Hovhaness's reply was quite different. He pointed to the heavens above. His music, he said, was the result of divine guidance! Well, he too was in good company. Many great composers believed in the same source of inspiration.

Ruth later took on the responsibility of director of research and development for the orchestra, and she successfully designed a three-year program to bring a fully rounded musical experience to students throughout Washington State, a project approved by the U.S. Office of Education. In addition to pre-concert preparation for the students, a good deal of attention was given to preparing teachers in the use of special materials. The hope and the expectation was to discover and encourage new young talent and to give that talent an opportunity to perform both as a member of the orchestra and, if it were warranted, as a soloist. Ruth was the well-deserved recipient of the Steinway & Sons Award for Distinguished Service to Music and the Performing Arts.

Milton and Virginia Katims

I've always been amazed and fascinated by today's size of administrative staffs of performing arts groups, like the Seattle Symphony and the Seattle Opera. At last count the present Seattle Symphony staff was 42! When I arrived in Seattle, I found Ruth with a full-time director of ticket sales, Vera White, and a secretary. Grant Angle and Dick Cornwall handled publicity and promotion. Accounting and fund raising were contracted out. A short time later, Lucile Linden, who started as a volunteer, was added to the staff to take charge of the Family Concerts on a full-time basis. These programs were another product of the fertile mind of Ruth McCreery. They were begun just about the time I took over the orchestra in Seattle.

(We have devoted an entire chapter later on to the subject of the Family Concerts, an idea that has so much potential and importance to the future of music that it deserves a chapter of its own.)

With Ruth McCreery I always had to be prepared for the unexpected, but I confess it wasn't possible for me or anyone else to be ready for one incident in particular. Early one afternoon she put on her coat and quietly said to Vera White that she was leaving the office a bit early, because she had some things to do. It was a bit unusual for Ruth, but Vera didn't give it a second thought. Ruth returned to the office a week later with an explanation of where she'd been. She had gone to the hospital and given birth to a baby girl, Marcia! None of us had any idea that Ruth was pregnant. That was vintage Ruth McCreery!

She was never interested in dwelling on the past, saying, "It's much more interesting to think about the present and plan for the future." After her years as the very creative manager of the Seattle Symphony and one who helped create and execute Washington State's innovative Cultural Enrichment Program, Ruth left to develop her own Arts Unlimited agency from her apartment on San Francisco's John Muir Drive. She joined a five-year project as consultant for the National Endowment of the Arts in a nation-wide survey on the status of U.S. symphony orchestras. The motivation, as usual, was her profound interest in children and their vital role in the future of the arts.

Her credo could be stated this way, "The children must become accustomed to having the arts as a natural part of their lives. They are the fountainhead not only of tomorrow's performers and teachers, but also the source of future audiences."

Ruth felt strongly that the need for music for the young is more imperative than ever. She fairly shouts, "I not only believe in midnight basketball, but also in midnight chamber-music concerts – symphony concerts. At the rate things are going now, I'm quite sure that the three Bs are headed for oblivion."

Ruth (Mrs. Hugh Edison McCreery) is an ideal example of what scientists have known for a long time: some individuals maintain alert and inquiring minds well into their 80s and 90s if they continue to exercise their minds. Like all muscles, the brain needs to be exercised or atrophy will set in. Intellectual functions do not decline, as was once believed. Having new experiences, reading new books, following current events, socializing, staying involved, and keeping the mind active are the best predictors of those who are going to continue to do well. The biggest mistake many people make is to retire and decide they don't have to think any more. Of course, education is a never-ending lifelong passion and process.

*V*irginia: During our years in Seattle, just before the symphony season began, we put on a wonderful ball called Symphoneve, which was designed to raise money for the orchestra. Many other cities do the same.

Symphoneve is glamorous, gives everyone a chance to wear their most handsome apparel, and is a great deal of fun. I've been head of and been involved in many of the parties. Once we invited Hubert de Givenchy to attend and bring some of his fabulous collection. That event landed the party in full-page photos in *Life* magazine. Givenchy, an elegant man, used many of our own glamour women as models. We served great French wines, had a gourmet French menu, and danced to a super band.

Milton and Virginia Katims

On another occasion we had a Greek evening, with many of us forming a circle and dancing to the music of Melina Mercouri and her "band." Later on we invited the extraordinary Italian fashion designer, Emilio Pucci, to attend a Symphoneve and show off his wares. That happened after Milton had conducted in Florence, Italy, where we met Emilio and invited him to Seattle.

Many of the fashion designers are eager to attend cultural events if they can show off their clothes. One year we invited Pierre Cardin to a Symphoneve, and he brought some fabulous clothes, but what I really remember is how the little designer seemed to reach only up to my nose by standing on my feet when we danced and whirled around the floor.

Another time we arranged a truly French evening and called it "A Night in Monte Carlo." Of course we had gambling, which seemed quite daring at the time. Our symphony president, Gordon Scott, was so worried that the police might drop in that he manned the gaming tables himself.

I entertained a great deal during Milton's tenure with the Seattle Symphony. He would come home after a concert, saying, "We were sold out again." I would counter with, "No wonder, they've all been to our house for dinner."

Early on I started a group I called "Symfunics." It was designed to attract young single professional men and women to become interested in symphonic music. Milton and I met with the group once or twice a month and talked to them about the music to be played in upcoming programs. We played recordings or tapes of many works, and we often had the artists who were to solo with the orchestra come to our home for those Symfunics meetings. We would talk about the music and play excerpts, as well. These meetings were fabulously successful. I finally added a "Wids and Divs" group (Widows, Widowers, and Divorcees).

Chapter 24
A Conductor's Art and Life

Milton: At one of my kibbutz concerts with the Israel Philharmonic years ago (1953), a newly arrived Yemenite asked what the conductor was doing on the podium. When he was told that the man with the baton actually added no sound to the music as he waved his baton, the fellow shrugged his shoulders, and asked, "Who needs him?"

Many decades ago, New York City had a short-lived conductorless orchestra. But that's not entirely accurate. The orchestra actually did have a number of "conductors." With the musicians seated in an elliptical configuration so that each player could see the concertmaster and/or the head of his section, the concertmaster gave the signals when to start and when to stop, as well as to indicate the tempos, much like the first violinist of a string quartet. The players were all fine musicians and had no difficulty starting, staying together, and finishing together. But there was one very serious flaw in the performances — they lacked the imprint of one individual's musical ideas. I cannot overemphasize that an exciting, inspired musical concept cannot be the result of a committee's thinking and feelings.

Only one glaring exception comes to mind – and that was very temporary. Immediately after the retirement of Maestro Toscanini and the dissolution of the NBC Symphony, the orchestra's players determined to remain and perform together. They chose an appropriate name – Symphony of the Air. With a conspicuously empty podium in front of them, they performed a couple of Carnegie Hall concerts. Being fresh from 17 years under the very demanding and highly disciplined baton of Toscanini, with his ever-exciting musical concepts still strong in their minds, hearts and fingers, their performances were remarkably good. But that wouldn't last!

The reality? A symphony orchestra cannot survive as a democracy. By its very nature, an orchestra must have a single leader – a leader who can't help but be a bit of a despot, hopefully a benevolent one. In his excellent book The Grammar of Conducting, Max Rudolph points out that conducting "is a very complex job." I would add that it is also an "esoteric" occupation. Rudolph writes: "The conductor must be a trained musician who knows how to work with and convey his musical intentions to a large group of players by means of physical signals."

But while it may be possible to easily and quickly explain these visible mechanical aspects of conducting, those elements are merely the tip of the iceberg. The vastly greater substance of the art of conducting lies beneath the surface. It embraces the infinite number of intangibles that defy precise description. This is the vast part that makes conducting almost impossible to teach.

Let's assume that a young, aspiring (male, for the sake of conversation) conductor is a good musician, that he has a good ear, that he has an adequate understanding of the capabilities of the various orchestral instruments, that he can read a score, and that he is comfortable with the established semaphoric system of conducting. But now consider just a few of the remaining challenges faced by the "teacher" (male, same reason) of conducting.

The Pleasure Was Ours

How does he begin to inculcate a natural physical coordination of ear, eye, and hand? How does he teach the ability to inspire a large group of players to respond to and help recreate the mental image he has of a piece of music? How does he help the young man (or woman, of course) arrive at the true tempo and the true character of a work that approximate the intention of the composer? How does he teach the elusive, but essential, elements of a conductor's being – his innermost feelings and, hopefully, his emotional involvement? How does he teach charisma?

Of all of the elements just mentioned, the most important for me is emotional involvement – the heart's being guided by the head. When I am playing the viola and my instrument is virtually a physical part of me, the musical experience is naturally very subjective. Being emotionally involved just seems to follow. However, the same is not true of conducting.

Dimitri Mitropoulos once told me that when he conducted, he felt almost like an outsider looking on much of the time. And so he made every effort to be a physical part of the music making. I'm quite sure that Lenny Bernstein must have been of the same mind. He was all over the podium, throwing himself in every direction and, at times, leaping off the podium.

At one of his concerts with the Israel Philharmnic, Lenny almost came to grief. It happened during his reading of Tchaikovsky's dramatic "Francesca da Rimini." At one climactic spot in the exciting score, Lenny lunged so fiercely toward the second violins that he literally flew off the podium.

After one of my guest appearances with the New York Philharmonic, Virginia and I were crossing Broadway behind a couple who evidently had just come from the concert. We could not help overhearing their conversation. The wife said, "Katims must have a different choreographer than Bernstein."

Husband, "Why, what do you mean?"

Wife, "Didn't you notice? Katims' feet never left the podium."

349

Milton and Virginia Katims

How can I describe what makes a really good conductor, let alone a great one? The moment an eminent conductor stands before an orchestra – before he even lifts his baton, he has already placed his imprint on the orchestra – as well as on the audience. Although relatively few in the audience may be aware of it, those few cannot help but sense a chemistry – an electric current that runs from the conductor to his players and to his audience!

I believe that the only way to learn how to conduct is to conduct! Call it on-the-job training, if you will. I was most fortunate in this regard. Conducting radio broadcasts made it possible for me to gain invaluable experience in my craft. When I started, almost every large radio station employed a staff orchestra. All broadcasts were live.

My association with Leon Barzin and the National Orchestral Association gave me many opportunities to learn my conductorial ABCs on the podium. On one of my very first efforts, I had been studying the "Beethoven First Symphony" from a miniature score in which an instrument is completely omitted from a page if it doesn't have a part to play. Because of that omission, at one point I mistakenly made a grand gesture to the trumpets, believing they were to play. They didn't, they pointed to the French horns. I didn't make that mistake again.

At WOR (Mutual Broadcasting System) in New York, I had to learn very quickly to conduct efficiently, to make every expensive rehearsal minute count. I was given many opportunities to conduct the "Wallenstein Sinfonietta," the "Symphonic Strings," and other programs. I didn't realize at the time that I was actually grooming myself for the move to NBC and Toscanini's fabulous symphony orchestra, as well as for all the symphonic doors that would open for me.

When the guest-conducting invitations began coming with greater frequency, I soon discovered the need to recognize the unique style of each orchestra. My first unfortunate brush with French musicians came in a broadcast concert I conducted in Paris for Radio Diffusion. I was in no way prepared for the complete lack of discipline that made a shambles of that encounter with the French players.

The Pleasure Was Ours

(In an earlier chapter I related the incident a few years later in which a French audience booed my playing Tchaikovsky's "Romeo & Juliet" instead of "Rachmaninoff Dances" because the music originally scheduled failed to arrive in time. French audiences are not much different than their musicians, it appears. They deserve each other. As if that weren't enough of an irritant, no one warned me that the French musicians did not acknowledge understanding one word in English! And my French was pitiful.)

It was very different in Japan – 180 degrees different. There, the players who understood English quickly translated my words for their colleagues. In Tokyo, where I spent six weeks guest-conducting the Japan Philharmonic, I was fortunate to find that a long-time friend, violinist Louis Graeler, at one time a member of the NBC Symphony, was concertmaster of the Japan Philharmonic. When we met before my first rehearsal, he briefed me on the mores of working with an Asian orchestra. "Never be critical of a player in front of his peers," Louis cautioned. "Always precede any request or suggestion with some positive words of praise."

I certainly appreciated his words of advice and heeded them to my advantage. The Japanese musicians were extraordinary in many respects. I was also most impressed with their ability to mimic precisely what they had just heard. At times during a break in a rehearsal, I would pick up a viola and play a passage or two from a sonata or a concerto. When I returned the instrument to its owner, he/she would amaze me by playing the same passage with exactly the same bowing and fingering. I couldn't do that if my life depended on it.

Although I really enjoyed making music with the Japan Philharmonic, I found one aspect somewhat disconcerting. When musicians play, the shades of emotion evoked by the music are usually reflected in their facial expressions. Although the Japanese musicians played beautifully and were no doubt emotionally involved, none of it was reflected in their facial expressions, which remained quite immobile. Some years later in Shanghai, I discovered that this wasn't true of the Chinese musicians, whose faces mirrored the emotion of what they were feeling.

Japanese concert audiences, too, are quite special. Throughout a performance they are incredibly quiet, nary a cough nor a sneeze can be heard. At the concerts, with my back to the concertgoers, of course, I was never quite sure the people were still there. Also, I was concerned that at the end of each work the response was rather tepid. I didn't know whether or not they liked the performance. However, at the end of the concert they more than made up for their quietness, and my concern would turn to joy.

In a way they were somewhat like the audiences I had found in Israel, where on three separate visits I spent six weeks conducting the Israel Philharmonic. The Israelis, however, did not wait until the end of a concert to respond to the music. They let the conductor and musicians know how they felt right from the start. When I followed my piano soloist, Shura Cherkassky, onto the stage of the large outdoor theater in the Tel Aviv suburb of Ramat Gan, I could see the people in the audience settling back in their seats with smiles of pleasurable expectation, as they awaited the familiar opening chords of Tchaikovsky's "B-Flat-Minor Piano Concerto." But when Shura and I began the much less frequently played "G-Major Concerto," (a specialty of Cherkassky) I distinctly heard groans and disappointed sighs of, "Oy vey!"

When American tenor Jan Peerce sang with me in the same arena, the audience greeted him with wild applause and whistles. Jan held up his hand and addressed the crowd, "In America, when people whistle in the concert hall, they express approval. But in Europe whistling is a No-No. What do you mean?"

The Israelis promptly responded with vociferous applause, sans whistles! I have always admired and felt very close to Israeli audiences.

Years before the Mann Auditorium was built in Tel Aviv, the Israel Philharmonic rehearsed in the Ohel Shem, which was simply a very large room with a stage at street level in a congested section of Tel Aviv. When concerts were going on, automobile traffic was rerouted away from the area. But we had no such luxury during rehearsals. All of the barred windows had to be left wide open because of the excessive July heat and the absence of air-conditioning in those early days. Braying donkeys in the street added their counterpoint and vocal complaints to the orchestration. Curious street urchins, with eyes filled with wonder at the mysteries of a symphony rehearsal, clung to the bars on each open window. But I loved having them there because they were very quiet and in no way added to the clamor coming from the street.

Once, in complete frustration at having to repeat a request I had made of the double basses several times, I lost my cool and began yelling at them, Toscanini-style. Then I heard one of the bass players say to his desk-mate, "Vus schreit er, der meschuginah?" ("What's that crazy guy yelling about?") I started to laugh, and that broke the tension. With my blond Swedish wife, Virginia, sitting in the hall, and my own ethnically ambiguous name, they had no idea that I could understand simple Yiddish!

Standing on the podium in front of the Israel Philharmonic was like facing 96 conductors. They all knew everything better than I did. I would not have been surprised to find that each player had a baton hidden up his sleeve, or one not hidden at all. But I suppose that's true of almost every orchestra. I'm sure the ego of every good musician leads him to believe he can do as well, if not better, than the man on the podium.

My first two trips to Israel were in 1952 - 1953, very early in the life of that young democracy. I was impressed by the vital place of music in the life of the new nation. In fact, music was an absolutely emotional necessity. I found remarkably sensitive responses in the most unexpected places. Taxi drivers were particularly knowledgeable and surprisingly accurate in their assessment of performances. But of course, I should not have been surprised. At this early date there were comparatively few Sabras — native born. Most of the audience had brought their taste with them from Europe.

Milton and Virginia Katims

One of the greatest challenges in Israel was the need to repeat the same program 11 or 12 times because of the amazingly large number of subscribers in Tel Aviv. It is obvious that the audiences were different each night. But my concern was to keep the orchestra interested and on its musical toes – to make each performance seem like a first.

Each orchestra has a personality of its own, and I was aware of this, particularly in moving from one country to another. But one aspect is very much the same no matter where a conductor goes: The first few minutes of the first rehearsal are the most important moments with any orchestra. It is during this time that the orchestra and the guest-conductor make a judgment of each other. Someone once pointed out the similarity between this process and that of a rider mounting a strange horse. The first moments establish who will be the boss.

I once experienced a ludicrous variation of those "first moments" at NBC when I was called upon in an emergency to conduct a very large jazz ensemble. The regular conductor, "Hot Lips" Levine, was ill. As I took my place in front of the large group, all of whom knew me as a musical "square," I must have looked somewhat uncomfortable because one of the players sang out, "Don't sweat it, Milt! Give us a downbeat, and get the hell out of the way!"

My first rehearsal with the Philadelphia Orchestra started on an unusual note. It was an unseasonably warm September day. Before stepping on the podium I removed my sweater. Suddenly I felt a blast of cold air coming up from the floor of the podium. I had no idea that Eugene Ormandy, the Philadelphians' regular conductor, had had a three-quarter-ton air-conditioning unit attached to the bottom of the podium. As I retrieved my sweater, Dave Madison, the assistant concertmaster, quipped, "They must have it set at the guest-conductor pneumonia level"

I began the rehearsal with Brahms' "Fourth Symphony," forgetting that the Philadelphia Orchestra played with the "organ" or slightly delayed response to the beat. I was accustomed to the Toscanini immediate response. I waited to hear the first two notes before giving the next beat. Anshel Brusiloff, concertmaster, quickly yelled, "Keep going, keep going! We'll be along presently."

I seem to have had more than my share of unusual happenings with the Brahms' "Fourth." One of the most unforgettable of them came in Seattle. Because I don't grip the baton tightly, it flew out of my hand when I gave a very strong upbeat in the Passacaglia, the final movement. The baton flew straight up into the air. Every head in the orchestra went up with it – and, I imagine most of the heads in the audience, too. I continued conducting and caught the errant stick with my left hand as it came down. To this day I still meet music lovers in Seattle who remember the night I caught the flying baton – but, not surprisingly, they can't remember what music I was conducting at the time.

Other works in the symphonic repertoire have provided unique memories. The first one that comes to mind is Respighi's "Pines of Rome." An unusual amount of movement on the part of certain players is required during the performance of this fascinating work. In the second section, the Catacombs, the solo trumpet player goes offstage to play a distant sounding solo passage. In the next part, Pines of Gianicolo, one of the percussionists goes off to play the recording of a nightingale. In the final movement, Pines of the Appian Way, six brass players walk on-stage to add their musical voices to the powerful ending.

After concluding a program with the Respighi in a Dallas Symphony concert, Virginia and I went to a reception. The moment we arrived the hostess hurried over to us and began to apologize for the lack of discipline in the Dallas Symphony. When I realized she was referring to the way the players were walking on and off the stage, I discreetly refreshed her memory of Music 101.

At a performance of "Pines of Rome" in the Hollywood Bowl, I asked the audio engineers in charge of the sound channeled through the six towers that they confine the sound of the nightingale to a single tower, the one next to the shell, in the middle of a large tree. It worked perfectly. After the concert, however, a couple of friends told me how much they enjoyed the Respighi, but did I hear that damned bird singing in the tree?

Another piece of music that is replete with anecdotal material is Tchaikovsky's "1812 Overture." The first time I programmed it in Seattle, I searched in vain for a small cannon to bring off the 11 or 12 shots indicated in the score. I finally settled for two shotguns, which two percussion players would aim into an empty barrel off-stage. I borrowed the two guns shortly before our first rehearsal and had them with me in the kitchen of our Laurelhurst home, which overlooks Lake Washington. Our daughter, Pam, was with me.

"You know," I said to her, "I've never fired one of these things." She suggested I take a shotgun outside, aim it at the lake, and fire it. So I did. But I failed to notice the psychiatrist who lived right below us was working in his garden. At the sound of the gun he shot up from behind a huge rock and shouted, "What the hell do you think you're doing, Katims?"

I responded meekly, "Oh, I'm so sorry. I was just auditioning this shotgun."

After a performance of the Tschaikowsky "1812 Overture," a well-known Seattle dowager stormed into my dressing room and heatedly berated me for tampering with the Tchaikovsky score by adding the cannon shots! But, at least I didn't lose my audience the way Leopold Stokowski did many years ago in a Mexican town. At the sound of the first shot, the entire audience, convinced that another revolution had started, dashed out and fled into the hills. Then there was the experience Erich Leinsdorf had with the Rochester Philharmonic in the Eastman Theater. At the sound of the first cannon shot, three students hidden in the rafters in the ceiling of the theater emptied three bags full of pigeon feathers, which floated down on the audience.

Virginia's mother was always fond of reminding us that "music will open many doors." She was so right. For me, it has opened doors in some 15 countries on five continents and has brought me into close contact with great artists, whom I profoundly admire. The joy of making music with them has been immeasurable.

The Pleasure Was Ours

In every city in which I have waved my baton or played my viola, music has introduced us to the most interesting people – people who shared our love of music and whose lives also would be incomplete without music. Having had the joy of making music for a livelihood makes me the most privileged man alive. I have a confession to make: I would have done it all free of charge!

Top left inset: 12 year old Danny soloed with Katims and Israel Philharmonic

Gifted maestro of the Chicago Symphony Daniel Barenboim (also a fine pianist)

Chapter 25

UnThemely Variations, Untold Mini-Tales

The Seattle Opera House

Milton: My primary motivation in working hard to build a proper hall for the orchestra to play in was to make possible an adequate income for the members of my orchestra. Adding concerts for the symphony to play was a slow process. But a new hall would make possible opera and ballet performances almost immediately, increasing the earnings of the musicians. My next step was to negotiate an umbrella contract with the musicians union, which would cover all three-symphony, opera and ballet.

For the opening of the Opera House, the unanimous choice for the most appropriate opera was, of course, "Aida" by Verdi. The glorious music of this dramatic score was constantly coursing through my heart and mind. Shortly before leaving New York, I had assisted Toscanini in one of the first televised concert performances of the opera, and I could hardly wait to be a part of the first performances of a stage production of "Aida" in the new hall.

We put together a first rate cast: Gloria Davey in the title role, Sandor Konya as Rhadames, Irene Dalis as Amneris, Robert Merrill in the part of Amanasro, and Harry Horner was stage director. Because the hall was still to be completed, the U.S. Navy gave us permission to set up the very large pieces of scenery on Pier 91. That was where all of our initial rehearsals took place. No expense was spared. And so, despite three sold out successful performances, the symphony incurred a deficit of $90,000.

Raising that money to pay off the debt was the genesis of PONCHO, the brainchild of jewelry businessman Paul Friedlander. It has been going strong ever since. Each year this popular auction benefit for all of the cultural organizations in the Northwest raises more than a million dollars.

During those first years, the Seattle Symphony continued to produce operas and I continued to conduct. I brought stage director Glynn Ross to Seattle to help me. One of the next operas I conducted was "Carmen" by Bizet. Singing the title role was Gloria Lane, who not only had a glorious voice, but also was quite voluptuous. I remember because so many of my friends (men) moved up to the boxes and the balcony to have a better view during the performances. I soon decided that if the opera were to flourish and the symphony to continue its growth, the opera and the symphony should be separate entities, tied together only by the musicians. The symphony board agreed with me. I believe the growth of the two organizations has confirmed my thinking.

Igor Stravinsky, Composer

Besides Van Cliburn as piano soloist, as a major attraction of the symphony concert celebrating the opening of the new Opera House in Seattle in 1962, I invited the legendary Russian composer, Igor Stravinsky, to conduct his popular "Suite From the

Firebird." An unexpected, but welcome, bonus was my being able to spend many hours with him that day. Quite naturally, almost all of our conversations were about music. I say almost because of the second of two very important pieces of advice he gave me.

The first was: "In performance, always accent the unexpected." He was right on. I have followed that advice since that day. Just as Accent added to food heightens its taste, accents strategically placed in music give added excitement to a performance. The second piece of advice Stravinsky gave me was: "Always drink the most expensive Scotch." And he set an example by starting to drink Chivas Regal at 9 in the morning! (My friend John Erling, program annotator, reminds me that there are more expensive brands of Scotch.)

Having Danny Kaye drop in on the morning rehearsal was another unexpected bonus. (We had first met when he came to Seattle to conduct a benefit concert a few years earlier and had invited me to his home in L.A. for a home cooked Chinese dinner.) As we sat talking with Stravinsky, Danny told us that his family name was really Kaminsky and I revealed that my grandmother's name was Katimsky. That's all Danny needed to set him going into one of his famed rapid-fire tongue twisters. Stravinsky -Katimsky and Kaminsky.

Jack Benny, Violinist(?), Comedian

One gift that I prize very much is a mug inscribed: "For Toasting Milton's "Tinth" (signed) Jack Benny, November 5th, 1964." He was such a delight to work with when he came to do a benefit concert for the symphony. And he really could play the violin. To kid around on the fiddle the way he did, you have to know what you are doing.

Milton and Virginia Katims

Leonard Bernstein, Conductor, Composer, Pianist, Teacher

As we've written earlier, Virginia and I were great admirers of the multi-gifted Leonard Bernstein, conductor, composer, pianist, and teacher. Of all his great talents, I would, without hesitation, put his inspired teaching at the top! When he devoted a broadcast to a single work, like the "Beethoven Fifth," he would begin with a set of instructions to help his listeners concentrate fully on the music. I remember how faithfully Virginia followed his instructions. She disconnected the phone, shut the window blinds, sat in a comfortable chair, and emptied her mind of all extraneous thoughts in order to make room for the great music and the verbal program notes she was about to hear. Lenny was just great!

Across the years I periodically programmed Bernstein compositions, which I admired very much. When I conducted his "Kaddish Symphony," which calls for a narrator, I was fortunate enough to coax Lenny's beautiful and gifted wife, actress Felicia Montealegre, to narrate the work. Her performance was eloquent. When she visited our home, she admired the glorious view of Lake Washington, the Cascades, and Mount Rainier. She was enraptured. She said it reminded her so much of her native Chile.

One of Lenny's disappointments was his not being fully accepted by critics as a composer of serious music. His great creative versatility may well have been the reason. The niche into which most critics cast him was as a great composer for the musical theater, with "West Side Story" the crown jewel. When I told him that his "Serenade for Violin and Orchestra" had received rave reviews when I conducted it with Isaac Stern, he wistfully said, "You do better with my music than I do."

When Lenny last visited Seattle with the New York Philharmonic, we hosted a party for him and the orchestra's leading players. While most of the guests were drinking wine, Lenny asked Virginia not to give him wine, but straight Scotch in a wine glass. The stem of the wine glass she chose was a replica of the voluptuous statue of Bacchus,

*Milton with
Igor Stravinsky,
opening of Opera Hosue
in 1962*

*1962 – In the
new Opera House*

*Milton with composer Aaron
Copland in Paris after performance of "Appalachian Spring"*

A Brahms viola-piano sonata with Abbey Simon (University of Houston)

the god of wine. At one point during the evening, Virginia noticed Lenny fondling the figure of Bacchus. Virginia, who is given to posing bold questions, asked him, "What gives Lenny?" His reply? "You know my problem, Virginia. I can't make up my mind which way to go."

We took Lenny to a wine-tasting party on the top floor of the old Frederick & Nelson building after store hours. When leaving, I escorted Lenny to an elevator that was programmed to take us non-stop to the street floor. However, it made an unscheduled stop on one of the middle floors. Before I could stop him he dashed off the lift, saying, "I've often dreamed of being in a situation like this and being able to shoplift!"

He saw a plastic banana on a display and pocketed it. When I observed that he'd be leaving town, but that I'd be staying to face the music, he put a $10 bill atop the display and we headed back to the elevator. When I related this incident to Bill Street, then president of Frederick & Nelson, he chuckled and said a cleaning lady was undoubtedly $10 richer the next morning.

Many years ago, during one of my visits with my parents in Hollywood, Florida, I was introduced to Lenny's father. Naturally Mr. Bernstein and I spoke about his enormously gifted son. I was particularly interested in his early childhood. The conversation stopper was when Lenny's father said, "How was I to know he would turn out to be Leonard Bernstein?"

Aaron Copland, Composer

Among the friends who made their way into my tiny dressing room after I conducted a broadcast of the Radio Diffusion Orchestra in Paris was, to my amazement, composer Aaron Copland, whom I had known since I was ten years old when he and my older brother, Herman, had been high school classmates. (Herman brought Aaron to our home one day after school. I recall his sitting down at our Mason &

Hamlin grand to play a short piece he had just written. It was "Kitten on the Keys.")
My program in Paris had included his popular "Appalachian Spring."

After the others left, Aaron remained so we could have a short visit. He liked my
performance of his music, but he questioned the way I had conducted one particular section of the suite – a section in which the challenge to the conductor is considerable because of the constantly changing meter. He wanted to know why I conducted it the hard way, observing each change in meter. When he told me that he ignored
them and simply conducted the entire section in 4/4 time, I was tempted to murder
him on the spot!

Leopold Stokowski, Conductor

My very first meeting with Stokowski was when he was assembling the
American Youth Orchestra for a tour of South America. Saul Caston, first trumpet
of the Philadelphia Orchestra with "Stokie," suggested that I get in touch with the
Maestro with the thought of my joining the Youth Orchestra as solo violist and assistant conductor. At that time I had achieved a modest reputation as a pretty good violist and conductor. After a brief phone call, I was scheduled to meet Stokowski at his
apartment the following day.

At the appointed hour I knocked on the door of his apartment and heard him
respond with, "Just one moment!" And then, "Come in." When I opened the door
and looked across the foyer to the living room, I saw him sitting in a large armchair,
which resembled a throne. Two shafts of blue light from opposite ends of the large
room met perfectly at his immaculately coiffed head. They had the effect of creating
a light blue halo on his head. After recovering from my mild shock at the scene that
confronted me, I told him that Saul Caston had recommended that we meet to consider his inviting me to join his orchestra as solo violist and assistant conductor.

Stokowski completely ignored the assistant conductor bit and asked when I could audition (viola) for him. (That jarred my ego quite a bit.) I suggested that my work as a free-lance violist in New York City and my work at WOR (Mutual Broadcasting) as both violist and conductor should obviate the need for an audition. I have never forgotten his response! He said, "You obviously are doing very well! You go your way, and I'll go mine."

The next time we met was when I had been playing viola at the first desk of the NBC Symphony for a few years and Stokowski was the guest conductor. It was as if we had never met! Nonetheless, now playing under his direction, I was more than a little impressed with his tight hold over the orchestra, almost immediately putting his unique imprint on us, the most important elements being beauty of tone and transparency of sound. (Terry Teachout succinctly summed up Stokowski's unique genius in a *TIME* {12-13-99} article in the following sentence – "Conducting Dukas' 'Sorcerer's Apprentice' in the original 'Fantasia,' Stokowski hypnotizes an anonymous band of Hollywood studio musicians into sounding like the Philadelphia Orchestra.")

But he was given to unforgivable exaggeration! The nth degree of this kind of music making was when we began to rehearse the Prelude from "Tristan & Isolde" (Wagner). The vastly exaggerated slow, wide vibrato that he requested from the strings should have been marked vomitoso! Joseph Gingold, the first violinist sitting right behind the concertmaster, decided to really let him have it. He played with a wildly tasteless vibrato. Stokowski stopped the rehearsal and turned to Gingold, asking, "What is your name, sir?" "Gingold, Joseph Gingold." "Mr. Gingold. You are the only one playing as I asked."

In his programming with the NBC Symphony Stokowski departed from his usual proclivity to perform far out contemporary scores. (He didn't even program one of his great Bach transcriptions.) One of the composers he espoused was the German Karlheinz Stockhausen. I recall when Virginia and I were captives of a 95 minute work by that German composer when we were at the University of Houston. I use the word captive advisedly because we were part of an audience in the round, with Stockhausen presiding over a huge tape deck with manipulated (prepared) tape in the center. There were four soloists – two singers, a clarinetist, and a trumpet player. They stood at the four points of the compass. We, the audience, sat in a complete circle around Stockhausen. After about five or six minutes I had had more than enough, but we could not move without causing an international scandal. After all, I was Artistic Director of the School of Music presenting the famous composer.

The following day, when I reported our experience to a British professor on my faculty, she asked if I knew what Sir Thomas Beecham replied when asked his opinion Stockhausen's music. He said, "Stockhausen? I have never heard any of his music. I've stepped in it!!"

For the following tale I'm depending on the veracity of one of the pages at NBC who told me this story. During the period that "Stokie" was married to Gloria Vanderbilt, she was taking part in an NBC radio program. Whenever there was a script change, this young man would deliver the altered script to Gloria. One day as she was coming into the foyer of her apartment building on Park Ave, she met the courier stepping out of the elevator. He told her that he had just left the new script with her grandmother. (He had not recognized the famous old conductor who answered the door in his bathrobe with his long white hair completely disheveled.)

Zubin Mehta, Conductor

One of the most flamboyant of Leonard Bernstein's successors at the helm of the New York Philharmonic was Zubin Mehta, who conducted with almost the same measure of excitement and emotion as his predecessor. In

Portrait of Maestro Katims by M.E. Smith

*Composer Morton Gould
& dancer-choregrapher
George Ballanchine with
Katims after a perform-
ance in Lincoln Center
(New York)*

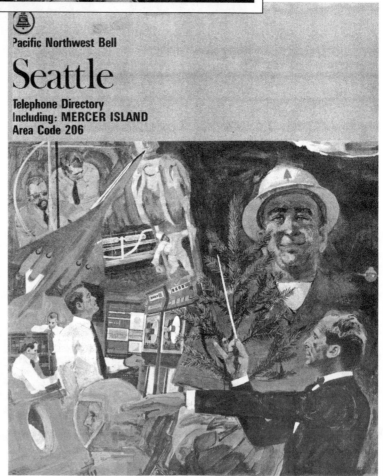

*15th anniversary as
conductor of the SSO
(Milton's portrait on the cover
of March 1969 phone book)*

my years of friendship with Zubin, we carried on a running feud over which of us was the better ping-pong player. Each time we met, we resumed play.

Our casual, ongoing "tournament" was a virtual tie when we finally stopped competing. I don't remember who was ahead at the time. But I do remember the last game, because we played mixed doubles. Zubin's partner was a very attractive, young pianist, whose name I can't remember. My partner was the well known concert manager, Kazuko Hillyer. Unlike the usual concept of a Japanese woman as a quiet-spoken, sedate lady, Kazuko was the most aggressive woman ping-pong player I've ever seen. Thanks to her, we "slaughtered" Zubin and his pretty partner. Zubin's quip after he had been the victim of one of Kazuko's bullet-like passing shots, "Look at her. Women's rib!"

Arthur Fiedler, Conductor (Honorary Fire Chief)

In Boston where the Lowells speak only to the Cabots, and the Cabots speak only to God, everybody spoke to Arthur Fiedler! And he spoke to the world through the music of his Boston Pops! His recipe for success? A rousing performance of a Johann Strauss waltz is just as important as a Beethoven symphony. As he explained it, "A good slice of beef gives much pleasure, but a fluffy dessert gives as much and sometimes more pleasure."

Fiedler knew quite well what he was talking about – he was a gourmet. He didn't mind confessing that he once made and won a bet with a San Francisco newspaperman that he could consume a $100 dinner. (That would be no feat today.) And he chuckled delightedly because the bill actually came to $109! The dinner, which took three and a half hours to eat, ran the gamut from gray caviar and very fresh bay shrimp (brought to the restaurant by taxi from San Francisco Bay) through the main dish of pheasant under glass with wild rice to a fluffy dessert topped off with

Napoleon brandy, all accompanied by a marvelous French burgundy. It was a fantastic experience, but also a well-balanced meal.

For some fifty years Arthur Fiedler served up a well-balanced musical diet to the world and to Bostonians. He was born in Boston and played violin in their famous symphony orchestra when he was 20 years old. In 1929 he launched the first of the now well known Esplanade Concerts, free outdoor Pops presented on the banks of the Charles River. Then in 1930 he became the conductor of the Boston Pops, which, under his canny direction, delighted audiences for over 50 years. I know how much he delighted Seattle audiences when he guest conducted my orchestra.

The only compositions he had to avoid programming were those in which the orchestration called for a siren, because the sound of one stimulated his grabbing his fireman's hat and his honorary Fire Chief badge and dashing off to the scene of the fire!

Morton Gould, Composer, Conductor

My musical association with composer Morton Gould began when we were in our teens. Although we lived in widely separate sections of Brooklyn, music brought us together. Some years later when I was the solo violist at WOR, Morton, who had established himself as a conductor, composer and arranger, was engaged to conduct a series of programs at WOR. When I kidded him about his whirlwind career, I found he took special delight in telling me that he knew he had arrived when he walked into the corner drug store one day and heard the clerk whistling the Pavane from his "American Symphonette."

Morton was known for his slick ability to arrange familiar tunes in the style of a well known composer, like Mozart, Schubert, or Gershwin. Each of his broadcasts contained one of these arrangements. In one of his jazzier settings, he included a riff for solo viola to be played up at the mike. Although I tried my best to meet the jazzy challenge, I was mortified (I almost said Mortonfied) when he stopped me and said, feigning scorn, "Ye Gods! Milton, you sound as if you're playing a Bach suite!"

My next musical encounter with him came some years later when he wrote a viola concerto for me to premiere with conductor Frank Black and the NBC Symphony. As he completed each section of the concerto, he would invite me to his house to read through it to advise him if there were passages that would be impossible to play. Morton's father usually sat in one corner of the living room shaking his head and constantly chiding Morton with, "Why do you write music no one wants to listen to?"

When the concerto was finally finished, I played its world premiere on one of the Sunday broadcasts of the NBC Symphony, and it seemed to go quite well. The next morning I had a rehearsal with Maestro Toscanini, and he asked me if I had played the viola concerto the day before. I nodded, hopefully. He put his arm around my shoulder and said, consolingly, "You poor man."

Glenn Gould, Pianist

I had heard about the sensational Canadian pianist, Glenn Gould, long before I met and made music with him. Word of the up-and-coming talent came during my rehearsals with the New York Piano Quartet, whose violinist, Alexander ("Sasha") Schneider, had "discovered" Glenn and raved about him.

My first encounter with Gould came when I was engaged to guest-conduct the Montreal Symphony, with Glenn as soloist. As he began playing the "Bach D-Minor Concerto" at the first rehearsal I wondered what was wrong with the piano. With each note he played I heard a "tst, tst, tst" sound. I wondered if the piano technician had checked the piano before the rehearsal. It wasn't until I turned to ask Gould if he, too, heard that sound that I realized he was the cause. He was vocally articulating every note he played. I'd heard many jazz musicians doing that, but never a world-renowned piano soloist.

It was only the first of many discoveries I was to make about the quirky, but enormously gifted pianist. Not long after the Montreal concert, I invited him to appear with the Seattle Symphony. He played beautifully, but his behavior was not to be believed. For starters, I learned that he was either terribly absent-minded or didn't care a whit about his appearance. His concert clothing looked as if he had slept in it. Before going onstage I had to put him through a spot-check, making sure his shirttail was tucked in, that his tie was fairly straight, that his shoelaces were tied and, finally, that his fly was zipped up.

I quit trying to shake his hand after a performance. He was so sensitive and protective of his hands that the most I could do – or anyone could do – was to touch pinkies carefully. I grew accustomed to seeing him wearing gloves and a scarf around his neck, no matter how warm the room was. At the first rehearsal in the old Orpheum Theater, before he had played one note, Glenn complained that there must be a backstage window open because he felt a draft. I immediately called Bill, one of the stagehands and asked him to close that window. A few minutes later Bill was back to report that he had closed the window. There was no need for him to give me a knowing wink, because we both knew that there were no backstage windows in the Orpheum. I made a mental note to thank Bill for his instant acuity.

For each of his performances Gould brought along a folding chair, which he set at a such a low level that he looked as if he were sitting on the floor, and three wooden blocks to be placed under the legs of the piano. Oh yes, he also brought along a small prayer rug to be placed under the pedals to muffle the sound of his shoes on the wooden floor of the stage.

I'm not finished. Each time he came on stage, he placed a glass of water at the left end of the keyboard. Whenever there were a few bars of rests in the solo piano part, he would take a sip or two of water. And, if either hand was not busy on the keyboard, Glenn would also conduct. I'm quite sure he could have been a very effective maestro.

On one of his final visits to Seattle, Gould agreed to play a Candlelight Musicale with Virginia and me. In a fleeting moment of madness, I toyed with the sophomoric idea of substituting gin for the water in his glass on the piano. But I never had the opportunity. He canceled his visit, and I was fit to be tied. I thought it might be quite appropriate to add his name to those of Vladimir Horowitz and Oscar Levant in the well known jest suggesting a full-page ad for these wonderful artists: "Available for a limited number of cancellations!"

After the final concert with Gould in Tacoma, Glenn was collecting his belongings, folding chair, blocks, and rug. Virginia was idly watching onstage. As he was rolling up the rug, he caught sight of Virginia, who had a quizzical, Mona Lisa-like half-smile on her face. He said, "Don't laugh, Virginia. This is the best part of my act." I think that Maestro George Szell described Glenn Gould best – "The nut is a genius!"

Two NBC Symphonies?

During the last half-dozen years I was with Maestro Toscanini, I found myself in the unique position of guest-conducting both NBC Symphonies. Yes, I said both Symphonies. Each season I was engaged to guest-conduct the four weeks immediately after Maestro finished his winter schedule, as well as the four weeks before he returned in the fall. It's difficult to describe how different the orchestra was during those two four-week periods.

In the spring, right after Toscanini's winter series, I took over a great orchestra. But in the fall, after the orchestra had been in the hands of a different guest conductor each week, the orchestra was merely a good one. I felt that part of my responsibility in the fall was, in large part, to try to return the orchestra to the one with which the "Old Man" was familiar.

For one spring series I decided to include at least one American work on each program and to invite the composer to attend the broadcast, so that he/she could join me on stage to share the applause of the invited audience. One of my choices was composer Virgil Thomson and his "Louisiana Story." At the time, Virgil was living in the Chelsea Hotel on West 23rd St. and was happy to attend. On the same broadcast I programmed a second work by young American composer, Lan Adomian, then living in Mexico. He was unable to attend.

Virgil joined me on-stage after the performance to take his much-deserved bows, and I then went to my dressing room. There, Eddy Bachmann, the colorful leader of the second violin section, said, with the grin of a Cheshire cat on his face, "Milton, you are a man of great courage."

With an attempt at modesty, I replied, "Yes, I guess it was foolhardy to try to do such a difficult program with limited rehearsal time."

"I'm not talking about that, I'm talking about the courage it took to take a bow with Virgil standing right behind you."

During the 22 years I was music director of the Seattle Symphony, I must have conducted a thousand or more scores. Many of them stand out in my memory for one reason or another, but one of them begs to be remembered whenever nostalgia strikes. The occasion was the first performance in Seattle of Carl Orff's "Carmina Burana." Appearing with the orchestra and the Leonard Moore Chorale were soprano Iris Fribrock, tenor Robert McGrath, and baritone Morley Meredith.

The Orff work was an immediate hit with Seattle audiences. Its simple consonant harmonies, engaging rhythmic patterns, and imaginative orchestration made it immensely appealing. In fact, the audience was so attentive that not a cough or sound could be heard – until a point midway through. Surprisingly, stifled laughter, chuckles, and then outright guffaws could be heard coming from a small group of men sitting somewhere in the first half-dozen rows in the center section.

I could hardly wait for the end of the performance so that I could turn around and identify the source of the hilarity. I should not have been surprised to see six Jesuit priests sitting in the fourth row, center. They were the only ones who understood the Latin in which 'Carmina" had been sung. I smiled as I realized that they had been the only ones in the audience who appreciated the bawdy verses.

Another work comes to mind, but for a rather different reason. When I programmed Berlioz's "Symphonie Fantastique," I decided to try to find real bells, called for in the final movement (Dreams of a Witches Sabbath), rather than to use chimes. I needed two large locomotive or fire engine bells, which sounded C and G. They are used in the Dies Irae toward the end of the movement. Where to find them? A sympathetic music critic solved my problem. He wrote about my need in his column and disclosed my unlisted phone number. My phone started ringing like mad and I started auditioning bells over the phone. I was able finally to select two bells after listening to an untold number. The owners of the bells were invited to be our guests at the concert.

Daniel Barenboim, Conductor, Pianist

One evening as I sat before my television set, watching and listening to Yo Yo Ma play the "Elgar Cello Concerto" with the Chicago Symphony conducted by its music director, Daniel Barenboim, my mind did a rapid rewind to my first musical encounters with both of these abundantly gifted artists. By an interesting coincidence, both Danny and Yo Yo were about 14 years old when I first met and made music with them. With Barenboim, it was in Tel Aviv in 1953 when he appeared as piano soloist at a Youth Concert of the Israel Philharmonic, which I was conducting. With Yo Yo, it was in the Northwest a decade or so later when I invited him to appear with the Seattle Symphony in the newly created series Stars of the Future.

Although I must confess that I had no idea at the time just how far each young star would ascend in the musical galaxy, they did touch my built-in crystal ball to the extent that I recognized that the world of music would hear increasingly great things about these two precocious teenagers. (Later on when we spoke to Arthur Rubinstein about Danny, the elder statesman said, "Barenboim is one of the finest musicians before the public today." My next encounter with Danny was about 11 or 12 years later when Virginia and I heard him in a cello-piano sonata recital in Lisbon with his fabulous cellist bride, Jacqueline DuPre.

After the concert we were invited to a party hosted by a Portugese countess in whose home the newlyweds were staying. Their wonderful recital was matched only by the obvious joy they had in each other. They couldn't keep their hands off one another. At one point, I expected them to wind up under the piano. Virginia and I should have been embarrassed, but we weren't. (We remembered how we were at that stage of our marriage.) We didn't have to wait long for them to excuse themselves.

After that our musical paths diverged and we could only keep abreast of Danny and Jackie with news from mutual friends and the accounts we read in print. The tragic curtailment of Jacqueline's meteoric career and her life, because of multiple sclerosis, is too well know and too painful to write about here. I had the very unhappy experience of meeting her for the last time backstage at Carnegie Hall when she was in a wheel chair, no longer the exciting cello playing bride we had seen and heard in Lisbon. What a tragedy!

Elsewhere in these reminiscences we have related our continued friendship with Yo Yo. But, to return to my thoughts about the televised Chicago Symphony concert – I was so moved and impressed that I sat down at my word processor and tapped out a real fan letter to each of my young friends. About ten days later I received a phone call from Danny Barenboim. He told me how very much he appreciated my words of admiration. There was, however, one slight correction he wanted to make in what I had written. At the time of our first musical meeting, he was 12 years old – not 14!

Oscar Levant, Pianist, Wit

During my career as a violist, I played on more than one occasion with the pianist (and personality) Oscar Levant (usually playing Gershwin). At no time did I ever see him without a cup of coffee placed at the end of the keyboard and a cigarette dangling from his lips. I don't remember hearing him play any composer other than George Gershwin, obviously his specialty. The first time I met him, away from the performance platform, was in the office of Goddard Lieberson, president of Columbia Records. As Goddard introduced us, Levant extended his hand and said, "So you're the greatest living violist! Who else do you think is good?"

Pinchas ("Pinkie") Zukerman, Violinist

When Isaac Stern had a mild heart attack and had to cancel his performances I was very fortunate to have "Pinkie" Zukerman, an elegant violinist, step into the breach. Along with a solo concerto, he played the Mozart "Sinfonie Concertante for Violin and Viola" with me. He had never played it and practically sight-read it beautifully. The following season, when I went backstage at Carnegie Hall to tell Pinkie how much I had enjoyed his concert, I asked him if he would like to again play the Mozart with me. He said, "Sure, but this time you play the violin part and I'll play the viola!"

Milton and Virginia Katims

Ethel Merman, Broadway Star

During one of my summers at NBC, I conducted the orchestra for the Ethel Merman show. It was quite an experience in many ways. First of all, there was never any problem with balance. With her leather lungs we couldn't possibly drown her out. Then, too, she was great to accompany. She never threw me any curves. The way she sang at rehearsals was the way she sang at the broadcast. (Unlike the experience I had with a young pop singer on a Milton Berle show. She distorted the rhythm badly and had me so confused that I felt that I had never conducted before. When Berle came on again, he pointed at me and said, "If he's a conductor, I want a transfer!")

Preliminary script reading sessions with Ethel, the director, producer, and sponsor were fascinating experiences. The first time she read the script like a fourth grader just learning how to read. But then, after really becoming very familiar with and practically memorizing the words, there was a world of difference between that first very tentative reading and her finished performance. She was a real trouper!

I have Ethel Merman to thank for introducing me to gin and tonic and the 21 Club. When she asked what I would like to drink, I tried to appear sophisticated and worldly, and ordered a gin and tonic. When she saw the look on my face as I took my first sip, she said, "Here, give me that, I'll get you some gingerale!"

It was at this time that Ethel was rehearsing for "Annie Get Your Gun." I suggested that if she gave me a pair of tickets for her opening night, I would give her a half dozen tickets to my next NBC Symphony broadcast. Sure enough, she sent us two precious tickets for the first night. As for my symphony tickets, it was, "Thanks, but no thanks!

On opening night of "Annie," Virginia and I decided to send Ethel an unusual floral tribute. We paid the florist in Radio City about $30 (quite expensive for us at that time) and left it up to him to put together something unique and imaginative. When we went backstage after the performance to congratulate Ethel, we found two dressing rooms filled with floral arrangements! After searching both rooms, we finally located our "unique" tribute. It was a single small antherium enmeshed in some green leaves floating in a small dish with its tongue sticking out at us. Needless to say, Virginia switched cards with the closest gorgeous arrangement!

Framed

When Virginia Price Patty, a generous supporter of the Seattle Symphony and a fan of mine, decided to commission a portrait painter to make me stand still long enough for him to frame on canvas, she invited Virginia and me to dinner at her home. At the same time she invited the artist Howard E. Smith to fly up from Carmel, California to meet us. After a very pleasant dinner, filled with interesting conversation about our two arts, we repaired to Mrs. Patty's living room. Smith had brought along a few albums of photos of his portraits to give us an idea of his style of painting. As he opened the first album I heard him mutter, "Oh no!" We soon learned the reason. He had inadvertently brought photos of his paintings of horses. But that didn't deter me. I felt that if he could paint horses so beautifully, he could surely paint me. The result hangs in the Seattle Opera House.

Recognition Variations

Recognition, in whatever form it takes is always important to receive. Whether it's a fellow shopper in the neighborhood grocer commenting upon the previous evening's concert, or a subscriber coming back stage after a performance to give me a reaction to the music, or it's in the form of a letter with critical comments (good or bad), they are all confirmation that the third part (the listener) of the musical equation is actively playing his/her vital role. I'll not soon forget the night, after I had concluded a program with the "Beethoven 7th Symphony," and Virginia reminded me to take out the garbage when we returned home. I was still in my white tie but had removed my tails. A car stopped, the driver rolled down his window and called out rather loudly, "Maestro, the Beethoven was wonderful this evening."

I never did find out who that was, although it did make me feel quite humble. Having a portrait of me appear on the cover of the Seattle phone directory in 1969 gave me quite a charge. I felt an even greater one when, before we left Seattle for Texas, Gov. Dan Evans appointed me the State of Washington Cultural Ambassador.

Eugene Ormandy, Conductor

Conductors do not usually fraternize. They don't have reasons to get together the way instrumentalists do to play chamber music (or to talk about conductors). But there are exceptions, as the time I was invited to guest-conduct the Philadelphia Orchestra and I met with Eugene Ormandy a few times. (I'm not mentioning the one time, a few years earlier in Amsterdam, when I went backstage after a concert by the Philadelphia Orchestra and told Ormandy how much I envied his playing on that Stradivarious of an orchestra – how much I would love to play on it. His response was to tell me to build my own Strad.)

I admired Ormandy's conducting. It may not have been as visually flamboyant as others, but it was very solid and dependable. It had to be to retain, for 33 years (probably the longest tenure of any conductor I can recall), the extremely high level of virtuoso orchestral playing established by his predecessor, Leopold Stokowski! Among his other attributes, Ormandy was an excellent accompanist. I always wondered how he was able to do it, considering the delayed response of the orchestra to his beat.

Orchestra players are constantly quoting, and often writing down mala-propisms, unintended humor uttered by their conductor. Recently, I received several pages of such remarks made by Ormandy. Here are a few:

"We can't hear the balance yet because the soloist is still on the airplane."

"Why do you insist on playing while I'm trying to conduct?"

"Even when you are not playing, you are holding me back."

"If you don't have it in your part, leave it out, because there is enough missing already."

Critics

When two or more performing musicians get together, the conversation invariably gravitates to a discussion of music critics. I was curious to learn (once more) how the word "critic" is defined in my *Webster Dictionary*, but settled for my American Heritage version. It reads: "One who analyses, interprets or evaluates artistic works. A fault finder." Farther down "criticism" reads: "The act of criticizing – esp. adversely." How diametrically opposite these highlighted words are from the description by W. H. Auden, British born American writer and critic. His words about criticism read: "Positive comments should be in appreciation, not advocacy. Negative comments should be silence!" (The exclamation point is mine.) It's quite obvious which of his two hats Auden was wearing when he wrote that.

Although I am not an anthropologist, I would hazard a guess that criticism is as old as man himself. The very first critic must have been a primitive man commenting on the cave wall paintings by his cave mate – or expressing his opinion of the other fellow's singing voice. Skip a number of centuries and you find the man responsible for the myriad of printed critiques that followed his invention of the printing press – Gutenberg. (This reminds me of the NBC Symphony rehearsal when Maestro Toscanini was so furious at how things were going that, at one point, he shouted, "Damn that Guido D'Arrezo for inventing notation!") (What an enormous burden of responsibility that early Italian bears.)

It's comparatively easy to write negative criticism. To tear down doesn't take too much know-how. It is not unlike the few seconds it takes to implode a structure which took years to plan and build. Human nature, being what it is, responds to and prefers reading bad news – negative reactions. Critic's reputations have been built on negative reviews. One prime example of this is the (in)famous critic, Claudia "Acidy" Cassisdy, who wrote for the *Chicago Tribune*. Her critiques were so nasty that quite a few artists refused to perform in Chicago. They had no wish to be exposed to Claudia's claws.

On the other hand, to write positively about a performance, the critic, in addition to having good taste, must have enough knowledge about the particular instrument (or voice) and the style of the composition being played to intelligently analyze and evaluate why the performance was good. I even go farther and say that the writer should have personal experience with the instrument about which he/she is writing. (I am well aware of the old bromide of not having to be a chicken in order to recognize a rotten egg!) Even though I am a violist, and as a conductor I have a fair knowledge of all instruments, if I were to be writing about a cellist, I would defer to my wife Virginia who has long years of experience playing that lovely instrument.

We musicians have a very easily explained concept of critics. If a review is bad, we say that the critic obviously doesn't know anything. If the critique is favorable, we say that the reviewer has great discernment. It's well known that the general public relies heavily on the printed word. This has been the basis of quite a few jokes –those who have to wait until they see the write-up before they can tell you how or whether they liked what they heard. So often, after a performance I received phone calls from people who had obviously just read the review (which by this time I had memorized) and they used phrases from that column.

The Pleasure Was Ours

One of my favorite reviews was written by George Bernard Shaw, when he was writing music criticism in London. After hearing a performance of the "Racozcy March," he wrote that it aroused him to such a degree of excitement that he felt like charging out of the theater and capturing Trafalgar Square single-handedly. Of all the reviews I have received over the years, one that I remember most vividly was when I performed the "Bach C Minor Sonata for Viola and Harpsichord."

The harpsichordist, Yella Pessl, who had edited the sonata, invited me to play it with her in New York's Town Hall. (Before that I had played it only with piano – then most recently with Bela Siki on a CD, along with the "Bach Three Gamba Sonatas.") In Town Hall I desperately tried to scale down my sound to the harpsichord level – without success. Finally I decided that I would just play and forget about trying to achieve a balance. In the *New York Times* the following day, there was a review of the concert by the chief of the music page, Olin Downes. He wrote that I "played very well, but sounded like the Bull of Bashan surrounded by a flock of mosquitoes!"

Famed cartoonist Saul Steinberg decides to make a G clef juggler out of Katims

Chapter 26
Music on Wheels

Milton: Family Concerts played a pivotal role in our constant efforts to build an audience for the symphony in Seattle. In fact, I believe that they and the Youth Concerts were the most important parts of the orchestra's schedule, and perhaps the most significant contributions we made to the musical life of Seattle. The Family Concerts had an immediate effect on attendance at the regular subscription series, while we had growing evidence that the Youth Concerts were building the audience of the future. Their format has been duplicated by many symphony orchestras. "Family Concert" is conducted by Skitch Henderson in Carnegie Hall.

Two unique factors marked the Family Concerts. One was that the orchestra reversed the usual process and traveled to the neighborhoods, where the programs were played in school or community auditoriums or even gymnasiums. The other was that each concert was an independent undertaking, in the manner of a mini-symphony setup. Each neighborhood program had its own committee, including a general chairman, a funding chairman, a publicity chairman, etc. It was a sort of "do-it-yourself" concert series. Each Family Concert chairman had a direct line to Lucile Linden, the extremely capable Seattle Symphony staff member, who did a superb job of guiding them.

In the 15 or so urban and suburban areas in which the orchestra played, each area raised its own necessary funding, set up a nursery hosted by Girl Scouts, provided ushers for the concert, took care of publicity, and hosted the post-concert reception. Since the concerts were usually held at neighborhood schools, the concertgoers didn't have to pay for parking. The nursery made it unnecessary for families to pay for baby-sitters. The cost of the tickets was minimal, and a special group rate rewarded large families. Finally, informality was the key word – informality of dress and informality in the way the concerts were presented. Since I used a microphone to provide verbal commentary, no printed program notes were needed. It was a series made in musical heaven.

Aware of the resistance "highbrow music" might engender in people who had not been exposed to the classics at home or in school, I assembled programs that would be attractive to the uninitiated. For the most part the programming fell midway between regular symphony fare and a pop concert – music the concertgoers would recognize or would sound familiar to them. An obvious example was the overture to Rossini's "William Tell." From their childhood, most of the listeners would readily recognize the part of the overture known as the "Lone Ranger" music.

I looked forward to talking to the audiences, introducing each piece with whatever words I felt would add to their enjoyment of the music. Please note that I said "enjoyment, " not "appreciation." I have always preferred calling Music 101 a course in enjoyment, not music appreciation. In my remarks I carefully avoided any technical language. But on one occasion I knew of no alternative.

We were about to play the set of Charles Ives' variations on the well known tune, "America," in a transcription for orchestra by William Schuman. I was sure the audience would have difficulty with one particular variation, the one that is simultaneously in two keys (called polytonality). I decided to take that variation apart. I had each section of the orchestra play separately, in its own key, and asked the people in the audience if they had any problem with it. Each time they shook their heads vigorously, indicating "No." But when I put the two parts back together and turned to the audience to ask the same question, the response was an overwhelming "Yes!" With tongue in cheek, I suggested that they use their left ear to listen to the players in one key and their right ear to listen to the players in the other key. I'd be willing to wager that the next time they encountered polytonal music, they would react like the two elderly ladies, mentioned earlier, after hearing Stravinsky's "Rite of Spring" the third time.

One of the major pluses of the Family Concerts was that they involved the people as active participants in each community. One year we conducted a competition for young – and not so young – pianists in each area. The winner appeared as soloist with the orchestra at the concert in his or her neighborhood. The music we chose for the first competition was a movement of the "Grieg Piano Concerto."

Another year we invited two young string players from each community to sit in the orchestra during the performance of one work on the program. A third innovation was to invite aspiring conductors to wield the baton in a piece at the end of the program. It was usually Sousa's "Stars and Stripes." These and many other ideas contributed to the great success of the Family Concerts. The ideas were not mine alone. I had wonderful partners in the neighborhoods and on the symphony staff.

One particular concert stands out in my memory, although it was not a neighborhood Family Concert. It was a special concert in the Opera House, albeit with a lite program in the Family Concert style. The final work on the program was a medley of Gershwin tunes, which called for a large chorus. Following the suggestion of one of my colleagues in the orchestra, I invited the choirs of Garfield High School and Bellevue Community College to join forces in performing the medley with the orchestra. They were happy to accept my invitation and started to rehearse the medley. Shortly before the final dress rehearsal, I decided to attend one of their rehearsals at the school. Although they were singing commendably well, I was appalled by the lack of any discipline. The students sat sprawled nonchalantly in their seats, caps backward on their heads, paying scant attention to their teacher-director, and obviously ignoring my presence.

I didn't say a word – I decided that it was not my place to make any comments at that time. A few days later, at the final rehearsal with the orchestra in the Opera House, I was in the middle of going through one of the orchestral works when the chorus arrived. They were noisy, giggling and engaged in loud conversation. I immediately stopped the orchestra, whirled around, and in the loudest voice I could muster, I shouted, "Quiet!!! Where do you think you are – in school?" There was shocked silence. After the rehearsal one of the young men in the chorus came up to me and said, "Ya know – you're sump'n else!!"

During my final two years with the Seattle Symphony, we undertook tours to Alaska, playing thirty-five concerts in one week on each tour. Yes, I said 35 in one week! Impossible? We merely reversed the biblical admonition, "Go ye forth, and multiply." We went forth all right, but we divided instead. After the initial concerts with the entire orchestra in Juneau, Anchorage, and Fairbanks, we broke up into two string ensembles, three woodwind quintets, two brass quintets, a percussion group, and a piano trio. Each group played a pair of concerts in two different locations. My associate conductor, Joseph Levine, conducted one string group and I took the other, also into two communities.

Funding of these musical safaris in the Far North was achieved with the help of the Alaska Arts Commission, the National Endowment for the Arts, companies and corporations doing business in the states of Washington and Alaska, and individual angels. With no need to depend on ticket sales, it was possible for each community to keep the money that came into the box office – to earmark those funds for some future cultural event. It was more than a traveling adventure. It was an ideal plan for taking the classics to people who might never be able to hear live music. I was immensely proud of everyone involved.

My first string orchestra concert in Alaska was at Bethel, a tiny hamlet on the southwest shore of the state. When I arrived at the school gymnasium for the Youth Concert in the afternoon, I found the orchestra's chairs set up at one end of a very large room and all of the children sitting on the floor at the other end, more than 50 or 60 yards away. I immediately requested that the teachers move all the youngsters much closer to the orchestra, suggesting that the children sit close to the instruments of their choice. I wanted them actually to feel the vibrations of the instruments and to sense that they were an important part of the whole music experience.

One little fellow elected to sit on the floor right in front of me. That was OK — until we started to play and he began to imitate me. I didn't mind that, but when I realized he had no sense of rhythm and that his erratic waving might cause some confusion, I solved the problem by exaggerating my movements, walking around as I conducted, moving in such a way that he had to inch around to my back in order to avoid being stepped on. It worked. When I could no longer see him, he was no longer a problem.

I have another remarkable reason for remembering Bethel. At the evening concert, I was absolutely amazed to find an audience of 900. The entire population of the town at the time was 1,100! Can any city in the world top that concert-going percentage? The one negative aspect of the Bethel concert was that after the concert, when we arrived at the tiny airport for our trip to the next town, we found that the plane's motors were completely frozen and we had to wait hours for them to thaw out.

We finally arrived in Sitka, a colorful Alaskan town that retains much of its Russian origin and influences. At the afternoon youth concert I was disappointed to find a thick curtain completely covering the back of the stage. I was sure it would absorb much of the sound of our string ensemble, which it did. I asked Dick

Montgomery, our stage manager, to remove the curtain before the evening performance – no matter what was behind it.

After acknowledging the welcoming applause of the audience that evening
when I walked on stage, I turned to the orchestra and, of course, to the backstage
area. The sight that met my eyes stunned me. The entire back wall of the stage was
one very long picture window. And what a picture met my eyes! A snow-capped
mountain and a large body of water in the immediate foreground. No mortal scenic
designer could possibly create as gorgeous a backdrop as Mother Nature had provided. Its beauty momentarily stopped me in my tracks. I turned back to the audience,
awestruck, and told them that, because of this wholly unexpected beautiful distraction, I wasn't sure I'd be able to keep my mind on the music. But I did. And that
rugged audience gave us an ovation equal to the gorgeous view!

Chapter 27
Cutting the Umbilical Chord

Virginia: During his 22 year tenure with the Seattle Symphony, Milton received many invitations to take over the music directorship of other orchestras. The first offer came from the Houston Symphony Orchestra shortly after we had arrived in Seattle. Unknown to us, Tom Johnson, then manager of the Texas Orchestra, flew to Seattle to "scout."

Tom attended a couple of Milton's rehearsals before going back stage to introduce himself. Of course, we knew his name. He was an esteemed and knowledgeable manager, and Milton invited him to lunch at our home. On the way home Milton pointed out the mountains, which were out in all their glory, the lakes and Puget Sound. Tom's reaction? "Take away the mountains, the lakes and the Sound and what do you have?" Texas has oil!

During lunch Tom and Milton made plans for guest-conducting appearances with the Houston Symphony. At the time the Seattle Symphony had nowhere near the number of concerts it would soon have, and Milton was able to get away for the

Houston dates. We didn't know that Houston's music director, Ferenc Fricsay, the distinguished Hungarian conductor, was the center of a bitter controversy. The fracas had divided the city's music public into two equally vociferous halves. Fricsay had requested that the Symphony board undertake an ambitious five-year plan to enlarge the orchestra (something every conductor wants). He also requested more scheduled concerts and the purchase of fine old Italian instruments for all the string players in the orchestra – quite a large order!

All the demands sounded too dictatorial, too socialistic to the wealthy Texans, and Fricsay was released from his contract. Into that messy situation walked Milton, unaware of the battle in progress. Hubert Roussel, a distinguished Houston critic, admired Milton's conducting. Ann Holmes, who wrote for the other newspaper, was a great fan of Fricsay. Despite the ruckus, Milton was so successful in his guest appearances in Houston that Tom Johnson engaged him to tour with the orchestra for a couple of weeks. He also offered him the music directorship of the orchestra at a salary that was about $10,000 a year more than he was earning in Seattle.

We thought hard and long about the offer. Finally, we decided we would be traitors to Seattle if we were to give them such a short trial. After many hugs and farewells to the many new friends we had made in Houston, we returned to the Northwest, to what had already become our home. Fricsay's successor at the helm of the Houston Symphony was the renowned Leopold Stokowski.

Rochester was the next city to make a bid for Milton as its permanent conductor. When he guest-conducted there, we loved the people we met. Evidently the love was returned – they offered him the post. Milton's manager, Arthur Judson, showed up for his concerts and tried hard to persuade him to accept the offer, pointing out its proximity to New York City. But while the Rochester Philharmonic was quite good, only half of the players were professional, the other half were students at the Eastman School of Music.

Milton felt that the Rochester situation would not work because of the temporary status of half the orchestra. The turnover at the end of each year would make him feel like a football coach having to constantly train new players. Once more we left new friends with hugs and farewells. Before we left, the orchestra board invited Milton to return to Rochester the following season. By that time, however, I had begun to wonder about the severity of the winters there, despite the bonus it offered in being so close to New York City. We again said "no, thanks," and headed back to Seattle. The Rochester board tried to entice Milton a third time, but he and I were both tuned to Seattle and wanted to get on with our musical lives in the Northwest. Rochester eventually found its new conductor, the celebrated Erich Leinsdorf.

Next it was Indianapolis' turn to beckon Milton. Its symphony board charmed us tremendously when Milton guest conducted there. The head of Eli Lilly, the huge pharmaceutical company, invited us to his beautiful home to view his El Greco paintings, while another distinguished gentleman hosted a memorable party for us in his wine cellar.

Milton and I began to find in Indianapolis something rather special. We phoned Arthur Judson in New York, because we valued his opinion. When we reached him, his advice was in the form of a question, "Why would you want to move to that wide spot in the road?"

We couldn't think of a clever answer, but decided that he was the person who could best advise us, so we tearfully said "au voir" once again to new friends we had made. The next call came from the Motor City. Milton's first guest-conducting date with the Detroit Symphony was a huge success. The orchestra's concertmaster, Mischa Mischakoff, a long time friend and colleague who had been in the same position with Toscanini's NBC Symphony, paid Milton the highest compliment he could have received, "You reminded me so much of the 'Old Man.' "

When he was invited back to Detroit the following season, I felt that if Milton were offered the conductor's post, he should accept. I told him, "We've been in

Seattle 15 years – long enough! Detroit is a fine orchestra, and it's well supported. Let's not outstay our welcome in Seattle." But it was not to be.

For his concerts in Detroit, Milton had programmed two very splashy works, Vaughan Williams' rather modern sounding "Fourth Symphony" and Respighi's "Festa Romana." He also decided to change the seating plan of the orchestra by bringing all the violins together, his favorite setup. We had no idea that the orchestra's conductor, the distinguished Frenchman, Paul Paray, was in town, living in the same hotel we were in – and that he was being replaced as music director. Paray was upset when he heard that his orchestra seating had been changed.

But that wasn't all. For reasons we didn't quite understand, the two rousing compositions Milton programmed had left the audience a bit stunned. Neither of the works had been played in Detroit for a very long time, although I wasn't sure why that should have been a problem. But, Milton and I were told that Thomas Schippers, a gifted young conductor, wanted the Detroit position himself and he had been sitting with the city's principal music critic. Alas, I could foretell the outcome. The president of the board was well disposed toward Milton, but he also seemed nonplused by the way things were going. The inevitable soon became obvious. Detroit was not to become our next home.

A short while later, the board president of the Baltimore Symphony phoned Milton to offer him the conductor's post, "We've heard only good things about you, Maestro. Our orchestra is a good one, and I think you will like us. Certainly, we will like you."

Milton replied, "I appreciate your offer, but I really cannot accept it without conducting the orchestra myself and finding out whether we like each other. It would be more advisable for me to come and guest-conduct at least a couple of concerts."

"No," the president said. "We would like to settle this now." Milton thanked the board president for their interest, but declined the offer.

The Pleasure Was Ours

For me, the bottom line on conductors' careers is very simple: After ten years, move on!! It is always a good idea to leave before a situation turns into a hassle. It's best to leave while the reviewers are still on your side, because audiences inevitably use critics as their musical barometer, no matter what. (As the old story goes, the classic reply of a man, when asked how he liked the concert, was, "I don't know. I'll tell you after I read the morning paper.") Of course, if your name is Milton Katims, you never want to change. You feel comfortable, you like your home, you fall in love with Mt. Rainier and you enjoy your audience. Are all Maestros like that? No! Most of them are constantly looking around for other opportunities, anxious to see if the grass is really greener elsewhere. But Milton? He likes the same thing for breakfast every single day!

After Milton's 20th year as Music Director and Conductor of the Seattle Symphony, we began to be aware of negative vibrations from a few members of the symphony board. I was also puzzled that certain members of the orchestra had turned rather cool as I greeted them backstage. The recently appointed manager seemed to avoid both of us. (Many of our friends warned us "to watch him closely – he was a real Machiavelli") It was no surprise to learn that a small anti-Katims faction was still in the orchestra. (The group that had wanted to retain their co-operative was still there!) That inevitably happens with every orchestra, whether it's the New York Philharmonic or the Podunk Symphony. There are always dissidents. Even in the legendary NBC Symphony, there were players who hated Toscanini!

The Seattle Symphony continued to play good concerts to large audiences. Lou Guzzo, a knowledgeable reviewer with a lifelong background in music (a former violinist), wrote positive reviews, but I began to feel tension in the air. After 20 years, years which had flown by so fast because we had been so deeply involved in building an orchestra and promoting the cultural ambience of Seattle, we finally realized that even with the charisma of a Cary Grant or Jimmy Stewart as conductor, audiences want change! How could we have been so unaware?

397

Milton and Virginia Katims

During this period the president of the symphony board, a man who was a big supporter of the arts, came to our home, sat down with us and quietly said, "Milton we appreciate all you have done for the orchestra and for Seattle, but the board and I think it's time for a change. We would like to appoint you Conductor Laureate and have you return to conduct two or three concerts each season." I thanked him and he left without any response from Milton. I suggested that we have a serious talk about our situation.

"Milton, 20 years is too darn long to stay in one spot, especially in our profession, no matter how many friends and admirers tell us otherwise. Let's move on! We, too, need a change. Let's get over this romantic nostalgia – forget Mt. Rainier and face facts! It will be therapeutic!"

ON TO HOUSTON

*V*irginia: Fate stepped in! We received a phone call from Houston, Texas. It seems that they, along with much of the country had heard about l'affaire Katims in Seattle. Two long time musician friends whom we admired, Moreland Kortkamp (pianist), and Clyde Roller (conductor-oboist), asked Milton to consider accepting the position of Director of the School of Music at the University of Houston. We had never even thought of the academic world. In the meantime we had to leave for New York where Milton had another date to guest conduct the Philharmonic. With two cross-country flights we had plenty of time to think.

We decided to try academia! It had been great to have a fine success with the New York Philharmonic and now we were visualizing our return to Houston, to new responsibilities and to all of our wonderful friends there. Milton thought it might be very exciting to become involved with the School of Music, and I was already dreaming of having intellectual discussions with the erudite members of the university faculty!

398

The Pleasure Was Ours

In Houston, Milton was interviewed by the dean of arts and sciences and the president of the university. We were impressed by the possibilities and the people we met. "Let's go for it," Milton said to me, and I agreed. After making arrangements for a place to live in Houston, we flew back to Seattle to pack and prepare for the major move from the Northwest to Texas.

Milton: When I told my university friends in Seattle that I had accepted an invitation to become director of the University of Houston School of Music, I received vital advice from two of them. Sam Krachmalnik, conductor of the University of Washington orchestra warned me to be sure to stand with my back against a wall whenever I was in the midst of academic types. William Bergsma, then director of the University of Washington School of Music, advised me that the most important qualification of a director was to be an expert "Geld Getter" – that is, a damn good fund raiser. I found Bill's advice to be right on, but (thankfully) I never found a need to heed Sam's admonition.

Virginia: Dr. Hans Lehmann and his lovely wife, Thelma, two of our most stalwart friends in Seattle, arranged a beautiful farewell brunch in our honor at the Rainier Club. Dr. Lehmann had been instrumental 22 years earlier in advising a much different Seattle Symphony board to engage Milton. The party was truly a balm to our hearts and wounded feelings, because so many of our longtime friends and supporters were there.

We patched up our wounds, said good-bye to the city we had loved so much, and set out on our new adventure. On the road, Milton roared past my old Buick in his yellow Corvette, and we both headed for the great state of Texas. It was a long trip, but we managed to keep pace with each other until we reached Houston. We found San Felipe Road, where our new town house awaited us, and we parked our cars in front. I hopped out, got a whiff of the unbelievable heat, jumped right back into my car, and drove off toward the freeway.

Milton came up behind me, pulled alongside, and shouted, "What do you think you're doing?" I shouted back, "I'm heading back to Seattle! I can't live in this climate!" Of course, I was joking. I was now laughing, but he wasn't. Not yet. We turned back to San Felipe Road and stopped once more in front of our new home. It turned out to be luxurious, surely one of the most attractive dwelling places we'd ever had.

*M*ilton: We arrived in Houston in late August after a fabulous trip from Seattle. Traveling by car had permitted us to enjoy the fantastic natural wonders of Bryce and Zion Canyons in southern Utah and the Grand Canyon in Arizona. Although I had already experienced the heat and humidity of Houston, I felt I was in an oven when we got out of our cars. But now, at least, unlike on our previous visit, we had the ubiquitous benefits of air-conditioning in our town house, our cars, and my office at the university.

On a previous trip, when I knew I'd be leaving Seattle, I had met with University of Houston President Hoffman, who had shown me a mockup of the future university. I shocked him when I told him bluntly that I didn't like it! Where, I asked, was the future School of Music building? My reaction evidently had the desired result. A new Music Building eventually was added to the plans, completed and dedicated September 1997.

I was able to gain a few more concessions. One was to change my title to Artistic Director of the School of Music, and to have the university appoint an administrative associate director for me, because I had absolutely no experience in the academic world and I wanted to devote all my time to creative efforts. Dr. Robert D. Jobe was chosen, and I couldn't have been happier. He had all the know-how and experience in academia that I lacked. We worked well together and in tandem managed to give the school the direction it needed.

The Pleasure Was Ours

Before we moved to Houston, Virginia had made an advance trip to find housing for us. When she called to tell me she had found a town house, I detected a somewhat resigned tone in her voice and asked what was disturbing her. She confessed she had chosen a dwelling because it was a bargain compared to the others, but that she had seen one fabulous town house she passed up because she thought it too expensive. I knew that Virginia would be in for a culture shock as she switched from being the wife of a symphony conductor to the wife of a college administrator. With that in mind, I told her to forget the cost and rent the fabulous house she had seen.

The choice certainly was worth it. When we walked into the town house with its terrazzo floors, high cathedral ceiling in the living room, and curved staircase leading to a Romeo-and-Juliet balcony, I knew we had made the right decision. It was a home we would look forward to living in.

My first day at the university went very well for the first hour or so. After meeting with the very pleasant and extremely capable office manager, Virginia Wilkinson, her equally capable assistant, Martha Phillips, and the rest of the staff, I sat at the large desk in my spacious office – and it finally hit me. I felt like an airline pilot who had been grounded! After years of making music around the world with baton and bow, and with the plaudits of thousands of music lovers still ringing in my ears, I now would be passing the baton (to coin a phrase) to younger musicians and literally watching them from the wings.

The transition would not be an easy one, but I told myself to quit reminiscing, accept my new status, and do the best I could. At first I concentrated on the methods I would use to help the new generation of aspiring musicians. But then a disturbing thought kept nagging me: Would there be places for all these young people in the world of music? I didn't worry about the gifted ones; they would surely find their way. But what about those with a burning desire, but with lesser talent? Would they all be forced to go into music education and thereby perpetuate mediocrity? Of course, some of them might turn out to be excellent teachers. But what were the odds?

401

Milton and Virginia Katims

As I reflected on the differences between the music director of a symphony orchestra and the director of a music school – as well as the similarities. – my choice was obvious. I had to concentrate on the similarities, not the differences, and use my experience accordingly. As with the conductor's role, I quickly realized I would have to concentrate on funding and visibility. I had to attract the best musicians to the faculty. Although the school was part of a state university, there never was enough money to do all the things that needed to be done to turn a good school into a great one.

Dollars were required to provide scholarships to attract gifted students to the school, as well as to pay the salaries of the top-grade artist-teachers the faculty would have to have. A school is only as good as its faculty. I'd say the same is true of an orchestra, despite what Maestro Toscanini once said, "There are no bad orchestras. Only bad conductors."

A word heard often in music schools everywhere is "appreciation," as applied to music. I never wanted audiences merely to appreciate my music. I wanted them to enjoy it. With that in mind, I tried to change the wording in the university catalogue – from Music Appreciation 101 to Music Enjoyment 101. However, I had not reckoned with the rigidity of academic tradition. I did not succeed!

Nevertheless, I did succeed in another area. I proposed that the school should take all the steps necessary to institute a doctoral program. It wasn't easy, but the disciplines leading to a doctorate in music are now an integral part of the School of Music.

Perhaps one of my best contributions to the school was in the realm of music education. I was astonished to discover that this most vital subject wasn't taught in the School of Music at all, but in the College of Education! I decided it had to come under our roof and started pulling the appropriate academic strings to make it happen. Since the time many years ago when I took a couple of courses at Columbia University's Teachers' College, I have been critical of the way music education is taught. The educators, I found, were much too concerned with methodology – the way it was taught, rather than what they were teaching. It was a sweet success for me. Music Education is now a part of the School of Music, where it always belonged.

Although my principal responsibility was to guide the music school, I couldn't abandon my baton and viola after all the years I had devoted to them. I enjoyed making music too much for that. When the Houston Symphony invited me to guest-conduct, I welcomed getting back on the podium. Many of the orchestra members had played with me on the two tours I had guest-conducted years earlier, so the return to the podium was made that much more enjoyable. At one pair of concerts I programmed the Mozart "Sinfonie Concertante for Violin and Viola," with the brilliant Oscar Shumsky playing the violin and with me, as usual, the viola and conducting – a dual role I've enjoyed dozens of times with as many different violinists. Meanwhile, playing chamber music with members of the faculty kept me practicing and performing, as well.

Another of my most rewarding pursuits was to combine coaching and performing, which I did by scheduling master classes devoted to the "Bach Six Solo Suites" in my own edition for viola. I took advantage of my friendship with many fine artists with whom I had made music and invited them to give master classes at the school. Among them were violinist Joseph Gingold and cellist Leonard Rose. All these activities added immeasurably to the visibility of the school, to say nothing of the great value they were to the students.

One word I heard often in the academic world was "priority." I was made to understand very quickly that, with the finite number of dollars available to the school, I had to decide how best to spend them. It was imperative that I learn to prioritize my spending. Having to make such decisions with funds that were never adequate brought me to seek financial support in the private sector – the "geld getter" (money getter) ability Bill Bergsma had mentioned.

Milton and Virginia Katims

Virginia was fantastic in the way she helped me, as always. She quickly acquired the same reputation in Houston that she had enjoyed in Seattle – the hostess with the "mostess" they soon called her, this time with a Texas accent. She gave fabulous parties in our beautiful town house to help woo potential donors for the school. General Hirsch and his wife, Winifred, were our honored guests one evening. Virginia engaged a very attractive belly dancer for the festivities and gave her instructions to pay special attention to the general. Evidently she did a fine job, because the following week I was told that the general had put the School of Music in his will for half a million dollars!

When I joined the School of Music, I already knew several members of the faculty – the two who had coaxed me to take the school job Moreland (Kortkamp) Roller, a fine pianist who had played many concerts with Virginia, and her husband, Clyde Roller, conductor and oboist, who had been associate conductor of the Houston Symphony while he worked at the university. Others were: Fredell Lack, a fine violinist and a great teacher; John Druary, tenor, who had appeared as soloist with me in Seattle; and Albert Hirsch, a fine pianist, whose reputation had preceded him. Hirsch had been accompanist for the great Emanuel Feuermann and for many other renowned artists.

One of the school's brightest lights was the celebrated American opera composer, Carlisle Floyd, who held the distinguished M. D. Anderson Professorship and was the composer of the popular opera "Susannah." In association with the Houston Opera Company, he directed the activities of the Opera Workshop. When I succeeded in obtaining funds to hire a director of public relations, it was Carlisle who recommended the delightful and very capable Miriam Strane. I should qualify that – we were given half a public relations director, because we had to share Miriam with Sid Berger, chairman of the Drama Department next door.

I confess to borrowing strategy from my longtime symphony experience – raiding another university's faculty for an artist I coveted for the School of Music. When the dean informed me that another distinguished professorship, the Cullen Professorship, was available for our faculty, I decided to lure a long time friend, pianist Abbey Simon, from the University of Indiana at Bloomington. The grapevine had informed me he might be interested in a move. He had also been on the faculty of the Julliard School of Music in New York.

At my invitation he came to Houston to have lunch with the dean and me. He told us he would join us, provided two conditions could be met. One was that he would not have to attend any faculty meetings and the other was that he would be able to continue to fulfill his concert schedule without interruption. I agreed to the two conditions, also telling him that it would be in our best interest for him to continue teaching and performing at Julliard because it would add to our school's prestige.

Not long after Abbey joined our faculty, he and I created the annual January weekend piano festival, which brings distinguished pianists, like Claude Frank and Lillian Kallir, to the campus for a weekend of master classes and recitals. It has continued to flourish. I was also fortunate in coaxing the great Greek mezzo-soprano, Elena Nikolaidi, to join our faculty.

At the same time I extended the faculty with full-time teaching of the viola, cello, trumpet, tuba, and tuba. This required not only more superior artists on the faculty, but more money to pay them. One of the dean's secretaries once asked me how I managed to be so successful at raising funds for the school. I told her that I rely strongly on "conversuasion."

But Virginia could not for a moment abandon her first love – music – and her cello! This love, plus her keen interest in bringing good music to children, naturally led to her forming a piano trio, with pianist Sophia Gilmson and violinist Shukada, to play concerts in the schools throughout the metropolitan area of Houston for young audiences. Being very articulate, and also very good on her feet, Virginia assumed the responsibility for providing vivid vocal program notes. In her one-woman war against omnipresent deafening rock, Virginia sought to provide the children with a choice – a positive alternative in great music.

She wanted the children to share her love of music and they were very responsive. For one series, the trio programmed a piece by Claude Debussy. Virginia promptly bought a good copy of an impressionist painting by Monet. Before playing the piece, she painted a word picture of the friendship between the two French artists – how each, in his own art, created an impression in sound and paint, rather than something resembling a photograph. It worked well until the day they played in a school with a very diverse group of youngsters. Virginia finished her little talk and sat down, prepared to play, when a boy in the back row stood up, waved his hand while shouting, "Miss Virginia, Miss Virginia!" "Yes?" "Can you tap dance?"

Chapter 28
Finale

*V*irginia: We spent eight good years in Houston. The people were gracious and generous. They appreciated what Milton brought to the University of Houston's School of Music. Best of all, he apparently enjoyed his work.

However, I noticed that after he did some guest conducting - two concerts with the fine musicians of the Houston Symphony, an appearance with the Norfolk Symphony, conducting and playing the solo viola in the Mozart Sinfonie Concertante with violinist Joseph Silverstein, and another with the Birmingham Symphony - he would return home completely refreshed, a new man! I realized that despite his accomplishments as Artistic Director of the School of Music, he really needed the fulfillment of being a full-time performing musician. The Dean agreed and released him from his contract.

And so it was time to say "au voir" to our many Houston friends. Then came the big question: Where did we want to call home? My first thought was Monte Carlo, a beautiful place to live, with wonderful tennis players, who live there because of the advantageous tax situation - not that our own interest in continuing to play tennis had the remotest connection with that.

It was also natural for us to think of returning to live in New York City, Milton's hometown, with its abundance of cultural fare - a great orchestra, opera, theater, and all the arts - a virtual university! But then I thought of the extremes of winter and summer, and Milton thought of the brusque quality in the culture and the expense of living fairly decently in that large city. We both thought of unique, beautiful La Jolla, where I adore walking on the lovely beach. It would be a sort of homecoming for me because I had been brought up near the beach in San Francisco.

But then we realized that our hearts were with our wonderful daughter Pam, her fine husband Patrick, and our two very special grandchildren, Michelle and Bryan, in Seattle. We missed them so much and wanted to share in the joy of watching them grow up. There was no way we could include our wonderful son Peter in our plans. He, a true citoyen du monde, is now living in Australia, constantly searching for his roots.

And so we returned to Seattle, in the beautiful Northwest, where our condo is right next to the Burke-Gilman Trail and we have a spectacular view of Lake Washington and the Cascade Mountains. I'm on the trail almost every day, communing with nature, and hopefully, keeping my body somewhat trim with race-walking!

*M*ilton: There are only a few more words of mine to conclude this tale of our two lives in music. I agree with Virginia that the best place for us to relax (?) and enjoy our "retirement" years is in Seattle. (Despite our daughter's coming to us one day and suggesting that it might be a great idea if we were to move to some other attractive place, so that they could all come to visit us!) All of the other places do have their attractions and we probably could be quite happy and comfortable in any one of them. But having spent 22 years helping to shape the cultural environment of the Northwest, it was natural for us to return to Seattle with the curiosity to check on its progress during our eight-year absence.

The Pleasure Was Ours

Its physical growth has been more than matched by the growth of the quantity and quality of cultural organizations. When we first arrived in Seattle, there were only two entities, the Seattle Art Museum, nurtured by Richard Fuller, and a regional symphony orchestra, sorely in need of artistic direction. Seattle Opera and Northwest Ballet came into being with the growth of the Seattle Symphony. There are now many regional orchestras, small orchestras, chamber music series and groups. Where drama was once the sole province of the university, there are now a number of companies headed by the Rep. Intiman and Act. Where there were no professional sports, Seattle now hosts the Seahawks, the Mariners, and the Sonics. And two (count them) new stadia being built! All competing for the entertainment dollar!

Physical progress has brought with it all of the usual negative aspects - a burgeoning population causes gridlocked freeway and streets, real estate problems, environmental needs. But at the same time, the influx of people from other parts of the country has brought with them their tastes, habits and needs - supporting the ever-increasing cultural activities. During our eight year absence there was obvious growth. The orchestra, with new faces (Ilka Talvi, brilliant concertmaster married to equally gifted violinist, Marjorie) and some welcome older faces, has grown impressively and is a delight to hear in their new Benaroya Hall. Seattle Opera, guided by Speight Jenkins, is now one of the leading opera companies in the country.

The University of Washington School of Music has a director in Robin McCabe (fine musician and pianist), whose inspired leadership is very evident in the musical activities of Seattle. Mt. Rainier and Mt. Baker, all of the bodies of water, and the mountains are still in place to be viewed, visited and valued. So, on balance, it's understandable why we decided to return to the city we call home.

We settled into a modest condo, suitable for our retired lifestyle, as we looked forward to our traveling to places in the world to which our music-making had never taken us. Before we set foot on the road, it's such a comfort and convenience to be able to hand our keys to our delightful neighbor, John Vibber, and know that all of our junk mail (and bills) will be waiting for us when we return. Also, our modest art collection and our instruments will be safe during our absence.

There's another helpful John in our lives – John Dermody. He's a tall, soft spoken retired engineer who spends many hours working in Seattle's aquarium, but always finds time to tote our loads of used newspapers down to the trash bin. He also has our hearty appreciation.

We are also in debt to the genius who gave us e-mail. That's not to overlook Alexander Graham Bell, who provided us with voice to voice communication. Between the computer and the telephone we are always able to keep in touch with friends near and far. Just the other day we had a phone call from Robert Schulman, who now lives in Louisville, Kentucky. When he lived in Seattle, Bob was the stringer for *LIFE* and *TIME* magazines. He was responsible for Virginia's full page photo in *LIFE*, and for *TIME* carrying news of my activities with the Seattle Symphony. We enjoyed looking back and brought each other up-to-date on our current doings.

We have enjoyed the pleasures of nostalgia as we've recalled the experiences we have poured into this book. Now we enjoy the company of a congenial group of friends. We even have the fun of being on the courts of the Seattle Tennis Club two or three times a week, when my accommodating opponents periodically succeed in hitting my racquet!

Our lives are comparatively quiet these days. Virginia and I enjoy our view of the beautiful garden and swimming pool below us. We look forward to going to concerts, particularly when long time colleagues, or exciting new comers, are performing, or when a special favorite piece of music is programmed. But I must confess that quite often I would like to be on that podium, baton in hand, doing my thing with the many wonderful artists with whom I have had the pleasure and the privilege of making music.

The Pleasure Was Ours

Many scores are still churning about in my head clamoring to be brought to life: Brahms – Mozart – Beethoven – Debussy – and the sublime passions of Bach. Along with the noble aspects of Bach I keep recalling how he fared at the hands of a young student who was asked to describe the great Leipzig master. The young man wrote: "Bach was an important German Baroque composer who had many children. He kept a spinster in his attic to practice on."

I don't mind it any more when Virginia occasionally chides me with, "This condo feels like a motel – when are we checking out?" As soon, I tell her, as we have exhausted all the storybook memories of the greatly gifted artists who have so intimately touched our lives. Who could be more fortunate than we have been?

The authors on a recent South Seas Cruise

Coda: Milton
Memorable Mail

During my career in music that has stretched across almost six decades, I have received many notes, cards and letters. Most of them have long ago been read, enjoyed and set adrift. A few have been put into a green leather accordion folder which was given to me many years ago by Maestro Toscanini. The inscription in gold, hand-written lettering reads: Merry Christmas and Happy New Year – Auturo Toscanini

This first letter is one of four I received from the great Spanish (Basque) cellist
Maitre Pablo Casals – Don Pablo

February 4, 1970

Thank you very much for your letter. I am happy to know that you are so active and doing wonderful things in music. A couple of years ago, I think, I received your recording with the Seattle Symphony of the "Dohnanyi Suite" and the "Hindermith Metamorphosis" on themes by Weber. I was surprised at the high quality of the orchestra and I admired your conducting very much.

I hope your activities as conductor are not making you abandon too much your viola. I think it is good that you publish your edition of the Bach Suites for viola. I thing that the idea of a preface is an excellent one, because it is natural that one can never play the same way. The basic ideas are probably the same, but it is not possible to play this music, or in fact any music, the same way every time. This is the main reason for my not having ever agreed to do an edition of the suites, in spite of the many requests I have received.

Thank you for your kind thought of dedicating your edition to me. I accept with appreciation. Martita joins me in sending you and your wife our best wishes and affectionate thoughts. How I wish we could see you again sometime!

Pablo Casals

Here are excerpts from letters from three of my most revered colleagues:

Allow me to begin my letter with congratulations on your great talent and leadership.

Yours affectionately, Arthur (Rubinstein)

I look forward with great anticipation to our making music together once again. How fortunate Seattle is in having you there building up their orchestra and giving them the benefit of so much musicianship of international standards. Certainly there are very few today who have your background as performer and conductor.

Yours as ever, Isaac (Stern)

Dear Maestro,
Over the years I have played with some of the greatest conductors in the world... Very seldom has anyone given me more musical pleasure, or gotten more to the core of the music than has Milton Katims.

Most cordially, Claudio Arrau

When the Critics Circle of New York announced Ernest Bloch the winner of their award I decided to devote one of my NBC symphony broadcasts entirely to the music of the Swiss-American composer. Two weeks after the Bloch broadcast I received a handwritten letter from Agate Beach, Oregon, written and signed by

Ernest Bloch

I am so glad you did "Evocations," which is completely buried here in U.S.A. as are "Voice in the Wilderness" and the "Violin Concerto." I heard also the "Concerto Grosso No. 2" for the first time, and I must confess that I was really impressed and that it sounded splendidly, clearly, and was not too old-fashioned, as I feared... Well, you did a splendid job, Mr. Katims, and I am happy that a young conductor has such a grasp of my intentions, spiritually and technically, which is very rare. This encourages me to get along, in my solitude! I hope we can meet some day, and soon- Thanks with all my heart and most cordial greetings.

Ernest Bloch

Among the many American composers whose compositions I performed with the NBC Symphony was New Jersey born George Antheil, who had become internationally famous as the "bad boy of music" when his sensational "Ballet Mechanique" was first performed in Paris. This score created a furor with its anti-expressive, anti-romantic, coldly mechanistic aesthetic. I met Antheil through Ben Lees, who studied with him. However, the Antheil work I programmed with the NBC Symphony was the product of a composer who had obviously mellowed and in no way did it resemble his earlier compositions. It was his "Over the Plains." A few months after the broadcast I received the following letter from the composer.

November 16, 1953

This letter is long overdue. I wanted, at the first opportunity, to write my feelings not about your absolutely superb performance of my "Over the Plains," but about you, generally, as a conductor. Milton, you are the first young conductor I've heard in ten years who I would definitely bet upon. You have everything that makes a great conductor, and I've heard all of them. I talked to my close friend Virgil Thomson about this quite a number of times during the days I was in New York, and to everyone else I encountered of stature.

A great conductor, in my opinion, is made by two great qualities, which are irreducible. (1) He must have a feeling of the "grande ligne" of every composition, its ultimate architecture, and (2) he must have enormous elasticity 'within the bar." In other words, whatever he does within the bar must not be pedantic. These two qualities make a composition breathe and live as the composer would have them breathe and live.

This is what I wanted to write to you and I hope I am not too vague. Anway, this is not vague: you are a great conductor, and it is my hope that sometime in the future you will once again conduct a work of mine. The performance you gave of my piece was the best I've ever heard - and I've heard quite a few, even this year.

Thankfully your friend,   George Antheil

In April 1992 I came out of semi-retirement to play (viola) and conduct a benefit concert of the Seattle Symphony on the 30th anniversary of the Seattle Opera House. I have treasured a card I received from the orchestra a few days later.

April 16, 1992
Dear Maestro Katims,
Thank you Thank you Thank you We appreciate your talent, time and generosity.

The Musicians of the Seattle Symphony

During the many years of our metamorphosis from tough New Yorkers to webbed-feet Seattleites, we have enjoyed the warm friendship of the Congregational minister (now retired), Dale Turner. As you read the letter he sent me on my birthday you can readily understand why.

June 24,1992
   Happy birthday, Milton, and a belated thank you for the indescribably great concert on April 16th, and the gala celebration on the 30th in your home! They threw

away the mold when you and Virginia came into the world. You have gladdened the lives of literally millions of people with your musical artistry and loving spirit. It is not only wine that improves with age. It is Virginia and Milton Katims. By the year 2000 you will be at the height of your powers. I plan to be around to share in the celebration at that hour. It is a joy and privilege to call you my friends.
Love and gratitude, Dale Turner

No Memorable Mail would be complete without a Father's Day card from my favorite daughter, Pamela Artura

June 16, 1996 Happy Birthday to a Classic Dad!
    A classic indeed! And a rare one at that. What wonderful models both you and Mom have been for me over the years. Oh, the lessons I've learned, the gifts I've received, the blessings I've experienced. My heart has always known your unconditional love, your willingness to listen, and your generous spirit. Thanks for being my dad.

Much love, Pamela

Son Peter weighed in with a note of encouragement regarding his parent's memoir:
Byron Bay (Australia)
Dear Mom & Dad,
    In choosing a title for your book, don't you think it should reflect the instruments you play (viola, baton and cello) What do you think of *Under the Chin, In the Hand, and Between the Legs*?

Love, Peter
Note: We considered Peter's title suggestion briefly - very briefly - but discarded it because we felt that it was too salaciously misleading.

Milton Katims, Conductor/Violist

Milton Katims was called *"A Beautiful Musician - one of America's finest young conductors"* by Maestro Arturo Toscanini.
English conductor Sir Alexander Gibson called him *"A Living Legend."*
The London Economist labeled him "A Great Virtuoso."

Milton has guest conducted orchestras and performed as viola soloist in 14 countries on 5 continents. He served for many years on the Music Advisory Panels of the State Department and the U.S. Information Agency, as well as on the panels of the Ford & Rockefeller Foundations, ASCAP, and the Foundation for the Advancement of the Arts, which annually selects and recommends the Presidential Scholars in the Arts.

At NBC he was assistant to Maestro Toscanini and Principal Guest Conductor of the NBC Symphony, conducting more than 50 coast-to-coast broadcasts. As first desk violist at NBC for over 11 years, he also appeared as soloist with the orchestra performing the world premiere of the Morton Gould "Viola Concerto." Katims performed and recorded with the renowned Spanish cellist Pablo Casals and the equally well known violinist Isaac Stern. He appeared (and recorded) so often with the famed Budapest String Quartet that he became known as the fifth member of the quartet. (SONY {Columbia} RCA Victor, Vox, Pantheon Legends) Approximately 45 editions and transcriptions for viola have been published by the International Music Co. since the start of their association in 1944. These editions are to be found all over the world.

Milton has given viola Master Classes at the Shanghai Conservatory of Music in China, in Israel under the auspices of the Israel Philharmonic (which he guest conducted on three separate occasions) – at Northwestern University, the University of Houston, the University of Washington, and the Juilliard School of Music, where he was a member of the faculty.

As Music-Director-Conductor of the Seattle Symphony for 22 years, he raised that orchestra to major status. Among his many innovative programs was his creation of a series entitled Stars of the Future, which gave debut performance opportunities to gifted young artists whose names are now well known – Yo Yo Ma (cellist), Murray Perahia & Horacio-Guttierez (pianists), and Kung Wha Chung & Miriam Fried (violinists). While largely involved in the building of the Seattle-Opera House, Katims was co-founder of the Seattle Opera Association. Governor Dan Evens appointed him Cultural Ambassador for the state of Washington. He was Man of the Year in 1966 (his portait was on the cover of the Seattle telephone book in 1969).

In May of 1997 Katims received the Lifetime Accomplishment int he Arts Award from the Seattle Corporate Council for the Arts. For championing American composers he has received the Ditson and the ASCAP awards. He received the Columbia University Medal of Excellence in 1954, and also three Honorary Doctorates: Whitworth college, Seattle University, Cornish College of Arts. Katims' biography is to be found in about a dozen Who's Who, including the prestigious Grove's Dictionary of Music and Musicians.

Virginia Peterson Katims, Violincellist

Her beautiful tone and sustained legato established her as a cellist of top rank.
Her expressive face fascinates all who hear her. – Oklahoma
Her cello solos proved to be the high spot in the program. – Wisconsin
Virginia Katims won her audience immediately with her precise playing, and the ease
with which she accomplished it. The most difficult passages always found her serene.
Her bowing technique was superb! – New Mexico

Virginia was born in San Francisco of Swedish parents. She began her musical studies with the piano, and then decided to make the cello her major instrument. She wanted to play string quartets with her brother Harvey, a student of Ysaye, who was a prominent violinist-conductor with NBC in San Francisco. Virginia's first scholarship was with Michel Penha in San Francisco, followed by another with Sir Ivor James at the Royal College of Music in London and an Extension Scholarship at the Juilliard School of Music. In 1939 she performed as cellist at the New York World's Fair.

She subsequently worked with Alfred Wallenstein and Emanuel Feuermann in New York City, as well as appeared with orchestra and choral groups and in solo recitals. Mrs. Katims concertized with the Beaux Art Trio (Eudice Shapiro, violin, and Edith Farbman, piano). As soloist with the Bary Ensemble, she toured throughout the U.S.A. and Canada for ten years under the auspices of Community Concerts. From 1976 to 1984 Virginia performed in a series of Houston, Texas-based concerts for school children under the auspices of Young Audiences, and taught cello.

Mrs. Katims has since resided in the Pacific Northwest where her husband was the conductor of the Seattle symphony, with which she was a frequent narrator. It was in this venue also that she had appeared in many chamber music concerts to benefit the orchestra and with such artists as Isaac Stern, Leon Fleisher, Claudio

Arrau, Leonard Rose, with the Budapest String Quartet and her husband, Milton, renowned violist.

Virginia has written and published several articles for Seattle newspapers on travels with her conductor husband, on music in China and on Toscanini, and has served as a volunteer at Children's Hospital in Seattle. Her writings include her life-long love, poetry, which she has had published in *The International Library of Poetry* (Watermark Press – 2001).

The following is one of her favorites, as she wrote it in reference to both her present walking trail and that of her youth on Mt. Tamalpais in Marin County, California.

Nature's Reward

Have you ever been in a forest,
A forest cool and serene,
Where the trees offer murmur'd whispers
To the plants so moist and green?

Where the birds sing softly at twilight
And merrily chirp through the day,
That the hikers may, at noontime, pursue
Ever happy this way?

A forest delights and enchants us,
With its silv'ry babbling brooks,
Its mossy cov'ring of leafy green,
Its shady restful nooks.

If you feel that life is a struggle,
A struggle to live and be free,
Just visit some magical forest
That God has made peaceful for thee!

Critical Comments

Her cello tone is unusually rich and mellow. She brings zest and temperamental élan to her playing. Her success was an immediate one.
Washington, DC

Virginia Katims knew how to coax from her cello a beautifully rich tone and make it sing with color. She played with a temperament which animated her music with throbbing emotion.
Halifax, Nova Scotia

Virginia Katims is a cellist whose sensuous, lustrous tone, fluent, secure technique, and imaginative sense of beauty brought illumination to everything she played. It was a most satisfying delight to see as well as hear her.
Richmond, Virginia

True artistry, combined with a profound sincerity of feeling distinguished the inspired playing of this gifted cellist.
Sacramento, California

Beautiful tonal quality, with a wide variety of technique, a spiritual beauty in interpretation that was most satisfying.
Michigan

She presented a group of solos which not only displayed her beautiful tone, but also the artist's amazing fingering and bowing technique.
Pennsylvania

Coda: Virginia
Virginia has the last word!

Music has always been my heart, my mind, my soul, my very life! Tonight we are going to Seattle's fabulous Benaroya Hall for a concert. We're running a bit late, so that when we enter the hall almost every seat is occupied. Have they all come to hear the first rate Bavarian Radio Symphony's premier Seattle appearance, or to see the recently appointed maestro of the New York Philharmonic, the gifted Lorin Maazel? He, you know, was voted into his position by a large majority of the musicians of the philharmonic, a rare event. But, of course, they know Maazel's background, a top flight conductor, violinist, and composer.

The atmosphere in the hall is hushed, no conversation, no rustling of programs, not even waving to friends. What is going on? Maazel enters, jumps up on the podium, and after quickly acknowledging the applause, gives the downbeat for the dramatically impressive Brahms "C Minor (First) Symphony" – a work full of melody and nobility. The storm of applause that greets the end of the symphony recalls the maestro for several bows. We are all so emotionally involved that we need the intermission which follows. But few are leaving their seats, all rapt with anticipation – anticipation for Debussy's great "La Mer." It would have done your musical hearts good to witness the audience's reaction - swaying to the irresistible, undulating rhythms of the sea.

For the closing work Maazel fairly flies on to the podium, and with his entire body gives the beat for the infectious rhythms and melodies of Richard Strauss' "Rosenkavalier Suite." He doesn't merely conduct, he dances his way through the music, and so do we – resisting the impulse to leap into the aisle of the Benaroya Hall to join him.

Why is the hall so completely full of attentive listeners? They are here for that program, a program full of melody and consonant harmony and nary a piece of atonal new music — music to which one has to dutifully listen intellectually, recognizing the various aspects of the creative process, but yearning for a melody! This is purely, or not so purely, my reaction. Oh, yes — music has always been my heart, my mind, my soul my very life. Make it a part of your life, too!!!

~ Index ~

You may order

The Pleasure Was Ours:
Personal Encounters with the Greats, the Near-Greats and the Ingrates
by Milton and Virginia Katims

ISBN 1-56550-094-6
from your local bookstore, Amazon.com
or
directly from the publisher

To order copies directly from VBI by mail use this order form:

Number of books: ＿＿＿＿＿ at $25.00 per book $ ＿＿＿＿＿＿＿

Sales tax of 7.25% applies to books mailed to California addresses only:

Number of books: ＿＿＿＿＿ at $1.82 per copy $ ＿＿＿＿＿＿＿

Shipping and handling at $3.85 for first book
(add $2 for each additional book)

    ＿＿＿＿＿ books $ ＿＿＿＿＿＿＿

Total amount enclosed $ ＿＿＿＿＿＿＿

Name: ＿＿＿＿＿＿＿＿＿＿＿＿＿＿＿＿＿＿＿＿＿＿＿＿＿＿＿＿＿＿＿

Mailing address: ＿＿＿＿＿＿＿＿＿＿＿＿＿＿＿＿＿＿＿＿＿＿＿＿＿

City: ＿＿＿＿＿＿＿＿＿＿＿ State: ＿＿＿＿＿＿ Zip: ＿＿＿＿＿＿

Please send a check or money order (no cash or C.O.D.) to:
Vision Books International
775 East Blithedale Avenue #342
Mill Valley, CA 94941
Visit our Web site at www.vbipublishing.com